THE LONG BANANA SKIN

THE LONG BANANA SKIN

MICHAEL BENTINE

NEW ENGLISH LIBRARY
TIMES MIRROR

First published in Great Britain by Wolfe Publishing Ltd in 1975
© 1975 by Michael Bentine

*

FIRST NEL PAPERBACK EDITION SEPTEMBER 1976

*

NEL Books are published by
New English Library Limited from Barnard's Inn, Holborn, London EC1N 2JR.
Made and printed in Great Britain by Hunt Barnard Printing Ltd., Aylesbury, Bucks.

45002882 8

Contents

To all my children

Acknowledgement

I would like to thank Harry Watt for turning me from
a scriptwriter into an author

Foreword

The title of this book sums up what little philosophy of life I have managed to acquire.

It refers to the number of times that fate has neatly slipped my feet from under me and landed me flat on my back.

These numerous prat falls have taught me one thing.

It doesn't matter how many times you fall down–it's how you pick yourself up that counts.

1. It shouldn't happen to a Peruvian

I can honestly claim that I am the only Peruvian to have been born in Watford. It happened on January 26, 1922.

I also claim, with equal honesty, to remember back to at least my second year of life. This is not due to any remarkable ability on my part, but rather to the exquisite plan of having my tonsils removed while lying on a kitchen table in Folkestone.

You don't forget things like that; especially every time a throat specialist looks at the resultant damage and shakes his head in wonder that you can talk at all. His large fee helps to remind you.

I must admit that I don't remember my earlier circumcision but my brother remembers his clearly, probably because he had his done when he was twenty-two years old.

This strange decision of my parents to have one son done and not the other was apparently a whim. As we were not identical twins they could not have taken this unusual step in order to tell us apart. Tony was my elder brother, by six years.

Pop had decided to move from Watford to Folkestone because of a large pond in our garden. He felt that I would fall into it, which I did, almost as soon as I could crawl.

We had also had a plague of frogs that year and father had spent a fortune having them removed by a frog remover. As soon as the last one had been removed, and the expert had been paid and left, Pop read in the local Watford newspaper that, because of the unprecedented shortage of frogs, the local hospital was offering a shilling per frog for research purposes.

Pop had that kind of luck. He also thought of this as a sign and my attempted suicide clinched the matter.

We first lived in a large flat in Westcliff Gardens, and Folkestone hardly welcomed us with open arms.

Father, being a Peruvian, was looked upon with some suspicion, but that was something that he was used to. Mother, who was a wonderful mixer – by that I mean not of puddings but with people – soon settled in. Where she was happy Pop was happy, for he loved her dearly.

So much so, that, when Ma had her teeth out, Father went straight along to the same dentist and had his perfectly good set removed. This says a lot for Pop and damn-all for the dentist.

Come to think of it, our medical and dental advisers seem to have been a mixed bag. After all, you don't normally take very small boy's tonsils out on the kitchen table, especially if you are short-sighted. Judging by that naso-pharyngeal scar tissue of mine, our doctor must also have been blind as a bat or drunk, or perhaps both.

That's my kind of luck.

Almost as soon as I had recovered from that inexpert tonsillectomy I was back in trouble and pain again, having pulled over a large stone flower urn on to my feet. That put me out of action for a bit and I managed to live out the rest of that year without any major tissue damage.

This early acquaintance with the smell of chloroform and ether, and the accompanying smell of whisky from our doctor, gave me a lively interest in all things medical. Somehow I felt, even at that early age, that there was room for improvement.

My memory, as memories will, now deserts me for about a year, so obviously, nothing really disastrous happened to me between 1924 and 1925.

Mother settled down to her favourite hobbies, which were bridge and housebuilding, and Pop devoted a great deal of time and energy to golf. Not that Tony and I were neglected because we had a series of nannies, some lovely and one or two dreadful.

The children's nanny was Britain's secret weapon. Consider it for yourselves.

When the British Empire wished to include a new member nation, for what it could get out of it, the first thing it did was to send a British nanny to look after the eldest son of the Sheik or Rajah or Emir or what-have-you.

This formidable lady would take over and lovingly condition the young heir to the throne in the best techniques of Russia's great Doctor Pavlov.

Every meal time, or just before slipping into a secure sleep, the small person would get a short homily on how lovely the British were and how lucky he was to be going to Eton or Harrow or whichever scholastic prison had been chosen for him. By the time he could toddle he could sing *Rule Britannia* and was already, as they say, in the bag.

That the British nanny also managed to instil a sense of fair play and justice into most of these children is another feather in the grey caps of these wonderful and lovable ladies.

Nanny Ockenden and Nanny Newman were dears and we loved them with all our hearts. Not that we didn't love Pop and Ma as well – we did very much – but those two kind and warm souls still hold a cherished place in my memory.

Not so the other two, who obviously kept broomsticks parked somewhere. But thanks to my mother's vigilance their reigns of terror, once discovered, were short lived.

It wasn't that our parents were in any way disinterested in their sons. Having a nanny went with the income group to which they belonged and, in those days in Britain, these matters were rigidly observed.

Mother now spent every afternoon bar Sunday at the bridge club and it says a lot for her delightful personality that, although she won enough money to put Tony and me through Eton, she remained its most popular member for years.

Pop applied his whole energies to the Royal and ancient game of golf and, eventually, became the only Peruvian to ever win the cherished Borough of Hythe golf trophy.

He made models of the greens and worked out every angle, putting his theories into successful practice and even playing with a red ball in the snow. Pop never did anything by halves.

Ma was keen that Tony and I should both speak Castilian, as Peruvian Spanish is called. Pop set out to teach us, but he didn't get very far. The first sentence we jointly put together was: 'El Professor no tiene Pelo!' which means: Teacher is bald.

Pop was very much so, from his early twenties, and supersensitive about it; so no more lessons. He tried various remedies for it – I recall a sort of electric comb that gave your scalp minor shocks. Once Pop soaked his shining bald head in paraffin, on the strong recommendation of some well-meaning friend.

As he played round the golf course his partner kept sniffing the air and commenting on the extraordinary smell of lamps.

Not that Pop was a vain man, far from it, but he was touchy about his head.

We were slowly absorbed by a sort of process of bourgeois osmosis into the strata of Folkestone society designated for us. The town itself lay along the cliffs like a Victorian matron, dabbling her toes in the sea. The long lives of battlemented white boarding houses and hotels stood massively together, with their lace covered windows gazing out disapprovingly at the French coast opposite.

The layout of the town reflected its class consciousness. At the bottom of the cliffs lay the harbour, where the busy packets plied between Folkestone and Boulogne.

Tontine Street, with its Co-op and the practical everyday shops that lined it, ran back from the harbour and swept up eastwards, towards the Dover Road and the Warren. This side of the town was composed of a large orderly mass of terraced red bricks two-up, two-downs that housed the bulk of Folkestone's working population.

West of Tontine Street the Sandgate Road climbed up a series of steep hills winding past the Town Hall, and through the show part of Folkestone's shopping centre with its Wellsian department stores which could, so easily, have once employed Mr Kipps.

H. G. Wells in fact had worked in a draper's shop and hated it. He later called Sandgate High Street – the little line of shops running from Folkestone half way to Seabrook – the 'Street of Lost Hopes', because so many small shops opened optimistically and closed shortly afterwards.

From the shopping centre Sandgate Road now progressed majestically past the splendid avenues that crossed it at intervals – these had long lines of double roads divided by a central walk and flanked by fine chestnut trees that flowered so magnificently in the spring.

Parallel with this main road ran the Leas, which fronted the town on the cliff tops and provided a fine grassy promenade for visitors and residents to perambulate along. Most definitely you didn't walk along the Leas – you perambulated.

We children didn't though – we ran along it. No scooters, fairy cycles or other vehicles were allowed. David Tomlinson, who lived two doors up from our final home, was once arrested and carted off in tears, still in his Triang pedal car, for disobeying this strict ruling.

At the furthest western edge of the town the Leas came to an abrupt halt and fell sharply down into Sandgate beneath. There had once been a funicular railway that crossed Sandgate Hill but this had just been dismantled when we arrived. Somehow I still feel cheated by having missed it.

This end of the town was definitely the West end. Falling

back from the Leas until it stopped at Cheriton, it formed a beautifully laid out maze of tall, well-built, red brick houses of typical Victorian and Edwardian solidity; family houses, in the old sense of the word.

That probably sums up Folkestone's main function – it was a breeding place for the family as much as a retiring place for the elderly.

Here, between the wars, for twenty years the families raised their young, just nicely in time to see them decimated in the Second World War. With those cliffs in front, the illusion of a Lemming Society became irresistible.

Along the whole stretch of the seashore ran a lower promenade walk, reinforced by groynes which stopped the agonisingly pebbly beach from being washed away.

From the harbour to Sandgate Castle, in a great sweep around the base of the cliffs, the foreshore managed to contain a lifeboat station, hideously built in corrugated iron, a pier with its Indo-oriental pavilion standing high on Tay Bridge-type iron pillars, a roller skating rink where a gramophone repeatedly played *Valencia* and a seemingly endless line of pebble-dashed walls that backed the equally endless rows of one-room chalets that could be rotated to follow the sun.

Over all these hung a smell of ozone and seaweed and, in summer, a plague of wasps.

The real playground of Folkestone lay quite a distance to the west, round the circumference of the sandy bay that stretched to Dungeness.

This wide strip of golden sands was kept firmly in place by more groynes, while the sea itself was held back, from the low lying land behind it, by the massive sea wall watched over by its Martello towers. These round cannon-shot proof, redoubts had been built to stop the threatened Napoleonic invasion and some had been converted into houses.

Behind the wall lay the Romney Marsh – still one of my favourite places on earth. This will seem incomprehensible to someone who doesn't know this strange flat, apparently feature-less land, but it does have its own unique fascination.

Rudyard Kipling who lived till the end of his life at Burwash felt this magnetic attraction and so, in a far less expressible way, did I.

I spent many happy and wonderfilled hours, during 1929 and 1930, paddling in an elderly and leaky canoe along the reeded military canal that backed it.

The canal had been built to act also as an anti-cavalry ditch and to provide for the floating batteries of cannons mounted on barges – all to confound the little Corsican corporal should he ever try his luck against the Marsh.

Wild bird life abounded and the Marsh slept under the summer sun as the lambs grew up in the great flocks that roamed its saltings.

When fog or sea mist descended on it and the mournful sound of Dungeness fog horn wailed out over its billowing blanket, the Marsh took on a sinister aspect.

Smuggling always had been a traditional way of life, for the Marsh folk, and Customs and Excise men waged a ceaseless losing battle against the steady flow of brandy, silk stockings and other commodities that ran across the Marsh, sometimes under cover of the flocks of sheep that had made its name famous throughout the world.

The Marsh ghosts became all too apparent if you were camping, in a small tent, out on the fringes of the flat grassland. Mysterious lights and hushed voices mixed with the sound of muffled hooves to indicate there was a 'run' on.

The Marsh folk were also well versed in witchcraft and, since the time of the Romans who had originally drained these low-lying lands, many of them practised Christianity by day and the old religion by night. They were kind enough to young people like my brother and I who had the freedom of the Marsh under our bicycle wheels, but they would pointedly warn us to go home if the weather conditions were right for one of their other activities.

'Don't you be about after sunset – not with this mist rising, moy lad,' would be quite enough warning to pack up and get off those dyke-cut water meadows as fast as our young legs could pedal. In those days our parents knew we were quite safe on the Marsh roads as traffic was almost non-existent and the Marsh folk were well known to us.

Russell Thorndyke's marvellous creation *Dr Syn* gives a very clear picture of that strange unchanging area of Britain. 'Love God – honour the King – but first maintain the wall' is still the primary Marsh motto.

I saw as a little boy of four the gangs of Irish labourers with their strange songs as they laid the tracks of the Hythe and Dymchurch miniature railway, manhandling the lines and sleepers into position on the shifting pebbly shingle, while the crack and rattle of rifle fire sounded from the nearby Hythe School of Musketry ranges.

*   *   *

One spring night in 1929 I was smitten with appendicitis.

Tony had nearly died from peritonitis, the previous year, when our doctor failed to diagnose a ruptured appendix caused by a fast moving cricket ball. My parents were taking no chances this time and I suffered the indignity of a rubber covered finger being inserted up my rectum by a – till then – welcome new doctor.

My next clear memory is of a tea strainer, covered with gauze, being placed over my mouth and nostrils and once again the sickly sweet smell of chloroform wafting me out of my body. When I woke up I promptly burst my stitches with whooping cough, which I had managed to catch at the same time.

Minus my appendix, I recovered fairly rapidly in time to go to prep school for my first term. This was the same one my brother had attended, but he was on his way to Eton, so I never enjoyed his tough protection even for one term.

The school was efficiently run by a family plus an assistant mathematics master and a couple of part-time school mistresses.

The maths master was a kindly man, tall and angular, who had served in the Royal Navy at Jutland, and could be persuaded on occasion to tell us about this fascinating battle.

The two school mistresses were elderly sisters who taught us music and English and any ability to express myself in words stems from the small plump one's endless patience. The tall beaky one clustered us round the piano three times a week and we lustily sang 'The Fishermen of England' and other suitable songs for young people. Once she even included Eddie Cantor's *Making Whoopee* which she pronounced 'hoopy' but it only lasted one session.

The Headmaster, however, was my nightmare and my terror for six long years. Comparing notes with the few surviving boys who were at prep school with me our experiences were identical.

This brilliant man was impatient yet very gifted as a teacher. He could be immensely kind and tolerant to some boys who boarded with him and in one case I know of, supported a boy whose parents were in financial straits. On the other hand he could be a tyrant and this is mainly how he appeared to me.

My stammer, which largely stemmed from that savage assault on my throat, was bad when I went there – but by the end of the first year it was a major impediment in my life. That my parents never really grasped the situation is difficult to understand, but this strange and clever man was in a way, a Doctor Jekyll and Mister Hyde. To them his craggy towering presence was charm itself. To me he was my good friend Carl Giles's cartoon character 'Chalky' personified.

Perversely he encouraged my ability to draw and praised it lavishly, yet would stand me up on my desk seat and slap a ruler across the backs of my calves when, with my dreadful stammer, I failed to answer a question.

An odd man indeed and one that, at this stage of my life, I could have well done without. Yet for six years, along with a lot of other boys who had the same troubles, I had to be schooled by this extraordinary mixture of scholar and tyrant. But he did teach well and my love of the classics is due largely to him.

When the mood was upon him and he could relax from the worries, possibly financial, that must have plagued him, he would read to us. I forgive him anything for the way he read those books – clearly and fluently – he brought many authors alive and excitingly close to our minds. He would, undoubtedly, have been a great actor.

He persuaded Pop, who was also gifted as an amateur actor, to join him in a production of *A Midsummer Night's Dream* which the local amateur group was putting on at the Town Hall.

To achieve this the dramatic society had decided to build a false proscenium, which was constructed out of secondhand aeroplane fuselages from the surplus air force stores. These had been bought cheaply and were ideal for the light structure needed to provide the false front. However it was a bitterly cold winter and a virulent influenza bug was going the rounds. In trying to fit up the framework and cover and paint the proscenium, three members of the cast caught pneumonia and died.

Pop survived the virus and staggered on to play Peter Quince. He also scared the living daylights out of me because just before I went to bed I saw him come out on the landing in his full flowing robes and beard and wig. Thinking he was Jesus, who had come to get me, I yelled blue murder and refused all comforting. (One of those pseudo-nannies had often told me that if I wasn't a good boy Jesus would come and take me away.)

Our life in Folkestone was varied from time to time by visits from our distant family in Peru, their natural Latin affection contrasting oddly with the almost formal family relationships of my friends. I realised how much family life meant to my father

18

and his nephews and listened proudly while Pop chattered away in Castilian, a pastime he loved.

Antonio and Rosita, two of my favourite cousins were then just in their twenties and one night took Folkestone by storm by dancing a real smouldering tango at the big Christmas Fair, Rosita complete with a rose between her teeth. Little did the wildly applauding aficionados realise they were having the gentlest of mickeys taken out of them.

In those days we were living in one of Ma's 'spec' houses which bore the exotic name of Rimac. Wherever mother built a house it seemed others followed. Next door a new one was already three-quarters built and throughout the long summer of 1930, Tony and I had played happily on its site after the builders left for the day. We were so engaged when Mother brought round *The Twins* for us to look after.

These were two younger children who were dressed in Lord Fauntleroy outfits and were a trifle timorous. They were entrusted to our care while their parents visited ours for a rather formal tea over which they were discussing a forthcoming charity fête.

The only game the twins could possibly play in those velvet outfits would be hide and seek and we duly told them to hide, feeling it was all a bit of a lumber. They went off happily enough while we lazily counted up to a hundred and then went to look for them, but they really had hidden themselves well. Search as we might in all the local corners and spaces of a threequarters-built house, we couldn't find them. Then they gave themselves away – or rather the floor of the builder's loo in which they were hiding gave way.

What on earth had induced them to hide there in the first place is beyond me.

Guided by their shrieks, which were strangely muffled, we found them and while Tony bravely hung on to their desperately grasping arms I rushed off to summon help. I can still picture that scene as I burst into the drawing room and surprised Mother in mid-macaroon.

'Come quickly!' I yelled. 'The twins have fallen down the shit-house!' – and here I naturally used the words I had heard the builders use.

Their mother fainted and was ministered to by Ma while Pop and their father dashed to the rescue. By now the twins were both understandably hysterical. Tony wasn't quite strong enough to get them out but at least he had been able to stop them sinking

19

any further into the liberal depth of human waste that nearly no little inconvenience.

Covered in newspapers that Mother came hurrying over with, they were borne, weeping, away and driven odoriferously back in their brand-new and very expensive limousine.

Around 1931, Pop had an unusual experience at a seance which changed the life of the whole family.

A friend of Mother's was an ardent spiritualist and, finding that Pop had an interest in supernormal phenomena, took him along to a meeting which was being held in a private house near the R.A.F. station at Hawkinge. The woman who owned this house was a widow who had lost her pilot husband in an air-crash and regularly held seances to communicate with him.

Dad was a bit uncomfortable at first because he was, by nature, a polite and shy man, and wasn't too convinced by the banal messages which were being given to various other sitters at the meeting. He felt he wanted to leave.

Then the medium turned to him and told him she had a special message for him from a young woman who he had known years before. Pop murmured something polite and wished he was somewhere else.

The medium asked him, 'Does the name Bolton mean anything to you?'

'I'm afraid not,' said Pop.

'Wait a minute,' continued the medium. 'This young woman says you were in a play at Bolton.'

'I'm very sorry, I don't understand the message,' said my father desperately. 'Perhaps it's for someone else!'

'No,' said the medium with complete conviction. 'It's for you. The young lady says you'll understand the significance of Bolton when I tell you that there isn't a play going on on the stage, but an auction.'

Pop said afterwards he felt as though ice water was being poured down his spine.

'Yes,' he said hoarsely, 'I know what she means now.'

'Good,' the medium continued. 'Now she says: Thank you for what you did for her and she is very happy that she is the one chosen to bring you into our movement.'

Pop left in a daze, remembering to thank the medium and this mysterious young spirit. When he told the story the next day he included my brother and myself in the listeners, as he felt it was so important.

On the face of it the name Bolton and a stage with an auction on it doesn't mean much but Pop's story brought it into a different perspective.

When he was a young man before the First World War, he and another South American student had met and fallen under the spell of a young actress. They were so taken with her that, during the summer holidays, they had joined the third-rate touring company of which she was the leading lady.

The play after a short tour had not attracted sufficient funds to be able to continue and, at Bolton, the company had gone bust. This was in 1910, long before the days of the actors union Equity and the manager had absconded with whatever funds were available, leaving the company stranded.

It had been decided, at an emergency meeting of the staff and players, to hold an auction on the Saturday afternoon to try and raise sufficient money to get the company back to town. Pop and his friend had telegraphed their guardian in London and had received a money order by return.

At the auction they had bribed one of the stage staff to bid for the leading lady's personal belongings and had left them with a short note in her dressing room. They had then shyly boarded the train back home and had never seen her again.

This then, Pop explained, was her rather unorthodox way of thanking them.

As I have already explained, my father never did anything by halves and we were all soon plunged into an intensive programme of psychic research. While Pop avidly absorbed every known work on the subject, Ma was told to invite a seemingly endless stream of mediums and clairvoyants to our home.

A special room was set aside for these meetings and a complicated series of electric communication machines were designed and built by my fascinated father. These ranged from a simple morse key connected to a buzzer to a very complicated piece of circuitry that could flash letters up on a screen. We solemnly sat round these strange machines for six months while we held hands and sang hymns.

In view of Father's voice, which was a little like a broken foghorn, we then switched over to a gramophone and a selection of non-secular music. I always remember Ernest Lough's boyish treble singing, *O, For The Wings Of A Dove*. I could hardly forget it – it was regularly played every time we sat in seance.

Nothing happened at all until a medium suggested that we needed magnetising, whatever that meant.

This medium brought along a friend who must have been a

powerful magnet, because almost at once the furniture started to move.

It's strange, but although all of Pop's splendidly devised and executed gadgets refused to buzz, knock, light up or whatever they were designed to do, the table on which they were placed rocked violently about – and even took off and circled the room – while we hung grimly on to it.

This didn't do my nerves, already taut from school, much good. I can honestly say I didn't sleep too well during those early days.

I was kept out of the more alarming seances that took place next door to my bedroom but of course I was fully aware they were taking place and hid under my bedclothes while various mediums went into noisy trances.

However I was allowed to sit at the sunny afternoon seances that took place in daylight, in contrast to the weekly affairs which were held at night. During these I watched in wonder the procession of Red Indians, Chinamen and Zulus that seemed to make up the bulk of the guides.

I suppose for every genuine medium we must have had a dozen phoneys or, to put it at best, people who had convinced themselves they were in a trance. One day, however, when my brother was controlled by some strange powerful being, I really became quite alarmed.

Tony had fallen into a deep sleep and was breathing heavily when quite suddenly he got up and started speaking in a vibrant foreign voice. I knew all my brother's voices and accents because it was a great game with us to talk nonsense in apparently foreign tongues or imitate the radio personalities or movie stars that were our special heroes. But this voice was quite unlike anything I had ever heard and I was sure Tony was really under the control of some other being.

I have never held a seance in my own home and my children have never been encouraged to either, because I think the whole business of psychic research, without proper control, is like letting a child loose in a power station control room.

However, we knew very little about this whole business in those days and Pop really thought he was doing what was best for all of us. Either we were well protected by my father's sincere innocence and his undoubted ability as a research scientist or we were just plain lucky. None of us went mad and none of the furniture got smashed up.

All this paranormal research activity of Pop's caused Mother no little inconvenience.

Apart from the home being constantly filled with weirdos of various kinds, her social life suffered considerably. Folkestone being a small town, gossip was its great recreation and news of Pop's interests was seized on readily and maliciously and spread like a prairie fire. Apart from the bridge club where Ma's skills were sought avidly, and she was much in demand as a partner, she found herself gradually becoming a social outcast.

To offset her sudden loss of social popularity, and to make sure that this didn't affect Father's researches, she looked for other outlets for her boundless energy. She found one of them in breeding budgerigars.

Like Pop, Mother also was capable of concentrated efforts and soon a large aviary had been set up in our back garden and was rapidly becoming stocked with bird life. So successful did she become in this new field of activity that within a matter of a few years she had won many coveted prizes at the great annual cage-bird show at the Crystal Palace.

Ma also got a parrot licence, which was slightly harder to obtain than a firearm certificate for a machine-gun. The reason the authorities were so strict on the importing of parrots was the danger of the then incurable psittacosis – a virulent, parrot-borne disease that killed practically every time. Somehow Ma got the coveted licence and was soon busily breeding these exotic birds. We also had a special flight aviary filled with South American species like the black masks and parrotlets of the Peruvian jungles.

Pop also became interested and started to breed the songful roller and border canaries and dawn at our home broke with a raucous and melodious birdsong never before, or probably since, heard in Folkestone.

One family of our long-suffering neighbours were the Tomlinsons. Four boys ranging from their early to late teens. Peter and Michael were Tony's great chums while mine were Paul who was my own age and David who was a few years older.

David and I wrote a play called *Dope* – with an intricate and puzzling plot, sparked off by my having been given a blank cartridge pistol and David having acquired a bald wig. This he wore in his character as the villain while using his own hair as the hero. As he forgot to take the bald wig off in the third act this confused the audience, which luckily consisted only of our two families and friends. The pearls, I remember, were hidden in a peeled vegetable marrow of notable proportions. It was that kind of a play.

Ma now added a whole litter of Scottie puppies to our menagerie which with our cats, rabbits and guinea pigs, surrounded our house with a strange animal smell.

Much later, Tony brought his art master to dinner. What he made of us is difficult to imagine. We had never met an artist before and naturally expected something a little different and I'm sure he had never met a family quite like ours. To make things worse our oldest Scottie, who was incontinent, had done her worst under the dinner table without being observed. The upshot of that strained dinner party was that the art master thought the smell came from us and we thought it came from him.

My great friends, apart from Paul and David, were Kit and another David. The one the son of a radiologist and the other the son of a retired naval captain.

Kit and his family were outdoor types who rejoiced in all things sporting and healthy, especially sailing, and frequently hauled me along to act as supernumerary crew. Kit also, I remember, had an odd habit of eating the grease off his fairy cycle. He said it was delicious but, having tried it, I feel it must have been an acquired taste.

David however was a loner, a keen ornithologist and solitary tree climber, for which sport he fitted special spikes to his ankles and shinned up tree trunks like a monkey.

I was very fond of them, and they were among the very few people I didn't stammer to when I was speaking.

David once gave me a pair of young jackdaws he had found in the woods that surrounded Folkestone. They stayed happily with us for two whole years, even though we didn't clip their wings.

In 1936 Ma acquired a West African Quaker parrakeet which lived indoors with us, unlike the other birds, because Mother wanted to train it to talk, which it did quite fluently.

It lived inside a cage and was violently anti-social until, one day, it caught its foot in the wires of the cage and hung there until Pop rescued it. From that moment on, Pop alone could do anything he pleased with it. Perched on his shoulder, it accompanied him all around the house.

Tony tried to coax it up his arm which it obligingly climbed and then neatly punched a piece out of the back of my brother's neck, like a feathered ticket collector.

The menagerie grew, and Tony sent me a lovely cartoon from

Eton of our front door being opened by a gorilla, dressed as a maid with the caption: 'Welcome home, Master Tony!'

These animals all lived in perfect harmony. By now our house must have been fairly well populated with spirit entities, but none of the animals showed any of the terror of the unseen so beloved by writers on psychic phenomena.

Only once did one of the cats react savagely and that was to the domesticated parrot who gave as good as she got and was only separated from her attacker after a long battle.

During the scuffle the cat nearly lost one ear and the parrot most of her chest feathers. For days the poor bird brooded silently while Ma fed her on brandy and milk. After a bit she perked up and only accepted the brandy neat.

That bird must have been the first alcoholic parrakeet in living memory. Stoned out of her mind, she would hang upside down, swearing drunkenly to herself and then, cursing, fall flat on her back on to the sawdusted floor of her cage. She also refused all solid nourishment unless a spoonful of her favourite tipple was added to her water pot.

As her feathers took a long time to grow back and Pop feared the cold Channel winter could carry her off, he indulged her whims and turned her into a contented parrot anonymous.

2. My father the moon worshipper

From 1924 onwards we all looked forward to our annual visit to Mother's English relations at Westcliff, Southend. Mother's family were sturdy yeoman stock from Essex though her grandmother was originally Dutch.

In our slabsided Austin saloon we would set off for Gravesend Ferry, and a long and perilous journey it seemed in those days, winding along the narrow roads through the lovely Kent countryside.

Pop was a skilled and careful driver but had the habit, that I inherited later, of muttering curses at motorists who behaved – he thought – foolishly. As in my case, this was probably a way of getting rid of tension. After all, when you are driving your family you bear a heavy responsibility.

The roads were much less crowded in those days, and motoring really was a very pleasant pastime. Many of the country roads still had horses and carts and the odd farmer jogging to market in a pony trap.

Ma had tried her hand unsuccessfully at learning to drive and had bent the car both times, bringing herself to a state of tears and my parents nearer divorce than at any other time in their many years of marriage.

Ma's family were a united and happy collection of uncles and aunts and cousins whom I dearly loved and with whom my shyness quickly vanished. Uncles Jim and Alf were glamorously joined by an uncle by marriage, Bert Woodbridge, who as an observer in the 1914–18 war had been the first man to shoot down Richthofen, the Red Baron. He had gravely wounded this top German ace and only a few months later Captain Roy Brown, a Canadian, finished the job.

We were immensely proud of Uncle Bert, who later was himself shot down by tribesmen while flying an Imperial Airways plane over Afghanistan in 1929. He survived the crash, but died looking for help.

My aunties were Nellie and Mary, the latter being mother's elder sister, and they were both loves.

I think the happiest days of my boyhood were spent with that sprawling uninhibited family of my cousins through the long lazy days of the summer holidays, racing each other in children-packed cars over the deserted roads round Shoeburyness and the marshy expanse of Essex. Even Pop forgot his usual caution and, muttering Peruvian curses, drove like one possessed.

Tony's closest cousins were the older ones, Audrey, Alan and young Alf. Mine were John and Joan, the younger set. We all joined in kite fighting, in the building of which splendid machines both Pop and Uncle Jim were experts.

As a matter of fact Uncle Jim was a card. He had a marvellously wicked sense of humour and his mobile mouth twitched as he gravely pulled your leg. He and Pop set each other off, my normally grave father becoming as potty as this lovely uncle.

The two of them in the First World War had been engineers with Pop concentrating on the aerodynamic side and Uncle Jim on the plumbing. In 1917, they concocted a safe double-decker bus.

London Transport, worried by the number of pedestrians who were being run over by these hard-to-stop buses, had offered a thousand pounds to the designers of a successful safety device for preventing careless pedestrians from being run over.

Uncle Jim and Father built a model bus and proceeded to fit it with various types of cow-catcher devices like the old-fashioned wood-burning trains in America.

They refined their design until they had perfected a device which not only gently picked up the wayward pedestrian but also deposited him safely back on the pavement. It worked perfectly on the little sandbag men that Mother and Auntie Nellie made for them and duly the two excited inventors got an interview with the head engineer of London Transport.

Hurrying up to town, they demonstrated their marvellous invention before a hushed audience of transport engineers. The little bus was a tremendous success – busily running along and picking up the sandbag pedestrians and depositing them safely sideways, one after the other.

There was, unfortunately, one slight snag which they had overlooked. Fitted with this splendid device the bus could in no way turn a corner.

27

Uncle Jim was also an inveterate practical joker, so much so that Pop often wondered about the design for the bus safety device. But none of Uncle's nonsense ever hurt anyone and he really was very much loved.

When Pop first arrived to meet his prospective in-laws, Mother was a bit concerned at the conventional Essex attitude to her marrying a Peruvian, and had confided her worries to her brother Jim. He winked, told her to leave it to him, and then went off into a corner and had a quiet word with Pop.

The upshot of it was that after a rather formal dinner with the starchier members of the family who had gathered, like a clan, to approve or disapprove of this strange South American suitor of Mother's, Uncle Jim addressed Pop:

'Well, Adam' – that was Pop's name – 'time for your moon worshipping.'

Pop nodded and followed Uncle Jim out into the back garden, where a full moon was shining.

Really the family should have guessed but, after all, there was Mother's fiancé calmly kneeling down and muttering gibberish at the moon.

Uncle Jim rose to the occasion magnificently.

'All join in the responses,' he said firmly. 'Adam's taught me them – just follow me.'

The far from enthusiastic but polite family now knelt behind Pop and Uncle, as Father intoned a sort of ritual chant which Uncle faithfully repeated and was followed closely by the acutely embarrassed family.

This would have gone on indefinitely if Mother hadn't appeared and exploded at the sight. But it broke the ice. Uncle Jim was scolded but remained irrepressible and, in his own way, irresistible.

A super uncle indeed!

3. Magnificent Pa in his flying machine

Southend was a boy's paradise in those days, with its great pier which you rattled along in electric trains reminiscent of the Hythe and Dymchurch railway carriages, its boisterous noisy sea front and, above all, its carnival.

Southend was also the popular resort for weekenders and day trippers from London and was as vulgar and honestly down-to-earth as you would find – immense fun after the stuffiness of pre-war Folkestone.

The whelk and cockle stalls, the mud football, the crabs and eels, perfectly suited the jostling paper-hatted crowds of laughing Londoners.

I loved it all and still look back on those days with a great deal of affection.

Folkestone, meanwhile, had been preparing an exciting innovation – gliding. The spectacle of two Austrians, Kronfeld and Magasuppé, wheeling effortlessly in their graceful gull-winged sailplanes, over the downs behind the town was breathtaking and I watched in wonder.

Lyons, the catering firm, had sponsored this remarkable display and from a large Lyons lorry, the *Stein Song* blared forth, interrupted at intervals by a commentary on the evolutions of these magic machines. Magic indeed they seemed to me because they had no motors and yet curvetted and circled, looped and rolled over the grassy slopes for what seemed like hours. They were launched by a Bungy rope of interwoven elastic like hugh 'octopus' grips.

At the end of the day the announcer warbled out over the loudspeaker that now the British would show what we could do. Duly, a rather ugly, squat machine of almost miniature dimensions was hauled out of a trailer and assembled by a small team of self-important experts.

In comparison with the Kronfield's graceful *Wien*, it didn't look too good, but the pilot got in it. The long multiple strands of shock absorber rubber were hooked on, and each side of the catapult thus formed was grabbed by four or five willing helpers.

Another three people hung on to the tail hook and we all leaned eagerly and patriotically forward to see this product of British engineering leap into the blue.

The tension mounted as the white-helmeted pilot called out – 'Walk!' – 'Run!' – and finally, when the whole machine was vibrating with the tension of the long-stretched cords – 'Release!'

The two groups of cord holders fell flat on their faces as the straining tail holders finally let go. Like an arrow shot from a giant bow, the little glider rushed along the downward slope.

We naturally expected the pilot to haul back on the stick and project the 'scud', as it was called, high into the air. But though he was obviously frantically attempting to unstick the glider it firmly refused to leave the grassy slope and eventually hopped across the road at the bottom and deposited itself splinteringly in somebody's front garden.

The pilot was, thankfully, unhurt. We all rushed down the hill to extract the scud from its resting place among the hydrangeas.

It later turned out that, in the excitement of rigging the machine in front of the impatient crowd, the mechanics had hooked up the elevator controls upside down so that the harder the pilot pulled back on his stick, the more firmly the nose hugged the ground.

Inspired by this fantastic display – that is to say, Kronfeld's and Magasuppé's not the scud's – a 'Channel Gliding Club' was formed with various enthusiasts, like Father, well to the fore.

As Pop was one of the few real aerodynamicists involved, the construction of the first primary training glider fell very much into his hands.

A kit, rather like a huge model kit, was purchased, and the work proceeded throughout the rest of the summer. It wasn't until the chillier airs of autumn had browned the leaves that the C.G.C.'s first machine was ready to fly.

The Bungy launch was still in favour as the safest method because towing behind a car had resulted in one fatality already at another gliding club.

Duly, the machine was rigged and ready but when it was finally complete, it looked even uglier that the little scud. It comprised a wing and stabilising surfaces connected by a sort of plywood skeleton framework, and the pilot sat on it rather than in it. The whole construction was held together and braced by a cat's cradle of wires and struts.

It looked squatly solid and anything but graceful. Still, it was a primary glider and you had to start somewhere.

After one or two launches, gingerly carried out by the enthusiastic but nervous catapult team, the Club felt the time had come to get it rather higher off the ground than the previous average of six inches.

They looked at Father. He, feeling that his own professional integrity was at stake, and probably the honour of Peru as well, strapped himself firmly into the hideous contraption. Carefully he tested the controls.

'Walk!' he called.

'Run!'

And finally, as the rubber cord twanged like a bass harp:

'Release!'

The tail group let go the hook. Off shot Pop, his cap reversed and held on by his goggles.

A short rasping skid over the grass and he was up. My father – the birdman!

Up he shot and then dived down – touched the grass for an instant and then hurtled up again – in two great swooping hops, to land in a long rustle of grass well down the hill.

As the excited Club members gathered round to congratulate him he must have made a few mental reservations, because never again did Pop take to the air in a glider.

Magasuppé went back to Austria but Kronfeld stayed on in Britain and became our leading sailplane expert, eventually dying during the war in the wreck of the experimental Armstrong Whitworth tailless giant glider. A brave and charming man who fought Fascism in his own individualistic way.

4. Your body between your knees

Our being sent to Eton had nothing to do with snobbery. My father could ill afford it and Mother claimed, rightly, that she paid our fees mainly from her bridge winnings.

The reason for going there in the first place was entirely due to Pop. When he had arrived in Britain, at the age of thirteen, he went to live with his guardian, Mrs Southery. This wonderful woman had been married twice: once to a Mr Hope-Jones and, on his death, to her second husband, a Mr Southery.

Pop spoke literally no English at all when he arrived in England in 1900. He had crossed the Isthmus of Panama on a mule, because at that time Ferdinand De Lesseps had died in the middle of building the Canal and the Americans had not, as yet, completed it.

Pop was naturally terribly homesick for Peru. Grannie Southery, as she was later known to us, was virtually Pop's mother – in *loco parentis* – his own having died shortly after his birth.

Her eldest son William was Pop's age. From the moment they met, they were like David and Jonathan. Bill Hope-Jones won a scholarship to Eton and Cambridge and Pop swore solemnly that, wherever Bill eventually became a schoolmaster, which was his chosen profession, Pop would send his sons, if ever he had any.

It just so happened that Bill Hope-Jones – or, as I knew him from the time I was a baby, Uncle Billy – became a master at Eton. If he had become a master at Pudsey Grammar School, we would undoubtedly have gone there and just as equally benefited from this exceptional man's marvellous influence on our lives.

To me Eton was like a breath of fresh air, after the long purgatory of my preparatory school. For my first half, anyway, I didn't feel the pangs of homesickness that most young people do when they are first sent away from home.

This British habit of sending their young away has always seemed a strange one to me but then after all, my family in Peru also had believed that it helped the development of character in children. Still, I have seen very young ones on main line stations being seen off by their parents, desperately trying to stem back the floods of tears that are breaking their small hearts.

Perhaps later in life it does help to have been chucked out of the nest so soon. I well remember in those first weeks in the R.A.F., in wartime, seeing young men, some years older than I was, silently crying their hearts out under the blankets, because this was the first time they had left home.

Which ever way you look at it, this question of sending the young away early is a puzzler and obviously doesn't suit all children equally. Some it probably even destroys. In my case I was so lucky to have the Hope-Jones family in charge of my house at Eton – Number One, Common Lane – known to us as M'Tutor's and, to the other twelve hundred-odd Etonians, as Hope-Jones's.

M'Tutor, a large tweedy man, still athletically built and as marvellously active as he was eccentric, had an arresting face which was wise, compassionate, strong and humorous.

If you think I'm going overboard about this extraordinary man, I am. To me Uncle Billy and my father were indissolubly one person. What one lacked the other made up for.

M'Tutor's family were as widely different as individuals in a family can be. All of them were brilliant.

Mrs M'Tutor, who had a strange way of emphasising her words, which I could only describe as a gift to an impersonator, had presented M'Tutor with five children, the eldest of whom was Kenneth, a remarkable combination of scholar and athlete, like his father, and whom we all wanted to emulate. Edward was a true eccentric and an academic of enormous appetite who devoured degrees voraciously. Ronald, another brilliant scholar, was a martyr to the most vicious migraine attacks I have ever seen. Elizabeth, a pretty and vivacious girl, could have chosen her career as an academic in many subjects. Susan, a wildly clever curly-haired girl of my own age, awed me by making cardboard models of complicated geometric figures.

All of them were as kind and loving as my own family and this, more than anything, explains why I wasn't homesick. I just loved them all.

3

M'Tutor, who was President of the Mathematical Society of Great Britain for more than twenty years, was obviously a brilliant mathematician, but he had the unique gift of teaching as well.

He gave you problems like:

'Chief M'Bamba, who presided over a cannibal island in the South Seas, measured the height of the tallest coconut tree on his domain by standing with his back to it and bending down, looking upwards between his legs. The angle he thus obtained was x degrees.

'Now, because of a sudden influx of missionaries to the island and the subsequent intake of this high quality protein by the cannibal chief, the girth of this worthy person increased considerably so that when he now carried out the measurement of the palm tree's height a considerable error of y degrees, caused by his sudden rotundity, became inevitable. Given the distance from the palm tree before ingesting the welcome protein as "z" feet find etc., etc.'

All M'Tutor's problems were as interesting and amusing, yet he never allowed any boy to presume on his good humour. His discipline was one arising from mutual respect between teacher and pupil.

The school itself was originally founded in the fifteenth century by Henry VI for scholars, and the College proper consisted of the classrooms and dormitories of the 'Tugs' as the scholarship boys were called. These buildings of Elizabethan brick formed three sides of the huge stone-cobbled quadrangle, with the large and beautiful Upper Chapel forming the other side.

The rest of Eton, including Lower Chapel and the houses in which we 'Oppidans' or fee-paying pupils, lived, had grown up round the College buildings and formed themselves into a small town, lying across the Slough to Windsor road and even spilling down into the long narrow High Street, where many small shops depended on the school for their existence.

The Oppidan buildings held the bulk of the 1,200-plus boys, and were divided up into about twenty-five houses, averaging thirty-five boys to each of them, with the College scholars making up the rest.

The whole school gave the impression of being the most expensive slum in Britain. But my entire picture of life there is, of necessity, coloured with images and memories of M'Tutor, many of which I shared with equally delighted school mates. For me, as my Uncle Billy, he remained unique, though I never once ever remember calling him that after I had arrived at Eton, or even right up to the year of his passing, in his eighties. I always called him 'sir' or 'M'Tutor'.

Twice during my school days he cycled, megaphone in hand, on his enormous pre-1914-war bicycle, straight into the Thames, while coaching the house rowing crews by pacing them along the tow path beside it.

Once he was arrested, at Bognor Regis I believe, for bathing in the nude, for he was a life-long believer in the healthy wonder of the human body. He delivered such a brilliant defence of his beliefs that it won him a fascinated magistrates' court and a very reduced fine.

During the First World War W.H.J., as he was known, had located by his own mathematical methods the whereabouts of Big Bertha, one of the giant guns that was bombarding allied targets from enormous distances. He was then an officer in the Royal Artillery, I presume. Eccentric as always, his boots were usually secured with string. For his brilliant services, and his never recounted bravery, he was awarded a decoration.

I remember asking him if he had received this at the hands of King George V.

'No,' said M'Tutor, thoughtfully. 'It actually arrived some time after the war, done up in brown paper and string, rather like a Yarmouth bloater.'

M'Tutor took a number of the boys in his house for what was known as Sunday Private, at which time he would read to us. Here was his only point of similarity with my former preparatory school headmaster. He read quite magnificently, such classics as *The Water Babies* and, sometimes, ghost stories by M. R. James, the provost of Eton at that time.

These ghost stories are still the most chilling and frightening things that I have ever read, and M'Tutor brought them completely to life. His object was not to frighten us, because he read them with a twinkle in his eye and told us, solemnly, to hang on to our chairs while he did.

The Water Babies or other great classics he would read, as completely absorbed as we were with the story until, suddenly, he would be overcome with some emotional passage and would cry quite openly. The book would immediately be taken from him by one of the older and more experienced boys, who would continue reading until M'Tutor had recovered his composure. Then Uncle Billy would continue to read on, quite unabashed by his emotional response to the words of the author.

That was the whole secret of M'Tutor. He was a completely honest and absolutely uncomplicated man of total sincerity and he expected everyone else to be the same. I don't know of one boy who was at his house, or up to him for maths, who doesn't share this view of him.

He lost his eldest son, the splendid Kenneth, at Dunkirk. The blow must have been almost mortal to a man as full of love as M'Tutor. I think I now understand fully myself what he went through. but he never let it interfere with his work nor let any bitterness affect him in any way. His example stood me in good stead, so many years later, and for that alone I could never thank him enough.

M'Tutor also believed, as Pop and I did, in the logical progression of the human soul after death.

'After all,' he said simply. 'It's such good logic – and such elegant mathematics.'

Eton itself I found a busy life and I never had time to be bored. There was so much to do in both work and sport. For any extra time you might have, there were so many other interests: Musical Societies over 500 strong, that gave rousing performances of *Acis and Galatea* and *The Revenge*; scientific conversations and Debating Societies, Astronomical Societies – the list is endless.

The masters, or beaks as they were called, were in themselves, another fascinating study.

They were all characters – from the Lower Master, Mr Conybeare, whose benign facial expression could turn to one of demoniacal fury at the blink of an eyelid – purely a nervous habit and not reflective of a character change – to Mr 'Jelly' Churchill, who reminded me of a very old tortoise, wrinkled neck and all, and who was so old that we believed he was immortal.

Don't get the impression that Eton wasn't tough. It was. And if you couldn't match up to it that was just too bad.

Early school started at 7.30, so you went to it, in winter, without breakfast and in the pitch dark. If you got down in time from your tiny room, for we slept alone, you grabbed a biscuit and a lukewarm cup of cocoa and your day had started.

Fagging and beating were part of the way of life, though I know M'Tutor was not in favour of the latter – but fagging never hurt anyone. Until you became an Upper boy, you all had to answer the cry of 'Boooooy!' that echoed through the house at intervals. You rushed madly along to its source where, if you were last to arrive, you were sent on some simple errand.

The beating by the house captain or library I resented, though

36

it was seldom unjustly used – and I set my mind to finding a simple chemical formula that would reinforce the natural resilience of my backside.

Together with another boy, who has since become a leading world industrial chemist, we came up with a preparation, the ingredients of which I swore never to divulge. This, when applied with a brush to the posterior formed a sufficiently flexible but impact-absorbing sheathing, that was proudly called 'Hard Arse'.

I merely saw it as a possible answer to temporary pain, but my friend, who obviously had the makings of a business tycoon – flogged it at half-a-crack – that is half-a-crown – a bottle. In modern coinage about 12½p.

Eventually this thriving business was discovered, and summary justice was once again administered, this time without protection of any kind.

We were beaten for different breaches of house or school regulations, and only major crimes entailed a birching by the Lower or Head Masters.

I remember once just escaping a beating by the head of my house. I eloquently proved that my pet tortoise had in fact not been dropped deliberately on to his head, which was fortunately protected by his top hat at the time, but must have either accidentally overbalanced out of my window box, where it lived, or had actually, due to loneliness during the mating season, committed suicide.

One of the biggest drawbacks to my time at Eton was naturally caused by my stammer, which was almost a total speech block. M'Tutor consulted Pop about it and, as a result, introduced me to a large ex-pupil of his called Mr Burgess. This extravagantly tall and impressive man was of early middle age and had studied speech therapy in Vienna. I also believe he later helped H.M. King George VI to overcome his appalling speech handicap.

In my case he took me, together with two other boys, through a series of speech exercises, which really do cure stammering. By using his methods, many years later, I have helped a number of very bad cases to cure themselves.

The trouble with all methods of speech therapy is that they take time to learn and this one probably takes the least time to acquire. It is so simple I will explain it here and you can judge for yourselves.

The stammerers' hardest hurdles are the consonants and the vowels, while the labials are much easier, and so it was in my case. K, T, D, B, etc., were hell to get out. The vowels also took a long time to get started.

Burgess's method was to put a sort of inaudible N in front of the consonants, in an ascending tone, so that you really said:

'N'can. N'do. N'bad, etc.' Not just flatly like that, but starting low and then raising the pitch of your voice to audibility, so that you finally hit the offending consonant, like a horse taking a jump.

The vowels you also approached in the same way – starting in low gear – this time with the vowel sound itself and then belting it out when you got up to your full speed. Words like 'owl' and 'eel' and 'ale', which before were almost unpronounceable, became quite easy after a bit of practice.

Invaluable if you needed an owl or an eel and indispensable if you were thirsty.

He gave us a new feeling of confidence in ourselves, by telling us that half our trouble stemmed from fear of people and made us picture important people who we might have to speak to as wearing only bathing shorts.

This certainly helped, though it did tend to turn you into a giggler, which might well bring the wrath of God down on you, especially if you were up in front of the Lower Master.

But it worked! Oh God! how blissfully well it worked.

We practised for about three halves, as the terms are called at Eton, and our improvement showed, in a kind of ritual speech which he taught us, embodying just about every difficulty the average stammerer faces. If I remember correctly it started: 'Ladies and gentlemen, all people in the whole world are crying for help!'

Burgess's method was summed up by him as: speaking with a swing and a rhythm and a pause and a run.

Finally, armed with the sentence, 'N'May I have a fish cake please?' I summoned up enough courage to enter the crowded Sock Shop, as the tuck shop was known.

Standing at the back of the crowd of milling boys – all busy ordering something to eat – I started my ascending N. Then suddenly, to a startled shopful of boys, my loud treble command rang out:

'N'May I have a fish cake please?'

'Corst you may,' said the amazed lady behind the counter. Beaming with pleasure, I ate the fish cake with every sign of relish, which was surprising, because I didn't really like fish cakes.

38

For the next month I ate one regularly every day, except Sunday, when the Sock Shop was closed – my appearance at the door being a sufficient signal for utter silence and then, together with me, a massed choir joined in my: 'N'May I have a fish cake.'

Eventually I graduated to multi-voiced renditions of, 'N'Banana split please!' and finally a triumphant chorale, 'N'Bangers and mash!'

The reason why we were all perpetually hungry wasn't due to an outbreak of Etonian tape worm, but to the immensely long time between after-early-school breakfast at 8.30 a.m. and lunch at two o'clock. Why? I never fathomed out!

Mass sport was never my cup of tea, but I enjoyed cricket, particularly bowling, and individual sport like Eton Fives, which is a hand-ball game played against a buttress and walls. M'Tutor, every year, played one game of fives, without wearing gloves – his tough hands, apparently, showing no visible damage.

Apart from the obvious school memories that everyone has, two things stand out clearly in my memory.

The first was the death of King George V, whose passing cast a pall of gloom over Windsor and therefore nearby Eton. The whole school moved up into the huge quadrangle, outside St George's Chapel, in Windsor Castle, to see the funeral procession which was the last time all the crowned heads of Europe and the World would ever be together, in one place. The long ceremonial cortège remains for me partly clear and partly hazy.

Eton supplied the guard of honour, within the courtyard, leading right up to the Chapel steps. Our O.T.C., the Officers Training Corps, in the distictive red-brown cloth uniforms and puttees, were supposed to stand at rigid attention, with the rifle reversed in front, and both hands laid crossed on the butt plate, while the head was lowered in military prescribed grief. But the odd eye peeked slyly out from below the down-slanted cap visors, to view, in schoolboy wonder, the unique procession of so many Kings, Queens, Princes and Princesses.

First came a small detachment of the Horse Guards – unmounted, at the slow march – in their plumed helmets and long cloak-like coats, with swords reversed.

Then, rumbling slowly over the gravelled asphalt, came the gun carriage, drawn by lines of bare-headed sailors, with the coffin seeming surprisingly small – for the King had not been a tall man.

Following this walked the four mourning sons – the Prince of

Wales and the Dukes of York, Gloucester and Kent, in the uniforms of the different services. Then I seem to recall a riderless horse with, quaintly, the boots reversed in the stirrups.

The Queen Mother, Queen Mary, and her daughter, in heavy mourning, passed us, dimly seen behind the closed windows of their carriage. After them came another carriage with the heavily veiled Duchesses.

The rest of the cortège was an alternation of walking Kings and carriage-borne black-veiled Queens, with a great long line of ambassadors and Maharajahs, Emirs and shieks, all shuffling along in that eerie silence, broken only by the snort of a horse, the creaking of the harness and the crunching of gravel, with the background of the soft weeping of the household staff behind us.

As we streamed silently back to school, I'm sure we felt intensely moved by it all, but then a thought flitted across my schoolboy mind, and I knew what that long procession of Kings and Queens and Princes and Princesses reminded me of – an endless Royal Flush!

However, even our young minds realised that we had see something out of history passing by, and that was indeed the last time for that extraordinary gathering of monarchs – many of whom passed so soon afterwards into the obscurity of exile.

The other memory I have was, not long afterwards, standing with the other boys in the library of M'Tutor's house in our dressing gowns, listening to Edward VIII's abdication speech over the small, oval, wooden-cabineted wireless set.

His voice comes back to me as he told us clearly and simply, in a breaking voice, why he was giving up his throne and I remember wondering what all the fuss was about – I still do, because I think he would have made a good King.

I never go back to Eton, now that M'Tutor is dead. When he left the school to which he had devoted his life, the Governors, or whatever they are, gave him a seemingly miserable pension. He had to continue to teach at Cranleigh. Even though this was the profession he loved – surely he could have been rewarded a little more handsomely for all the wonderful and unselfish work that he had done.

Another reason I never go back is that only a pitifully small number of us survived the war. Their names are among those carved on the backs of those many chairs in school hall, that had already acted as a practical memorial to all the Etonians killed in the First World War.

Among those who never made it home from the second holocaust was a boy at M'Tutors called Maudsley – who was blown up on the Eder Dam, while trying to destroy it with Dr Barnes Wallis's special spinning bomb. I remember him as a quiet scholarly type of boy, older than I was and a fine athlete. He wasn't the only one from M'Tutors to go – of my contemporaries at least a third were lost and more than that suffered major wounds.

Eton was no womb-like school that coddled and protected the young – far from it – its tough methods bred tough survivalists. To me, it was just another assault course to go over which is really very much how I had learned to look at my life, even at that early age.

In those days we wore top hats and short Eton jackets, with the wide white collar and black tie compulsory if you were under five foot tall. Tailcoats and narrower white collars and white bow ties were worn if you were over the regulation line of demarcation in height. As I started off under it and graduated to over it, this cost my hard-pressed parents two lots of clothes. Nowadays it is much simpler, I understand with the boys wearing the ordinary school cap and change coats and grey trousers and only wearing the other regalia for special days.

The top hat was the most useful of the old items, being a splendid place to keep ice-cream in summer, and white mice in winter.

The new topper had been produced by hand – by an Eton hatter who first put on your head a measuring machine, strongly reminiscent of something out of the Spanish Inquisition. This weird expanding device, made up of black rods in a hat shape, imprinted on paper, by means of needles, I think, the shape of the young head.

It really didn't seem to fit that well when you got it as most parents insisted on a size bigger to allow for growth and then you had to stuff the inside sweatband with paper.

Wearing it precariously at first on your youthful head, you walked blithely down the street – only suddenly to feel a violent impact and apparently suffer total blindness. This was caused by a skilled, heavy and older hand 'bashing' your top hat. so that it descended over your eyes and ears. Only the aid of a sympathetic passing boy rescued you from this frightening state.

The expensive top hat somehow survived this first assault and, somewhat battered, continued throughout your school life – I think, altogether, I had two.

Many of the boys were as eccentric as the beaks. We had one

lad who swam the Thames and tic-tacked a 'book', back to an enthusiastic crowd of punters on the other bank during the Windsor Races. Another young boy had a large and powerful frame that enabled him to object demonstrably to being beaten – by taking the cane away and upending and beating his older tormentor.

Then there was another lad of great wit and charm, who couldn't resist imitating the beaks and who was always being given endless lines to do because of it. An example of his method of handling these chores being:

'Boy! Stop imitating me and take two hundred lines.'

'Certainly, sir! A pleasure, sir! For you, sir – anything!'

'Boy! Take five hundred lines.'

'Five hundred it is, sir! Immediately, boy! I mean, sir!'

'Boy! You will write five hundred lines, twice.'

'With pleasure, sir.'

At this he would take out a worn pocket diary.

'Now let me see, sir. I have fifteen thousand lines for M'Tutor. Another twenty-five thousand lines, in round figures, for the Lower Master and a further forty-two thousand five hundred lines for sundry others. I can fit you in around 1968, sir! Will that be all right?'

Nine times out of ten he got away with it. He later died, most gallantly, in the Fleet Air Arm.

Another boy suffered from a loose sphincter ring and farted odiferously and repeatedly. What was worse, these effusions were silent and deadly to the unwary. The fight not to sit next to him was constant and, poor lad, we always sat him by the open window. But on hot days, even passing by that window on the outside was a job for quick feet.

I can't remember his name, nor would I be cruel to give it, but I recall his nickname was 'Oh, Jesus!' because that was the natural spoken reaction, when you found yourself, unwittingly, seated next to him.

With some beaks their eccentricity was anything but lovable. Anyone who has been up for Mathematics, to the deeply respected but much feared 'Bloody Bill', will remember this strange overtense man.

After my prep school experience I thought, 'Here we go again!' when this brilliant hawk-like being, of great height and lanky power, stood glowering before me at my first division with him with the question: 'Name, boy?'

I remained struck dumb – this being before my 'N' cure.

After my obvious visible struggle to get it out, he raised his eyes to heaven and said, 'Someone tell me the boys name!'

Immediately a chorus of Bentin! Bonkin! Burkett! – Baskett! and Blankett! burst forth. It was my first half and my name hadn't got around much.

'There seems to be some indecision about your name! Come here, boy, and write it on the blackboard.'

I got up, crimson with effort and did so, breaking the chalk in the process. By some freak of chance it happened to be the only piece of manageable sized chalk left.

'Bloody Bill' looked down at my name and the broken chalk from his enormous height and, trembling with an apparent irritation, which seemed to centre in his genitals, grated out, 'Bentin – odd name! – odd boy! – but you will be, while you are in my division – a good mathematician! Boy!'

And I never had any more trouble with him after that, as he took care to see that I was never put in such an embarrassing position again, until I could speak properly.

An oddball, I think one could appropriately call him; probably as frightened of us as we were of him.

The Academic standard was high at Eton if you wanted to learn, which I have always enjoyed doing, not because I was a goody-goody – but because I really got a tremendous kick from finding out.

If you slacked you could just about get away with it, for a time, but eventually you were found out and possibly 'sent down'.

Boys also mysteriously got 'sent down' from Eton, for various other reasons, mostly the subject of wild rumour, though one 'boy', genuinely was the victim of circumstance. His father, 'An Eastern Prince', had sent his small son to Eton, without anyone knowing that this diminutive youth was, in reality, about twenty-four years old! He looked about thirteen and had to wear jackets.

He possessed, so rumour also had it, sixteen wives and a white elephant. The theory was that the elephant was the reason he was 'sent down'.

So I spent my time at Eton absorbing knowledge and experience of tough discipline and hard work, while building up a healthy and fit body and a sound humorous approach to life and its attendant difficulties. I had, long ago, discovered that my ability to clown warded off a lot of wrath, if not pushed too far and I had, thank God, inherited my mother's strong sense of the ridiculous – especially where I was concerned personally.

I left Eton before my full time was up, only because financial conditions had deteriorated at home. When I found out about it, I didn't see the point of any further, and very real, sacrifice on my parents' part.

Uncle Billy, naturally, offered to board me for nothing. Pop, naturally, refused. And so with the many regrets from M'Tutor, who very much wanted me to run the full course, I left Eton. I was going to work full time with Pop, and to try and decide exactly what I wanted to do in life. This was obvious to me, if not to anyone else – I just wanted to work with my father, at anything he felt like investigating.

Though I had made many good friends at Eton – most of whom I was to lose in the war – I never regretted the final decision to leave early, a decision which, quite rightly, rested finally with me.

5. Things that went bump in the night

Absorbing knowledge from Pop was, for me, like putting blotting paper underneath a leaking bottle of ink. It poured out of him and I lapped it up. The marvellous thing about Father was that, as far as science was concerned, he never treated me like a child or a teenager but always as a colleague.

I was cramming for examinations at the time, and an hour with Pop was worth two weeks with the text books. His spectrum of knowledge was enormously wide and he had the enviable ability to extract the essence of things and then impart them concisely. It was wonderful to be home. I worked hard and, undoubtedly, I saw some wonders.

When I read *The Exorcist* quite recently I thought how frighteningly like our actual experiences with possession it had been. I discussed this at length, not long ago, with a well-known teaching psychiatrist, and he agreed that schizophrenia or split personality is totally different to the phenomena of possession I described. Here is one example:

Pop had become part of what he called a 'rescue' circle to help people who had got themselves into the sort of condition where, apparently, another entity had taken over their bodies and was completely controlling them.

One case I shall never forget was a publican in Dover whom I shall call L. He was a middle-aged man, of rather precise appearance, with a small waxed moustache, carefully brushed thinning hair, and so colourless a personality that he was almost invisible.

However, being a publican, he had to make something of himself to interest his customers and he found out that he had got a certain gift of prophecy. This was of a low-level nature, that is to say, worldly in the extreme and of a short time range. He could, for instance, predict the winner of the 3.30; unless he himself had a financial interest in the bet, in which case his own involvement would cancel out his emotional detachment and his prophetic power would cease.

To put it simply, this rather vain, normally practical and unimaginative man suddenly found himself the centre of interested attraction among the circle of customers in his pub. His vanity started to feed on his success.

'Come on, L, tell us the winners of today's races,' became the regular and eager demand. Usually he came up with one horse in the first three and, within a very short time, he was mentally asking for more and more information.

The odd 'inspiration' which had come to him became, because of his urgent insistence, an obsession. Slowly, in his own mind and even outwardly in his own appearance, he took on the mentality and personality of another entity. This entity was a very different one to his normally quiet rather insipid, but basically honest and precise self.

L. was never known to use a swear word, other than 'damn', before, but now he came out with every basic Anglo-Saxon adjective and noun in the whole dictionary of slang. He also became intemperate, whereas before he had been an extremely moderate drinker. This intemperance led to him becoming violent as well.

He had already developed his powers of prophecy by sitting in seance with his wife in the room above the saloon bar after the pub had closed for the afternoon, and was well on the way to becoming a case of total possession.

Up to now, according to medical science and contemporary psychiatry, here was a classic case of split personality – except for that extraordinary gift of short-range prophecy. Now the very real danger of dabbling with the occult showed itself in murderous rages – during trance. Upstairs in that commonplace room in Dover a demonic personality seemed to take over L. completely.

He smashed up the furniture and ordered his wife, whom he now often assaulted physically, to burn all the linen. He berated her with an unceasing flow of foul language and generally degraded himself to the level of a bestial sub-human.

At this point his terrified wife, who somehow had stuck it out till then – probably fearing scandal – went for help.

The local doctor could not help much. When he was called in, L. had returned immediately to his own personality and the doctor could only diagnose heavy drinking and advised him to stop.

46

In despair L.'s wife went to see a priest, who realised that there was something far more frightening than just an uncontrollable drunk.

Pop became involved when Eddie Partridge, a remarkable and truly saint-like local grocer, was also asked to help and he in turn roped in my father.

Eddie had been the subject of Pop's investigations, for some time. My father had become very fond of him and had great respect for this small, quiet, cheerful, Dover grocer, whose tiny shop sold everything from 'a needle to an anchor'.

Eddie, Pop, L. and his wife held a seance in the room where all the mischief was being made, and were helped by two well-balanced witnesses who were equally experienced in this sort of phenomenon. The sitting took place in broad daylight on a spring afternoon. Within a matter of minutes, L. had gone into a deep trance and was breathing heavily.

Suddenly, as Pop described it, the room became intensely cold – not an unusual condition, in paranormal phenomena and one which I had personally felt many times while sitting with Father. The intensity of this drop in temperature, however, was both rapid and alarming.

Immediately L. changed before their eyes.

With the added power of at least two other physical mediums present the entity manifested itself through L. at full intensity.

His thin ineffectual frame seemed to fill out and his rather scrawny neck swelled, while his face seemed to expand into a bloated travesty of his own features, which now took on a mottled colour.

At once the whole room, in Pop's words, 'stank of evil' and a rasping guttural voice, which actually seemed to reek of liquor, came vindictively from L.'s mouth. With every sort of vileness the personality heaped vocal filth on the circle of helpers.

Most people, confronted by this almost instant transformation, would have left at this point. But Eddie and Pop were very courageous men and their helpers were also experienced and resolute.

They let the entity take over L. completely and the trans-figuration became complete. In place of the quiet and nervous man sitting in the chair, was a big, brawling, drunken pig of a man, if you can grace such an entity with humanity.

Drooling, garrulous and truculent, with rolling reddened eyes and literally stinking breath, the entity came through completely, and took over the whole of L.'s body and mind.

By the sheer power of their spiritual forces, combined with their total lack of fear, the small rescue team confronted this daunting and offensive being with the power of truth and logic.

'I'm not dead!' the entity yelled. 'Look at me you bastards! I'm alive! I'm Old Pal, you – ! I'm alive, you – !' The entity continued pouring out a stream of invective while Mrs L., who had collapsed into tears, sobbed helplessly.

Then the entity tried to rise from the chair and grapple with them physically, but the tremendous positive force generated by Pop, Eddie and the helpers, seemed to bind it. This frightened the being controlling L. and the bullying tone soon gave way to a whining submission, which the rescue team knew was a sign that they'd won.

With simple but firm words, Eddie told the controlling force a few home truths and banished it from L.'s body. Within moments, in place of this foul abomination, there was L., sitting exhausted and limp in the chair.

When Pop woke him from his trance, L.'s gratitude was quite pathetic. Weeping uncontrollably, he joined the small group in a prayer of thanksgiving.

The coldness had left the room together with something else, as though a grey, chilling shadow had gone from their midst. Pop said he'd never felt so tired before and, after a short closing prayer, the circle broke up. Pop and Eddie left the sobbing L. in the hands of the helpers and his wife, who could hardly believe that the terrifying ordeal was over.

Schizophrenia or possession? The event took place more than forty years ago and I can only put down the bare bones of what happened, just as Pop told us the next day. The fact remained that, somehow, that poor bedevilled man was cured and would have been free of that terrible torment for the rest of his life, but for his own vanity.

The sad truth is that, after two or three months of grateful acceptance of his deliverance from evil, L. couldn't resist the many overtures of: 'What's the winner of the 3.30? Come on, old son! Lost your powers have you?'

Pop and Eddie had suggested that L. should change his job and give up being a publican – not that they suggested this job was in itself evil, but in L.'s case it just put too much temptation in his way. Had he been an alcoholic he would undoubtedly have complied with the suggestion, as that would have been plain common sense, but he honestly believed he had learned his lesson and could resist the return of such a condition.

The reverse, tragically, was the case, and L. found himself seeking the cause of his misery and degradation again.

He could indeed predict the winner of the races once more, but the cost was so terrifying that, this time, there was nothing anyone could do for him. A roaring, raging lunatic, L. was put away in the violent ward of the local asylum, where he was pronounced incurably insane and confined till his death, a short time afterwards.

In this case I wasn't an eyewitness, but I had met L. when Father had first been asked to help and I can confirm that his normal personality was exactly as I have described it. I accept, completely, what Pop told me had occurred and Eddie's later confirmation of it, because both of them were incapable of lying, or even embroidering the truth.

My own experience of a similar case was no less alarming and took place in 1937 in our own home in Folkestone.

This time the subject was a bridge-playing friend of Mother's, an early-middle-aged doctor called J. He had been for some considerable time in the Indian Army and had just retired and moved to Folkestone.

He was a nice quiet unassuming man, with a very good mind. He had recently married a charming girl and they were both delighted when they learned that she was pregnant.

He had, for some time, been intensely interested in the occult and had studied it extensively in India, though purely from an academic point of view.

On his return to England he had started to dabble himself, and had firmly believed that he was in complete control of his solitary investigations into the supernormal.

There lies one of the great dangers of this type of research: undertaking it alone and without assistance from people who have developed their own powers, slowly and carefully – themselves under constant observation and instruction from experienced researchers.

In Dr J.'s case it wasn't vanity, in any way, that led him to becoming involved personally with paranormal phenomena, but rather the sort of true spirit of the devoted researcher, that was my father's driving force.

He came to consult Pop on my mother's advice because, to his surprise and growing concern, he found that his control over the forces he believed he had contacted was becoming minimal.

The methods he used for communicating with the external entity were odd and original, to say the least. He had worked out a sort of code which involved his hands. Sitting alone, he had invited any outside intelligence to manifest itself by working his hands, which he held together in front of him with the fingertips touching.

He had chosen this rather unorthodox method because he could not move a table, nor did he wish to use either a ouija board or automatic writing. (In automatic writing, the entity seemingly manifests through your own hand which, holding a pencil or pen, scribbles at enormous speed on a block of paper.)

The code was simple – a sharp forward movement of the hands represented the vowel, one for A, two for E, three for I and a backward movements equally gave the consonants: one for B, two for C, three for D and so on. The extraordinary speed at which he did these movements was fascinating to watch and difficult to keep up with, but we could just manage to check with him, as he called out the letters and the words formed.

It was certainly an original and rather spectacular form of communication, if that is indeed what it was. Could it have been an expression of his own subconscious? Very possibly – until he started to test it out, fully, with predictive and prophetic applications.

His hands told him to go up to London on a certain train. Outside Charing Cross station, the London terminal from Folkestone, at a certain precise hour he would see a woman, minutely and clearly described, with a small dog.

To prove to himself it was just a manifestation of his own imagination, Dr J. duly caught his train and arrived in London – to be confronted, at the exactly predicted moment, with a woman, precisely as described, complete with a small dog.

He was to taken aback that, by the time he had collected himself, she had disappeared in the crowds around the station entrance.

This shook him considerably and he decided to leave well alone – but to his horror he found himself waking in the night, with his hands in front of him, fingertips touching and working away.

He had become possessed, or, if you prefer it, schizophrenic. But what a very unusual form of schizophrenia it was! In no way, other than in the uncontrollable behaviour of his hands in the middle of the night, or while sitting alone in his study, had this contained, intelligent and charming doctor been mentally affected.

When he came to see Pop about this phenomenon, my father

sensed immediately that here was a case of 'overshadowing', rather than possession and that Dr J. had indeed contacted and become attached to another entity.

Pop also picked up that there was nothing intensely evil, as there had been the tragic case of L. in Dover and my father knew how we could best help Dr J.

He enlisted the help of my mother, my brother and myself. In full late afternoon daylight, we 'sat' with Dr J.

I have since confirmed, with my brother, many of the details of that extraordinary sitting. As closely as we can both remember that scene, nearly forty years ago, here are the simple facts.

After a short prayer, Pop asked Dr J. to demonstrate, if possible, a contact with the overshadowing entity. Within a few minutes, the doctor's hands started to move at an increasing speed, backwards and forwards.

Dr J. spelled out the words, as he replied to Pop's simple questions. These related to who the entity was – name, age – type of person, his background, etc. Slowly there emerged a strange picture of an Indian in his late twenties who had passed on as a result of a violent death – his occupation being that of a professional wrestler!

At this point in the sitting, Dr J. passed into a light trance and an audible voice, quite different from his own, came from his lips. The language was not English and was obviously another tongue. This, again, could have been due to the Doctor's subconscious, because he spoke Hindustani fluently from his long service in India.

Then suddenly the whole sitting became electrifyingly alarming, as Pop asked. 'Can you tell us something about your death?'

Immediately the quiet unassuming Doctor hurled himself, without any warning, on to the floor and twisted himself into the most terrifying position that I have ever seen a live body assume.

In complete silence, other than Mother's gasp of astonishment, the body of Doctor J. seemed to completely dislocate his spinal column – then he screamed!

We were about to rush forward to help him but Pop ordered us back in a firm, commanding voice. In complete control of the situation, he knelt beside the tortured body of the Doctor and, laying his hands on him, said a simple prayer.

Doctor J.'s body untwisted itself and, at Pop's nod, my brother and I helped him back into his chair, noticing for the first time that his eyes were staring fixedly.

He sat in the chair for a minute or two, while Pop stood behind him and gave him healing. My father made certain passes with his hands, which apparently helped to remove the condition linking the two entities together.

Pop's voice once again was firmly commanding, as he forced the possessing being to leave the Doctor alone and to stop influencing his hands.

When the entity started struggling violently and weeping loudly, a thing absolutely alien to the personality of the intelligent and experienced Doctor, Father instantly demanded total obedience and his strong tone of voice and utter control of the proceedings seemed to put a rapid dampener on the being's resistance.

Then, in the blink of an eye, we all felt that something had left us – an actual physical feeling that something had gone from us, and there, sitting exhausted in the chair was the Doctor that we knew and respected.

He was totally unaware that anything had taken place at all.

The whole thing seemed suddenly so normal, that Mother suggested that we have a cup of tea. Pop took Doctor J. to the bathroom and made him run his hands, up to the elbows, under the cold tap while he completed certain simple banishing rituals.

When Doctor J. rejoined us, he was like a man reborn, to coin an old but apt phrase. The rather nervous and anxious man of an hour before had been supplanted by the cheerful quiet person of our everyday lives and we gave him a warm welcome back.

Possession or schizophrenia? Again, with only these written details to go on, it would be difficult for anyone, but those of us who were there, to judge. But I will never forget the terrifying position of that doctor's twisted body as the controlling entity acted out how he died, presumably during a wrestling match; nor that dreadful scream that was forced from his lips.

And how does one explain the fact that, having undergone that extraordinary physical experience, the Doctor felt no residual pain or ill effects whatsoever?

The predictive ability that he had developed through his hands, under control, is another odd thing to explain. The woman with the dog outside Charing Cross station, for instance?

The outcome was a happy one. The Doctor never again dabbled in the occult, though he continued to maintain a lively interest in the academic study of it and often assisted father in testing mediums. And shortly after the sitting, his wife presented him with a fine child (I'm afraid I cannot remember whether the baby was a boy or a girl).

Not all our paranormal experiences were as alarming, however. Mother, for instance, had a special way of dealing with phoneys, of which we had plenty. They had convinced themselves that they had supernormal powers, and they really deserved the shaking they got from Ma.

One I remember well was a self-opinionated and largely constructed lady who had set up business locally as a clairvoyant and who had been recommended to Mother by some over-anxious dupe.

I was sitting with them, when Ma pounced and the fake medium got the *coup de grâce*.

This florid woman had started off by going into an over-played trance threshold, with much heavy breathing and grunting and groaning, a travesty of even the most physical of mediums.

Then, presumably figuring out Mother's age fairly accurately, she started to whisper hoarsely: 'War! War!'

Ma's bright eyes, which could be so warm and humorous, hardened perceptibly, and her nose became 'beaky' – her description of this warning condition that she was on the warpath.

'War? Yes! What about the war?' said Mother sweetly, with just the right amount of interest.

'War! Lost in war!' went on the woman, feeling she was on to a good thing.

'Ah! Is that you, Obadiah?' asked Mother eagerly.

'Yes,' said the medium hoarsely. 'Obadiah! Obadiah!'

'How lovely to speak to you, Obadiah,' exclaimed my mother, warming up for the kill.

'And you too – lovely to speak to you – Obadiah is so happy – so happy here – speaking to you!' the medium continued.

'It's a real miracle,' declared Mother. 'What a wonderful thing, Obadiah, to hear your voice, at last!'

'Yes. Yes. Wonderful – Obadiah is so happy to speak to you,' repeated the large female phoney – burning her last bridge. 'As you say – a miracle!'

'I should think so too,' said Ma, in a cool clear voice. 'Obadiah's a dog!'

Mother had no mercy on the phoneys who battened on the grief-stricken, but was the most understanding and co-operative of people, when she was dealing with the all-too-rare genuine mediums who came to us. And she knew which was which. For the self-deluded she always had a courteous but firm attitude and quickly cut things short if she found them wasting Pop's time.

Her jolly and plump presence, with those arresting blue eyes and mobile mouth, so often crinkling with laughter, belied her appalling migraine attacks, which could lay her low for 48 hours of misery.

Ma was such a sudden victim of these vicious bouts that, in the early days of their marriage, a local doctor actually believed Father was poisoning her. One moment the doctor would see her well and fit – her ebullient self – and then, within an hour, would be called to her bedside to give her an injection to put her temporarily out of her obvious misery.

The attacks were at longish intervals however, and, after a two-day period of darkness, Ma would climb back to her usual pinnacle of good humour.

She herself had not yet had a 'mystical' experience, as it is fashionable to call it nowadays, but had witnessed an enormous amount of supernormal phenomena.

She firmly believed in survival and helped Pop throughout his long and arduous researches, with unfailing good humour though I knew how much it cost her in behind-the-back ridicule and bitchy gossip from the Folkestone circle of bourgeois society.

Pop's firm decision never to change his nationality from Peruvian to British, which many people had urged him to do, also caused problems. These started in the 1914–18 war, in which he was engaged on highly secret work for the Aeronautical Inspection Department, which he had helped to form, and followed him right through to the Second World War, costing Mother and Pop their home in Folkestone.

As an alien, Father had to register at the local police station, where he was domiciled. Because he was Peruvian, under the existing laws of that country, both my brother and I held dual nationality.

That's why I claim to be the only Peruvian ever born in Watford.

Pop's investigations into psychic phenomena also brought him under the due suspicion of the local constabulary. The abominable Witchcraft Act was still in force at that time, and even the most respectable of researchers could be scrutinised under its medieval charter. It wasn't repealed till long after the Second

World War, and Father was one of the stern fighters against this barbarous and uncivilised Act,

Ma's only true experience of pure physical mediumship actually happening to *her*, occurred during a sitting in 1938 at Eddie Partridge's house, which was really a part of his little shop. This particular seance was held in darkness, something none of us were keen on, as it did invite trickery. But both my mother and father fully accepted sitting in any conditions with Eddie and his vivacious wife Biny, because of the complete honesty of these lovely people.

At this seance, held in Eddie's back room in Dover, Pop and Ma and Eddie and his tiny wife were present. There was, I believe, one other sitter, who was well known to them all and who I think was called 'Pop' Walker, a seaman from Dover and a member of the local lifeboat crew; himself a wiry man but by no means large.

During the sitting various entities had manifested, among them Eddie's child guide.

Now I don't particularly go for child guides, as they are so easy to fake, but I totally and unreservedly accept Eddie's. He was himself such a marvellously uncomplicated person that, under a system of natural spirited law, where like attracts like, Eddie would naturally, as he did in his everyday life, have a very strong bond with children.

Mother had just been thinking, she told me later, how exciting it would be really to experience some form of physical phenomenon, like levitation, when she was whisked out of her chair up into the air – no mean feat, when you consider she was all solid woman. Then she was carried safely over the top of the table, round which they were all sitting, and finally deposited lightly on to the lap of the surprised sitter on the other side of it.

Her gasp of surprise brought the sitting to a close. When Eddie put the lights on, there was Ma, somewhat shaken but delighted by her experience directly opposite where she had originally been sitting.

To have performed this feat in daylight would have required at least four of us, because we tried it. In darkness it would have been impossible to do it without someone or something else being struck by her 'flight' through the air. I am certain that between them Pop, Eddie and the other sitter could never have done it successfully, for Mother tipped her scales at around eleven ston .

She also told me she felt no pressure, such as would be made by hands holding her; just a feeling of actually flying. I accept her word, unreservedly, just as I did Pop's and Eddie's and his wife's, when they described the experience to me to corroborate Ma's story.

Anyway, why should they all get together to fool me, a 17-year-old boy?

*　*　*

So, as the world rushed headlong towards those dreadful years of war, I passed my late teens in work and research with Father and the crammers – learning as much as I could about science, in every branch of it that I could lay my mind to and, in particular, what is now called parapsychology.

Pop always said I was educated off the back of cigarette cards, which is a very good description of my basic scientific disciplines in which there are gaps you could drive a double-decker bus through.

But I do have sufficient background, in general science, to just about cope with the many situations I find myself involved in outside show business. Whenever I need the gaps in my knowledge filled up, sure enough, along comes someone well qualified to do so and off we go again!

I think, probably, my main job in life is to act as a catalyst – to make things happen – or as some people prefer it – a short fuse!

The banana skin could well be some sort of safety device, in case I go too far in any one direction.

6. Signs and wonders

My brother Tony, with whom I have always had a treasured and happy relationship, also helped Pop with his researches, proving to be a powerful medium in the process.

Bro and I had enormous fun together, even though he was six years older than I, and he had taught me to draw almost as soon as I could hold a pencil. A fine artist himself, with an excellent pictorial imagination, Bro fascinated me with his abilities.

He was also a wonderful companion and the inventor of many games which we played together with great gusto. These ranged from model gliders and kite flying, through unconventional forms of cricket, in which he was a cunning slow bowler of great ability, to complicated indoor table-top manoeuvres with soldiers and sand trays, which would now be classed as war games.

Chess was a passion with him, and such small skill as I have with it today I owe to him. (Pop was a fine chess player himself and he and Uncle Billy often played multiple games blindfolded.)

The most extraordinary display of my brother's mediumship happened one summer's afternoon in 1935 or 1936 when the father of one of my preparatory school friends came round to see Pop about a personal problem.

Mr B. was a widower, compact and middle-aged, of orthodox Jewish parents. A man of great integrity, who was much respected in Folkestone.

I remember, on that particular afternoon, he had come to tea to discuss his concern over his relationship with his son Neville, a quiet, handsome lad whose quick mind, and shy willingness to do his share in any of our hare-brained pastimes at school, had made him one of my friends.

I wouldn't have joined the discussion except that Mr B. asked me for my own opinion of Neville who was, apparently, becoming rebellious, in direct contrast to his normal quiet obedience.

Mr B. was obviously intensely worried over the whole matter and I was treating it lightly. After all, Neville was growing up and, like all young lads, wanted to stretch his wings a bit. Pop was backing me up.

At this point my brother came in from bowling at the local cricket club nets. The conversation about Neville ceased as Tony joined us for a cup of tea.

Up to now the whole scene was really one of routine normality in any household. Then, in a moment, the whole atmosphere changed.

In the warm summer afternoon sunlight my brother simply sat back and went into a trance.

The whole thing was so sudden that I thought he had just closed his eyes but, within seconds, he started to breathe deeply and regularly. I knew that these were the signs of his going into a deep trance.

Abruptly his face took on a darker and older appearance and the room seemed to fill with a strong sense of presence – and peace.

Then, slowly and sonorously, my brother started to speak – in a language utterly alien to either Father or me.

Pop gestured to me to remain with them, but I was far too fascinated to be frightened. I knew all my brother's accents and pseudo-languages that we used for fun and this strange deeply moving voice was unlike anything I had ever heard.

Its effect on Mr B. was arresting, as he somewhat haltingly started to reply, in what was obviously the same language but not either as fluent or as unhesitating, as though he was searching for half-forgotten phrases.

My brother or whoever had control of his body, responded warmly to these replies and the conversation continued, in the form of a flowing dialogue from my brother's lips, and questions and hesitant replies from Mr B.

This must have gone on for some twenty minutes or so, while Mr B. was obviously totally unaware of anything, other than that extraordinary deep melodious voice and the strange language it spoke. All the time, however, tears were coursing down his cheeks and he was clearly deeply moved.

At the end of the conversation, for that is what it was, my brother rose from the arm-chair and, as Mr B. stood in front of him, he laid his hands on the small weeping man's head and gave him a blessing.

You didn't have to understand the language to recognise that from the gestures and the tone of voice.

Then Bro sat back into the chair again and, breathing heavily came out of the trance – completely unaware that anything out of the ordinary had occurred, and, obviously, somewhat embarrassed to find our guest now weeping uncontrollably and being comforted by Father.

Pop told Bro to go and have a cold wash and Tony sensed that something must have happened but, when I made to follow him, Pop signed to me to stay.

It took some minutes for Mr B. to calm down sufficiently to speak and then he said: 'Do you swear on your son's life, Adam, that your elder son has no knowledge of Hebrew?'

Pop quietly reassured our shaken guest that this was so and Mr B. turned to me: 'And you, Michael? Do you speak any Hebrew at all?'

I told him 'No!' and that the only Hebrew word I knew was 'shalom' which Neville had taught me.

'Then,' said Mr B., 'I have no doubt at all that through your elder son I have spoken to my Rabbi, who I knew and loved as much as my own father. He has told me that all will be well with Neville and this has convinced me for ever of survival. I can never thank you or your family enough for the miracle I have experienced here today.'

There it is, simply and factually stated, as well as I can remember the details. Tony, unfortunately, having been the trance medium, cannot confirm the facts, other than that he remembers the occasion, the fact that he came in from cricket practice and then nothing more, till he woke up to find Mr B. in tears and Father telling him to go and run his hands under the cold tap – a procedure Pop always recommended after a trance or healing session.

My father, and presumably Mr B. too, have both passed over, so there is one eyewitness left – me – and I can only say that those are the facts, as accurately as I can recall them.

Tony also had a terrifying experience at home in 1938, which happened by the strangest of coincidences.

He had been out at a late party, and didn't want to rouse the household when he returned in the small hours of the morning.

He let himself in with his key and gently crept upstairs and, rather than wake me up in the room that we shared when he was home from his studies at the Royal College of Art, he decided to spend the rest of the night in the small room at the top of the

59

stairs that Pop had set aside for psychic phenomena. This had been a bedroom but was kept sparsely furnished and spotlessly clean. It contained a curtained alcove for a medium to sit in during tests for physical mediumship, and a bed for the subject of the test to relax on, should he so wish.

As Tony silently climbed the stairs he was, of course, well aware of the use to which the little room was put, decided he had nothing to fear.

He opened the door and, in the pitch darkness of the room, he became abruptly aware of something small and white moving towards him. At the same time a strong smell of sulphur assailed his nostrils. Before he could close the door, the white sulphurous presence had hurled itself at him.

Tony gave a blood curdling shriek, which echoed from top to bottom of our modest home and brought all of us bolt upright in our beds, bringing Pop rushing out of his bedroom door, followed by Ma close behind, and sending me to the bottom of my bed and well under the bedclothes.

What had happened was that one of our Scottie dogs had developed a skin rash, and had made her back raw by rubbing it under the gas stove in the kitchen. Mother had applied the recommended ointment of sulphur and zinc, and then had bandaged the old Scottie's back with torn-up sheets. She finished by wrapping the dog up in a broad strip of this material and putting her, for the night, in the little room.

My poor brother nearly died of sheer fright when the dog, who adored him, smelt him coming, even over its own effluvium of sulphur – and joyously hurled itself at Tony's chest.

* * *

About eighteen months before the war actually broke out, we had seen a very remarkable demonstration of what was described as transfiguration mediumship. This again happened in full light – which is the most evidential form of paranormal occurrence for me, because it minimises trickery – and the subject under test was a medium from London called Mrs Balmer.

This very straightforward and ordinary person has left very little impression on my memory, but her strange gift has left a lasting one. I checked the facts with my brother, who witnessed her demonstration at the local spiritualist church, but not the one at our home. The particulars differ only in detail, rather than in essence.

The seance consisted of about eighteen people sitting in our drawing room. It was held on a sunny afternoon, with the medium seated in a wooden chair in the corner of the room. The sitters, who were composed mainly of interested and scientifically trained friends of Father's, together with their wives, were gathered in a half circle in front of her.

To provide photographic evidence Pop had one camera, Doctor J. another and Michael Tomlinson – David's elder brother – a third. They were, if I remember correctly, all using the then new fast panchromatic film – either in the form of a roll of film, as in Dr J.'s and Michael's cases, or made up as quarter plates, as in Pop's case. Anyway as near as Tony and I can recall there were three cameras to cover the sitting. Obviously there must have been plenty of light, or the film would not have been exposed, for none of the photography was being done by flashlight, a clumsy business in those days.

In due course Mrs Balmer went into a deep trance. Almost immediately, people began to exclaim as they saw or recognised faces forming over her own.

I can only describe what I saw, which was that the medium's face seemed to go out of focus and then another face appeared for a short while, then that in turn would blur and vanish, to make way for yet another. The effect was most startling and I closed my eyes several times to make sure that it wasn't some malajustment of my own vision. But, as everyone else was excitedly pointing out the different visual transfigurations, I can only assume I was seeing them too.

While Pop, Doctor J. and Michael took their pictures, the reactions of the sitters were most interesting, as the faces of small girls, a naval officer, an elderly woman and many others appeared superimposed on the face of the medium.

They were definitely not just the result of Mrs Balmer pulling faces, as their delineation was absolutely clear and so startingly different as to rule this out completely.

When you consider that the medium received something like five guineas for the weekend demonstration, she was hardly doing it for the money. With that gift, any showman could have sold out every seat in the Albert Hall.

When the hour-long sitting was over, we all had a buffet tea. Mrs Balmer had a rest and we compared notes.

One or two of the sitters had not seen a thing, other than the blurring of the medium's face. This apparently, is normal, as people are so different in their perceptive make-up.

The result we all waited excitedly for was centred around the photographs and their development. When these were compared, on the following day, the results were equally extraordinary and puzzling.

I can only speak for the ones I saw, those being Pop's half-dozen exposed plates and Doctor J.'s film. Michael's I never saw.

Both Pop's quarter plates and Doctor J.'s roll of film were fogged, as though by intense radiation of some unknown wavelength. Had the radiation been of a familiar one, it was so strong that material damage must have been done to the sitters in that room.

But, and here is the extraordinary thing, two plates of Pop's were clear and unfogged and two pictures out of Doctor J.'s roll of twelve exposures were also clear. These were the ones taken at the start and the end of the sitting – and, in both cases, they showed Mrs Balmer sitting in the chair. The ones exposed during the sitting, when the phenomena was taking place, were all densely and completely covered with fogging, as though they had been exposed to X-rays of great intensity. As this was impossible, for obvious reasons, the only other explanation was that the phenomenon itself produced some form of radiation which, while harmless to human beings, could fog photographic emulsions.

In this sort of way those immediately pre-war years passed for me, full of interest and fascination, and busy as could be.

With the rapid approach of the war itself, which many reckoned would indeed be Armageddon, naturally I felt a deep sense of disquiet and mounting tension – but reassurance was given to me in a strange and rather wonderful way.

I had been with Pop on a trip to Dover to see Eddie Partridge in the August of 1939. We had stayed late, while Eddie fascinated me with his simple explanations of the purpose of life and his descriptions of various exciting and unusual experiences, that he had taken part in.

He sensed that I was disturbed and strangely excited by the coming events that we all felt so strongly were about to happen and, late that evening, he asked Pop if he would drive us a little way out of Dover, because he wanted to show me something. The summer was far advanced and the night had that perfect stillness that is the all too rare blessing of this season in southern England.

Only a few miles away Eddie asked Pop to pull in, off the side of the road. Leaving the car, we proceeded on foot towards a small but dense wood.

The darkness was velvety and lit by starlight and a three quartering moon, with little or no cloud. The silence was so absolute as to be noticeably broken only by the sound of our own footsteps and our swishing passage through the late summer bracken.

Eddie went first, I followed and Pop brought up the rear. In this Indian file, we entered the wood without speaking. Somehow words seemed completely out of place.

In a few minutes, even in the darkness of the tree-packed wood, we had come to a clearing almost in the centre. Here the still starlit night was so impressive that I literally found myself catching my breath.

Eddie, whom I could see quite clearly in the moonlight, turned silently towards me. He smiled in that wonderful encouraging way of his and, somehow, indicated that this is what he wanted to show me.

An intense longing seemed to fill me and I knew that I was about to witness something natural and wonderful.

In the middle of the softly lit clearing, at a moment of utter stillness, Eddie gave a short low cry, halfway between a whistle and a word.

Instantly, every bird and beast and animal and insect that lived in that wood replied in a great chorus, that sounded like a shout of loving welcome.

It was so unexpected and so deeply moving that I found myself in floods of happy tears. I turned to my father and saw that he too was crying with joy as well.

Then Eddie laughed, a lovely happy chuckling sound that echoed round the clearing, and the bird song and animal squeals and barks and the chittering of the insects slowly stilled.

It was a moment of pure magic. My earlier sense of foreboding had left me, like a vanishing mist before the warmth of the sun.

I shall never forget that.

7. Three men in an ambulance

When the war came the Bentines were ready for it. I knew things were serious because Father had sawn the ping pong table in half and covered the windows of our front rooms with it. He had also stuck strips of brown paper over the glass itself which, as it was already in leaded frames, gave the inside of our house the lighting of a catcomb.

My brother Tony joined the army as a gunner. I, naturally, thought I would soon follow him, as a volunteer. But I was to find out that volunteering is one thing and actually getting into the Services another.

I clearly remember that first interview with what the Royal Air Force called an Aircrew Selection Board. It took place, up in London, in one of those imposing annexes to Adastral House, Kingsway. Spotty but spruce, I nervously took my seat opposite the three R.A.F. officers who comprised the Selection Board.

At first everything went well, especially the Old Etonian bit, because at that time the R.A.F. was extremely snobbish. The men in blue smiled benignly at this eager applicant – and I'm sure the fact that, as a child, I had flown with Sir Alan Cobham almost convinced them that here was Icarus reborn.

Then came the crunch – Father was a Peruvian. At this news a cloud seemed to settle over the selectors – they fidgeted uneasily. The senior officer present, an aged flight lieutenant, spoke in a voice of doom.

'You are not of pure European descent,' he said accusingly.

'Well, even in this light I can almost pass for white,' I replied brightly.

This pleasantry was greeted with stony silence.

'Thank you! We'll let you know,' said the elderly flight lieutenant nodding curtly at a warrant officer, who hurried me from the room.

From then on I volunteered about once every four months, at various enlistment centres around the country – pointing out that my brother was already in uniform, with the Honourable Artillery Company, and that surely this must influence my own acceptance into the Service. But each time we came up against Father's origins the axe fell and all was silence.

While I waited anxiously for news of the outcome of yet another attempt to enlist, Pop suggested that he and I should join the A.R.P. – the Air Raid Precautions organisation – and we duly presented ourselves at the headquarters, which was the Pavilion at Folkestone's cricket ground where we had often watched the great Australians playing at visiting Test matches.

As the A.R.P. weren't as particular as the R.A.F., we soon found ourselves issued with armbands, tin helmets, one-piece overalls and gas masks and told to get on with our first job, which was sand-bagging the pavilion building till it looked like a World War One dugout.

This nearly killed Father, who suffered badly from asthma and couldn't wear a gas mask for long.

We had been issued with a mask which was a cut above the ordinary civilian issue. The civvie mask was a cheap looking thing of thin rubber with a plastic window and a metal filter, all of which fitted into a cardboard box. Our model was a moulded rubber mask with goggle eye-pieces and an exhaling device which looked and sounded exactly like a child's 'raspberry' blower. It also had a moulded-in bit, which allowed a telephone to be used. This produced a marvellous effect with the exhaling blower.

'Operations here (Brrrp), speaking. We're sending a (Brrrp) right away. Stand by your (Brrrp), and we'll be with you in about (Brrrp) minutes. Roger and (Brrrp).'

This, with tin helmets and anti-gas hoods on our heads and oilskin overalls tucked into heavy rubber boots and anti-gas gloves, made the ideal outfit for sandbagging the pavilion.

I could tell Pop was having a bad time. The raspberries coming from his blower, as he exhaled, were followed by a muffled wheezing as he tried to inhale. I just got the mask off him as he was about to pass out.

At that moment the siren went: a chilling and mournful dirge. It was a false alarm, but Pop, who was a glutton for punishment, jammed on his gas mask as per our orders and dashed out with the first stretcher party. He returned shortly afterwards. On the stretcher.

5

That put paid to Father's A.R.P. career, but not quite yet to mine.

In all modesty, I must say that I took to the A.R.P. like a duck to water. Having some vague knowledge of anatomy and a reasonable memory I was soon given charge of an ambulance team, average age 18, including the driver. That is to say the one with the driving licence. We all three took turns at learning to drive it – quite unofficially that is – and nearly wrecked it because our ideas of ambulance driving were highly coloured by watching American movies. We only used two speeds – flat out and reverse.

Bell clanging, we would set off on various A.R.P. exercises. As soon as we were safely out of sight of the hospital, our old Army ambulance careered erratically along at a bone shaking and near suicidal forty miles an hour.

The last time we took it out remains engraved indelibly on my memory. It also put paid to my career as an angel of medical mercy.

The day's master plan called for us to patrol the Leas – the long lush grassy strip to Folkestone's cliff tops. The Leas were bordered on one side by a road that fronted the long line of white hotels and boarding houses and, on the other, by the steep cliffs that fell sheer down to the lower road and the pebbly beaches.

This lovely part of the seaside town was very popular with young and old alike, but was an obvious favourite with the many retired naval officers who lived in Folkestone. They could be found strolling along the Leas, gazing out enviously at the great ships passing up and down the Channel.

We had stopped the ambulance for a quick smoke. I reported back our position from a phone box. Then I set out to find a suitable volunteer to be an air raid casualty. Someone who would be public spirited enough to not mind being splinted and bandaged and driven back at high speed to our eager colleagues at the hospital.

That morning the Leas was nearly deserted but, eventually, an elderly naval type hove into sight. I stopped him and asked politely if he would help us out. His honest, tanned face watched me kindly as I stammered out my request.

Perhaps it was his sympathy as I struggled with the word 'casualty' that eventually won him over. It could just as well have been the devil himself that persuaded him to agree.

Within a few moments he was lying on a thoughtfully pro-

66

vided army blanket, his bowler hat clasped on his stomach, while we bandaged and tourniquetted and splinted him at high speed.

He even listened, with interest and tolerance, while I described his injuries – my stammer miraculously, as always, disappearing, in the heat of the moment.

'Fractured femur, due to bomb blast,' I rapped out, efficiently. 'Severed femoral artery – pressure and tourniquet applied, haemorrhage arrested.'

I carefully wrote these grisly particulars on a label and tied it to his top coat button, completing my job, as per the First Aid book, by marking the letter T, for tourniquet, with an eyebrow pencil on his forehead.

I stood up and took my position at the head of the stretcher on to which we had moved him.

'We'll soon have you safe and sound in bed, sir,' I said confidently. As the old gent smiled, I nodded my head crisply to my two mates. My tin helmet slid off my head, like the blade of some blunted guillotine, and smacked down with a heavy clunk, on the top of his head.

Without a sound he passed out like a light, breathing heavily through his nostrils.

For the blink of an eye I stood rooted to the spot, then some inner instinct – perhaps the devil again – took over. I bent down and diagnosed a possible fractured skull, certainly severe concussion and extensive bruising of the scalp. I actually wrote this on the back of the label attached to his coat button, while my two mates, speechless with shock, stood there trembling.

Apart from our shaken group, we were alone and it was the work of a few moments to hurriedly blanket wrap our casualty – or victim – and rush him into the ambulance.

This ancient vehicle had seen better days. So it came as no surprise when the stretcher stuck about two thirds of the way into the racks designed to take it.

As we pushed and shoved the reluctant stretcher our patient stirred uneasily in his unconsciousness and groaned audibly, indicating that something was wrong. We stopped our efforts and examined the stretcher closely – to find that two of our patient's fingers were now jammed immovably in the runners.

At that moment my nerve snapped.

'Get him to the hospital before we kill him,' I gasped – unkindly including the other two in my crimes.

Closing the ambulance doors as far as they would go, I pulled off my tie and knotted it securely across the handles. Then I dashed over to the phone box to warn the hospital that the casualty was real and in urgent need of emergency treatment.

As I got through to the doctor in charge I heard the engine, always a reluctant starter, churn over and fire intermittently. Then to my relief, the motor caught and was revved up hastily — while the fierce grinding of gears indicated the driver was impatient to get away.

'Get going,' I yelled, signalling frantically from the phone box.

At last the clutch went in, with a bang, and away swayed the ambulance, coughing and rattling as it rapidly picked up speed.

'They're on their way,' I croaked excitedly into the phone as the ambulance took the corner of Earls Avenue at high speed, lurching over madly, with screaming tyres.

Goggle eyed, I watched my tie tear apart. The two doors swung open. Like a torpedo from a submarine's tubes, the stretcher and its blanketed burden shot out and crashed into the base of Harvey's statue.

As I looked at the silent tableaux of the wreckage at the foot of the great physician's memorial, I knew somehow that I would never be a doctor.

Thank God this story has a relief-filled if not hilariously happy ending. The elderly naval hero survived to walk the Leas again. Such are the qualities of this sturdy breed that he forgave us — and even more amazingly didn't sue me for damages.

I shall always think of him as a perfect example of a noble soul, responding to that ancient cry of 'Forgive them Lord for they know not what they do'.

8. Positively for one week only

The A.R.P. experience had shaken me, deservedly, to the core. But within a matter of days, the plight of the Allied Forces at Dunkirk drove everything else from my mind. We could clearly hear the guns across the Channel, and even see smoke and flashes of explosions from Boulogne. Everyone flocked down to the harbour to help as the battered ships limped in.

As fate would have it, I had to go to London University to sit some exams and travelled up on a train packed with grubby and exhausted troops. Standing in the corridor I wondered why they were so quiet. Grey-faced with strain, the soldiers just slumped in their seats, smoking or sleeping. No questions were asked; none would have been answered. It made an eerie contrast to the rows of anxious friendly faces that lined the back yards and gardens of the houses we passed through on the long run-in from the London suburbs to Charing Cross.

It seemed that everyone cared deeply about these troop trains. Though the dirty and unshaven passengers were past caring about anything, the anxiously watching people waved little flags and shouted dimly heard greetings and blessings. It was so compelling that, ridiculous though it may seem now, I felt I had to do something in return, and waved and smiled back – not for myself, an inept and unsuccessful volunteer, but for all the 'real' soldiers, sailors and airmen of my own age who sat hunched up and battle-shocked inside the long lines of green Southern Railway carriages.

In London, I stayed with my sister-in-law and tried to keep my mind on the examination at London University. But my eyes kept straying to the balloons, tethered overhead in the great barrage that surrounded the key points of the City. Air raids continually interrupted our work, sending us to the shelters.

That balloon barrage of silver sausages glinting high over

London prompted a treasured remark from a serviceman who, miserably homesick for his sunny Australia after days of unceasing London rain, muttered, 'Why don't they just cut the cables and let the bloody place sink?'

Soon I was joined by my mother and father who, because Pop was an alien, had been forced to leave Folkestone. Apparently Father, though not an 'enemy' alien, was not allowed under the Emergency Regulations to live near the coast, have a wireless set or even a bicycle. Odd, because during the First World War he had been engaged on highly secret aeroplane development work for Britain.

Mother took it marvellously, even after having to sell our home and furniture for a fraction of what they were worth and move, at short notice, into a small flat in London. Pop didn't seem to resent it either. The only thing that really worried both of them was having to find suitable homes for all the birds and animals they loved so much. Somehow, with the help of good friends, the menagerie was satisfactorily dispersed. Rosie, our lovely housekeeper, who had now married a farmer, helped most of all, and took in our 'alcoholic' parrot and many other homeless little creatures. Dear Rosie, with her apple cheeks, great gurgling laugh and wonderful loving nature, also started something which later grew into the Great Pig Saga.

At the start of the war, her farmer husband, a male counterpart of Rosie, advised us that we ought to have a pig. They would raise the pig for us and eventually turn it into pork and ham, bacon and sausages. A practical thought in wartime.

We chose a piglet and, throughout the first years of the war, it grew and grew. Before we left Folkestone, it had already attained its maturity. But frequent visits to the farm had endeared the pig to us and none of us could bear the thought of its slaughter. So it grew larger and larger. Despite pleading letters from Rosie, neither Mother nor Father could sign its death warrant.

According to Rosie's husband this giant overweight monster could barely see out of its little eyes. He even hinted that it was cruel to allow it to live longer, as it now could only just stagger around the sty, breathing heavily as it supported its great swollen carcass on its grotty trotters.

My parents were adamant that the pig must live. And God knows how much food that monster ate before eventually the end came. In the last photograph of it, which Rosie sent us, it looked exactly like a huge pink barrage balloon.

One morning in 1942, the pig – after a last gigantic intake of nourishment – collapsed with a massive heart attack, expiring almost immediately. It was carried off with enormous difficulty to be turned into the lard which, by then, it totally consisted of.

* * *

Meanwhile, in London, I had been waiting impatiently for my call-up papers to arrive. Naturally, I had to get a job. The Local Defence Volunteers, to whom I had taken Pop's treasured guns, refused to have me enlist. So here I was, a fully trained shot, unable to fire one because even the Home Guard, as they became called, wouldn't use my abilities.

Eventually I found a job in Fleet Street. This I kept, until the Ministry of Information found, in 1941, that Pop was Peruvian and ousted me – pronto!

Keystone Press, one of the most famous photographic press agencies in the world, had taken me on their staff. The kindness of my first boss, Mr Bert Garai, his son, 'Young Bert', and all the friendly hard-working team at Keystone got some of the frustration out of me. Soon I was at work in the picture library, where, surrounded by a half a million fascinating news pictures, I began to learn this new and exciting profession.

The laboratory team kindly took my photographic education in hand. They soon showed me the ropes and what a thrilling place the labs could be on a rush job. The whole staff developing, printing and enlarging, at an amazing speed, to get the 'pix' pushed out by dispatch rider to the great daily and evening papers. At quieter times the whole place ticked over at a steady pace, providing thousands of copies of news pictures to buyers from all over the world.

I was thrilled with it all. But for fate and the Ministry of Information, I might still be happily working in the 'Street' today. But one terrifying Wednesday night the Luftwaffe came in strength. Even at Hammersmith Bridge, you could read a newspaper by the light of the great fires they lit in the city.

As the planes droned menacingly overhead, the Londoners fought their firebombs with sandbags and stirrup pumps while the fire brigades attacked the great seas of flames. The endless black smoke clouds glowed red underneath and sparkled with the distant explosions of the anti-aircraft shells. No one who saw it or took part in fighting the fire will ever forget that night and its aftermath.

In the morning – stunned with shock and lack of sleep – I

picked my way, with the weary fire fighters, through streets littered with glass and debris.

Keystone was a ruin – the picture library a mass of smouldering ashes, surrounded by the wreck of the lovely little square it once stood in.

My boss, a small dejected figure, was stumbling over the water soaked and burned out piles of rubble that had been the editorial offices and the labs. As tears glistened in the eyes of this kindly Hungarian who had become the greatest photographic journalist of his day, I wanted to hug him.

He had lost everything, including the priceless and irreplaceable negatives which were a unique pictorial record of the history of the past forty years.

It all looked so hopeless – yet within a few weeks he was back in business in borrowed offices; backed up by that marvellous staff of his, and, together, they rebuilt the press agency. I would have been a proud part of it all, but, by this time, the Ministry of Information had formed deep suspicions of a Press card holder whose father was Peruvian. Despite Mr Garai's protests to the Ministry, I was out of a job.

Which is really why I became an actor.

The theatre was the one profession where it didn't seem to matter what you or your father were, provided you weren't actually an 'enemy' alien – in which case you went straight into an internment camp.

I had heard, through a friend, that there was an audition for a play being held that morning in Greek Street. Just for something to take my mind off the Ministry of Information business, I went along. For once, my stammer didn't betray me. Probably because I wasn't an eager applicant for the part, I relaxed and read some lines from the play *Sweet Lavender* for the producer.

To my amazement, I got the job, though truthfully I must admit it wasn't in the face of much competition because only about eight other people turned up for the audition.

The producer, actor, manager and character-comedy lead combined was Mr Frank Forbes Robertson whose whole appearance and personality stamped him as one of the old actor-laddie theatrical school. A kindly, patient man whose rugged, mobile face and rich, plummy voice proclaimed him a kinsman of the great Johnstone Forbes Robertson. When he offered me the part, at eight pounds a week, of Clement Hale, the juvenile lead in Arthur Pinero's play, my incredulous acceptance was only to be expected. Suddenly, I was an actor, about to open at the Prince of Wales Theatre, Cardiff, in two weeks' time.

My parents were as amazed as I was, and I set out to learn my part – or rather the whole play. By the end of three days and nights of endless study I could literally repeat it all word for word. As a matter of fact, I thought you had to.

I suppose I should have guessed some of the dangers and pitfalls that lay in wait for me but, when I went to the costumiers and tried on the tight fitting Edwardian clothes with their narrow trousers and button boots, I could only wonder at the excitement of it all. Yet those same button boots nearly brought my barely-started stage career to an abrupt halt.

At the end of rehearsals, which, with the enthusiasm and sheer cocksureness of the young I had carried off reasonably well, we left for Cardiff. We arrived on the Saturday, ready for our dress rehearsal on the Sunday and opening night on the Monday – only to close six days later, after one of the most disastrous theatrical weeks I can ever remember.

It was unbelievable how many things went wrong. On the opening night the curtain stuck fast at the end of Act Two and refused to come down. The supporting juvenile lead got the worst attack of stage fright I have ever seen and sat on the sofa, opening and closing his mouth like a drowning goldfish. We bustled round him giving him his cue lines out of the sides of our mouths until, still wordless, he got up and left us.

The entire scene, somehow, was saved by the unconquerable Frank Forbes Robertson, who gave a short resumé to the audience of what the young man should have said – a stage device which would probably be accepted today without question but which, in those days, was a little startling to say the least.

Various other disorders of a minor kind also happened on that amazing opening night but I really stole the thunder with my own small disaster.

At one point in the play I had to change quickly from my pepper-and-salt, narrow-trousered tweed suit into full evening dress of the same style and cut. I made my exit as the play partially recovered from the second juvenile's stage fright and immediately started changing my costume.

To my horror, I couldn't find the button hook. The tightly buttoned boots defied every effort to undo them by hand. The narrow trousers were far too tight to get off over the boots and, as the cue lines for my re-entrance grew alarmingly near, I had only one thing left to do – I ripped my pepper-and-salt trousers up the seam, like a banana, and tore them off.

It was at that moment I realised that this was also the only conceivable way I could get my evening dress trousers on over those bloody immovable button boots. So I ripped them up, as well. Somehow I got into the full evening dress outfit and tidied myself up by tucking the bottom of my ruined trousers into my black socks, thought I still had to keep on the brown and white canvas topped button boots.

As I heard my cue I stood up, my folding opera hat flat in my hand, and entered, keeping well upstage behind the sofa to hide my unorthodox lower half.

The cast looked a bit apprehensive, because hiding behind the sofa wasn't a move that we had rehearsed. Of course, eventually I had to come out from behind my cover.

The audience looked on in stunned silence at the weird spectacle of a young man in full evening dress and cape with his trousers tucked into his socks and wearing brown and white button boots – seemingly about to go out for formal evening bicycle ride.

Then they gave a great roar of laughter which died off into a nervous silence as they saw the look of despair on my face.

For an instant I stood defying them and then, with great dignity, I took my stage partner by the arm and led her towards the exit.

Had I gone straight out of the door I might have got away with it but some devil of delay made me continue with the actions we had so carefully rehearsed. At the door I paused and jauntily flicked my opera hat to open it and placed it, nonchalantly, on my head. At that precise moment the hat, which had worked perfectly during rehearsals jammed, half open, and perched, lopsidedly, on my wiry hair. This, combined with my already strange appearance, completed the picture. I must have looked like Charlie Chaplin impersonating a demented penguin.

The whole house rocked with honest-to-God belly laughs. Only once since, when I split my trousers at the old Empire Theatre, Leeds, and for the first time in my theatrical career wasn't wearing a jock strap, have I heard such a sound.

9. Have tights, will travel

This first, shattering, experience of show business very nearly put me off it for life, but, by the time I'd got back to London – it was now 1942 – I was already addicted and ready to have another throw at it.

In *The Stage* newspaper, I saw that Robert Atkins, a well-known actor-manager, was holding an audition for a season of Shakespeare.

This took place at a pub in Soho, suitably enough, because Robert enjoyed a small tipple between viewing the applicants. Here was a man who was, in all things, completely different from my first experience of actor-managers.

Whereas Frank Forbes Robertson was tall and willowy, with an indefinable air of sadness about him, Robert Atkins was thickset and solidly confident, with his bright, humorous eyes peering out from underneath great bushy eyebrows and his bald head shining with rude health.

His great booming voice – 'Like an organ, old son! You must learn to use your voice like an organ!' – inspired me with respect and admiration.

Here, I felt, was a man I could trust to set me on the right road to theatrical fame and fortune. Dammit, I thought, if the R.A.F. won't have me, the theatre shall.

Robert looked me over, quizzically, as I finished reading the part of Demetrius in *A Midsummer Night's Dream*.

'Well, old son,' he rumbled, 'you've got a good leg for a pair of tights!' Then added briskly, 'Eight quid a week, old son, and not a penny more.'

I jumped at the chance and signed a contract then and there.

Almost before the ink was dry, Robert – who never wasted time at rehearsals or auditions – had me cast as Valentine in *Twelfth Night*, one of those Shakespearian characters that come on, as a messenger, and set up the plot of the play.

'If your Valentine's any good, old son,' he said, 'I'll let you have a bash at Demetrius.'

I was also to understudy a very experienced actor called Meadows who was to play Orsini in *Twelfth Night* and he, very kindly, helped me enormously with my job as his 'cover'.

Robert's main concern with me, however, was to reduce my rather high young voice to a more mature pitch. To do this he showed me how to breathe with my diaphragm, graphically hitting me on this vital part to illustrate his method.

'God gave you a bloody diaphragm, old son — use it!'

I tried hard and soon found it worked surprisingly well, dropping my youthful tenor to a sexy baritone.

We rehearsed solidly for two weeks and then set off to take the 'Dream' and 'The Night' on a tour of Manchester. This was not exactly a conventional, theatrical tour but more of an *al fresco* affair, as we played in open-air bandstands in Manchester's Parks.

Platt Fields, Wythenshawe Park and — believe or not — Boggart Hole Clough were the settings for my first 'bash' at the Bard.

The more I got to know Robert, who rather overawed me, at first, the more I liked him. This grew into a very real affection on both sides.

Under the gruff guidance of this Super Uncle — my stammer disappeared as if by magic. With my newly acquired diaphragmic breathing, I was soon playing Demetrius, the second juvenile lead in 'The Dream'.

Occasionally the weather got the better of us and the audience, mainly school children, rushed for cover, tightly clutching their school copies of the play.

Wythenshawe Park had an Elizabethan Mansion in its grounds, and on wet days we played inside the great gallery room. It was there that I heard Robert break up as a gushing schoolmistress twittered to him, 'Oh, Mr Atkins, I so enjoyed the "Dream" — your Bottom was simply enormous.'

Stories about this great man are still legend in our business, and you can always tell if someone who claims to have played with his company really has, because all of them can do a faithful impersonation of his unique voice. Even the girls like Helen Cherry and Dulcie Grey.

Here are a few examples of vintage Robert.

To a rather gawky actor: 'Don't walk on the stage like a rabbit with rickets!'

On another occasion: 'You made your entrance old son, walking like a constipated guardsman.'

One of his most quoted gems was while he was rehearsing a competent but effeminate young actor.

'Watch it, old son! That last gesture you made was untheatrical, unnecessary and, in your case, downright suspicious.'

Those weeks in Manchester seemed to fly by. We next moved down south to play Leytonstone Park near London and finally opened our main season at the famous open-air theatre in Regent's Park.

This stretch of bush-backed grass faced an auditorium which could hold well over two thousand people and made a perfect setting, 'if fine', for Shakespeare's fantasies. Robert had kept it going for years.

He once told me why he thought he'd never received a knighthood which we all felt he richly deserved.

'It was the toilets, old son!' he reminisced sadly. 'Yes, the toilets did me.'

'You see,' he went on, 'when the Queen Mother's equerry phoned me and said that Her Majesty would like to attend a performance at the open-air theatre, he always inquired about the toilet arrangements. After all, old son, even Royalty have to piss.

'Each time I had to give him the same answer: "You know very well what toilet arrangements we have, my dear sir. The same bloody old chemical ones we've always had."'

This was apparently too much for the proxy Royal ear and Robert never received the accolade. A shabby business indeed!

One matinée, laryngitis seized Meadows in its silent grip and I was 'on'. (By now I was becoming quite confident and found that I could actually 'hold' an audience.) To look older I wore a moustache and beard and added a few distinguished touches of grey to my hair, as well.

My first entrance was fairly impressive. Keeping my voice as low pitched as possible, I really did quite well – that is, until the final act when, drawing in a huge breath to cope with the loud tone of my performance, I drew in half my moustache as well.

This put me off my stroke and I got out of synchronisation between my lines and the accompanying action.

'You uncivil lady, to whose ingrate and unauspicious altars, my soul the faithfullest offerings hath breathed out that ere devotion tendered . . . ' I managed to get out, along with the half moustache, quite an achievement in itself.

Unfortunately, I directed this speech to Viola's brother and not to Olivia as I should have done. This inferred that I was in love with the brother.

I panicked a bit at this and my breathing got out of control, raising my voice to a much higher pitch.

Finally, to crown it all, my beard also came unstuck and fell off, leaving Orsino looking a sudden twenty years younger and nearly clean shaven.

But these were minor mishaps and I was thrilled when the whole company moved, at the end of the open-air season, into the Westminster Theatre, which, if not exactly a West End theatre, at least was only a bus ride away.

In this next production of *The Merchant of Venice*, Robert let me play Lorenzo, Shylock's daughter's lover. Robert, of course, played Shylock in a manner and style not noticeably different from his interpretation of Bottom or for that matter Sir Toby Belch. The reason was simple. Robert's massive personality swamped any part he played and made it unmistakably Robert.

As Lorenzo I played opposite the lovely Helen Cherry who was the tall slim Jessica. Helen was so beautiful that it quite made you catch your breath, and it became obvious that I couldn't top her slim height.

'You'll just have to wear lifts, old son,' said Robert kindly. 'Go and get some fitted inside your thigh boots, Michael.'

I went off to the costumiers and the mysterious lifts, great wedges of cork, were placed inside my boots.

When I wore them for the dress rehearsal I found I was, undeniably, taller than Helen by a good two inches, but the illusion was slightly impaired by the fact that I also looked as though I was leaning against a strong wind.

As I made my first entrance Robert bellowed from the stalls, 'Christ, old son, you're supposed to come from Venice! Not bloody Pisa.'

I managed to correct this slight handicap to my image, by learning to lean backwards as I walked forwards. No mean feat, I can tell you.

Only once did this technique fail me, and that was in the Elopement scene, where Lorenzo runs away with Jessica. For this part of the action, I had to cope with a sword, a cloak, another cloak for Jessica, the box of jewels that she had thrown me from the window, a lantern and a mask.

As I flung myself athletically towards her in the best style of

Douglas Fairbanks, Helen stood coyly in the doorway, dressed as a boy. She really did look stunning.

My line was:

What, art thou come? On, gentlemen; away! Our masquing mates by this time for us stay!

Normally I managed this almost balletic leap quite impressively but on this occasion, one of my lifts shifted in my boot, causing me to trip.

My mask slipped over my eyes and, with my sword neatly between my legs, I shot forward horizontally, blindly stretching out my hands in what looked exactly like a rugger tackle. I hit Helen around waist height and we both went flat, with me on top.

The effect was one of sudden rape and, to complete the illusion, a harsh voice rapped out, from the gallery, 'Wait for it, mate!'

Another minor mishap happened to a young friend of mine who was serving his apprenticeship with Robert, at the same time as myself.

This lad was called Dominic and was highly-strung and Irish with it. Altogether an excellent combination for a would-be actor.

In the 'Merchant', Dom played a small part, and also understudied Antonio. One night, the inevitable happened, and Dom had to go on for Antonio stricken with 'flu.

To make him look older I suggested he followed my Orsino example and wore a beard — I didn't suggest a moustache as obviously by now I didn't trust upper lip hair.

I'd lost my professionally made beard in the move to the Westminster, so we had to use crêpe hair instead. This strange piece of stage make-up consisted of tightly-plaited curly hair held in place by twisted string. When you unplaited it, the stuff seemed to be possessed of a life of its own.

Anyway, it defied both our efforts to uncurl it and finally we stuck it on in short lengths with a liberal helping of spirit gum, a sort of thick varnish. This gave Dominic an impressive Assyrian type of Van Dyke beard, tight and curly.

What neither of us knew, and the experienced Antonio of course wasn't there to tell us, was that heat was the only thing that straightened this type of hair and made it long, linear and manageable.

Dominic did extremely well in the first scene, but was sweating heavily with first-night nerves. The scene is played with

Antonio being fed the plot by a sort of double act called Salerio and Salanio.

Both of these characters watched, spellbound, as the effect of Dom's sweating became apparent. Quite slowly, the crêpe hair unwound, with his body heat, and his beard started to 'grow'.

The audience also became aware of this remarkable phenomenon, but not so Dominic. Carried away by the excitement of his big chance to show what a good actor he was, Dom was blind and deaf to anything but the sound of his own voice.

We watched breathless, from the wings, as that damned beard became longer and longer. Totally unaware of his plight, Dom finished his speech and made his exit – with the beard now a good six inches lower on his chest. The applause, let me add, was deafening.

Helen and I had our troubles as well.

One beautiful scene that we both enjoyed was the famous Moonlight scene and normally this really grabbed the audience. However, one night we were in for a surprise.

I had started the lines, 'The moon shines bright: on such a night as this, when the sweet wind did gently kiss the trees and they did make no noise.'

One of the 'tabs', a curtain, started to descend and kept on doing so till it lay, in a heap, in front of us with all the rope and tackle spilling down on top of its retaining bar.

Robert, from the wings, where he thought he was hidden from the audience, leaned right out into full view and bellowed up to the stage hand in the 'fly' gallery, 'I'll tear your bloody cock off!'

The audience shrieked with joy at this and the curtain whipped hurriedly upwards out of sight.

Amazingly enough, when the laughter died down, I went straight on with the scene.

It was all marvellous experience and I loved it – but that blasted banana skin was still lying in wait for me.

One night, in September, 1942, I was getting ready to go on when two R.A.F. service policemen appeared and accosted me.

'Mr Michael Bentine?' the corporal, a grim-looking man with square teeth asked accusingly.

My heart leapt with sudden joy – here at last, was my long-awaited call-up.

'Yes,' I said eagerly.

'You're a deserter,' continued the corporal menacingly, 'sixty-five days adrift.'

'What?' I gasped.

'Utter balls!' added Robert, who had come up behind us. 'This young man had been trying to get in the R.A.F. for nearly two years.'

In fact Robert had himself tried pulling a few strings on my behalf, also without result.

'My orders are to bring him in,' went on the corporal, adamantly. Then turning, to his tough-looking assistant, he continued, 'Take his sword, Fred. He might do himself a mischief.'

Robert really blew his shining top.

'I'll have you two stupid bastards shot for this!' he roared.

They were so over-awed by this outburst that at least they let me finish the performance. Each standing on either side of the stage, in case I made a break for it.

At the end of the play they marched me off to their staff car, with my trench coat slung over my doublet and hose, not even giving me time to change.

'Don't worry, old son,' said Robert. 'I'll straighten out this idiotic business.'

We drove off in state, with the rest of the cast waving like mad. At the headquarters of the Deputy Assistant Provost Marshal, in Exhibition Road, I was booked in as a deserter. When the ignominy and injustice of the whole affair hit me I turned nasty on them.

'Right!' I said. 'You treat me as a criminal – at least I'll be a Peruvian one. Fetch me the Peruvian Ambassador, pronto!'

I sat down, still in my Elizabethan costume, and flatly refused to say another word in English.

That really shook them. Thinking they were calling my bluff they consulted my documents and found, to their horror, that my father was indeed Peruvian.

'Bloody hell!' said the Corporal. 'He really is a wog.'

The Duty Officer, who had rather more common sense, was summoned. He phoned the ambassador who, of course, was a close personal friend of Pop's.

Within a matter of minutes the ambassador arrived, in a Rolls Royce. He was furious because he knew the full story of my unsuccessful attempts to join the R.A.F. and to him this was a direct insult to Peru.

'Not one – but not one! – British ship will enter the Port of Callao until the honour of this young man is satisfied!' he pronounced dramatically.

'Miguel Bentin is Peruvian – like all his family. I personally will be responsible for his passport,' he continued, clinching the matter.

The assembled R.A.F. police looked slightly green and humble apologies were made, together with an offer of transport.

'Señor Bentin will come in my car,' said the ambassador – and that was that. But I do claim to be the only British serviceman, for some three hundred years, to attend a defaulter's parade in a doublet and hose.

The next day I talked to Robert and decided that, as this was really a perfect opportunity to get into the Service, I should use it as such.

We needed a week to rehearse Dominic in my part, and then I went, by appointment, to see the Commanding Officer at the air crew reception centre in Regent's Park. This was a charming Group Captain, who had been a famous cricketer. What a change that interview made from the shambles of the night I was arrested.

'Do you really want to come into the Service?' he asked kindly.

I patiently explained that I had been trying to do so for nearly two years.

'When would you like to come in?' the Groupie asked, to my amazement.

'In about ten days' time if that would be convenient.'

'Certainly, Mr Bentin,' he said politely. He shook my hand and I was ushered out by his pretty W.A.A.F. secretary.

It was all a bit different about three weeks later when, with a twinkle in his eye, he bawled me out for not saluting him. But by then, of course, I was Aircraftsman Second Class Bentin, M. J., under training as aircrew.

Had I known the strange adventures that lay in wait for me, I wonder if I would have been as keen as I was to get into the R.A.F. Perhaps it was just as well that I didn't know.

We brand-new aircrew cadets wore a distinguishing white 'flash' in the front of our caps and were billeted in the numerous luxury flats that fronted the top half of Regent's Park. These blocks of smart modern apartments had been left empty practically overnight when the air raids hit London in 1940 and had since been taken over by R.A.F. Training Command to house the thousands of young cadets who were passing through this reception centre.

Although we didn't complain at the comfortable billets, it did seem a strange place to concentrate the Royal Air Force's most valuable long-term assets. I can't imagine the Germans doing the same thing in Berlin.

We were marched down to the local garage, which had been turned into the main stores, to collect our equipment. We tried to pack into our new kit bags a greatcoat of thick blue wool, an equally heavy tunic and trousers – battle dress had not yet been issued to cadets – shirts, collars, ties and underwear, socks and braces, a flat side cap, with the white flash in it, and finally, a pair of ammunition boots.

These 'bovver' boots felt at first like encasing your feet in cement but, within a few days of brisk marching, your blistered feet enjoyed their supple comfort and support. I even felt rather lost when I went back to wearing shoes. Indeed, I found the boots the most comfortable footwear I have ever tripped up in.

We had a haircut – or rather a quick run over the neck, back and sides which left me looking like a Romney Marsh sheep, ready for dipping and marking.

The 'Ablutions' as they were officially named, gave us the dip and the R.A.F. looked after the marking by issuing each of us with a number. I still recall the last three digits – 743 – because each week on pay parade we called them out before collecting the few shillings that made up our meagre pay.

On our first day at A.C.R.C. we were interviewed by the accountant officer, who seemed to be keen on reducing even this pittance a mite further by persuading us to allot part of our pay to our families.

The cadet next to me flatly refused to part with a penny. This upset the accountant officer, a beaky-nosed flight lieutenant, and he tried to persuade this somewhat older cadet to make some contribution.

'After all,' he said, righteously, 'those few shillings can buy your wife some of the little luxuries that women need.'

The mature cadet, who had just been clipped at the barbers, was fiercely resentful of the establishment at that moment. I felt him savour his revenge, as he said in a slow drawl: 'I'm allowing her £10,000 a year, sir, and that should be sufficient.'

Our eating facilities were a little unusual in that the mess was located in the canteen at the zoo, right next to the gibbons' cage. This gave us and the gibbons much pleasure, as we fed them, quite illegally, the scraps that we couldn't finish.

Rumour had it that along with the endless stew, grey mashed potatoes and huge 'doorsteps' of bread and margarine, we were

83

being given doses of bromide in our huge mugs of tea to keep us sexually placid.

Ever experimental, I quenched the overfed gibbons' thirst in many cups of the suspect brew. I still wonder whether they ever bred again till long after we left.

Every morning at 6 a.m. we were marched down to the zoo canteen, at a swinging 120 paces to the minute, oddly enough an exhilarating experience. In the pitch dark of pre-dawn, the airmen at the front and rear of the flights carried red lanterns to warn any traffic. It seemed a shame we didn't carry port and starboard lights as well.

Due to some bottleneck in the Initial Training Wings, which were to be our next posting after A.C.R.C., we did a lot of training in classrooms dotted among the apartment blocks. This consisted of elementary navigation, wireless telegraphy and morse code. There was also a quite horrifying lecture on venereal disease, graphically illustrated with a short film, guaranteed to put you off normal sex for life.

Morse code also became a much practised art and we got quite proficient at it – sending unbelievably crude messages to each other during the other lectures. All I can remember today apart from the dot dot dot dash dash dash, etc., of the SOS is the letter F, which went dot dot dash dot, and had the word association of FORNICATION. This subject was the main topic of conversation, as a change from aeroplanes, which we discussed endlessly.

'Shooting a line' – that is to say, exaggerating about such things as your exploits with women – was a popular pastime, though probably most of us knew a damn sight more about aircraft.

The drill instructors, loud-mouthed little men of corporal rank, who enjoyed a bedroom to themselves and a great deal of petty power, kept us busy with the endless marching and counter marching. We also looked after the pig pens which were, theoretically anyway, to provide us with pork products. In between we did a lot of gardening to help the 'Dig for Victory' campaign. Many of us were shipped off to a camp called, I think, Ludlow, to dig drains and build roads – a splendid training for these fit and bright young men who wished so ardently to fly.

Anyway, the R.A.F. kept us busy and we became very fit. Which is probably the real reason why I survived my next Service experience.

In November or December of 1942, a sudden switch of plans indicated that we might be going straight overseas, because of the increasing bottlenecks at the I.T.W.S. To get us ready for this we had an inoculation of A.T.T.T.A.B., anti-tetanus/anti-typhoid.

Another lad and I were on the end of the line waiting to receive our 'jabs' and I remember clearly seeing the medical orderly change over to a new batch of the inoculation serum, just for the last two of us. It was a fateful action for us both and very nearly a fatal one.

The corporal D.I., a repellent specimen, later had all of us scrubbing out the billets.

'It'll get your bloody arms movin' again,' he smirked, gleefully. 'A bit of suffering won't hurt you.'

I was delighted to hear later that – because of what happened to myself and the other lad – our mates threw him into the Regent's Park Canal and nearly drowned him.

About twelve hours after we had been jabbed, the two of us developed dangerously high fevers and went into convulsions. By some miracle, certainly in no way due to the baffled efforts of the medical officers, we survived.

The other lad was half crippled and eventually invalided out of the Service, to return to his craft as a cobbler in Weymouth. I was a physical wreck for months.

In extremis, I felt myself leave my body, as it lay on the sick quarters bed, and recede into an infinite blackness. My last conscious thought was one of anger and frustration and then my subconscious must have taken over.

I felt myself, with great clarity, tiny and naked, alone and awestricken, before the vastness of space time. I hung suspended between life and death, with all the pain suddenly gone and a total, peaceful acceptance taking its place. Then I seemed to be drawn back into my body, and slowly awoke – to an awareness of lowered voices discussing my soul.

As my mind cleared, I could now make out the words:

'No, no! It's my job – his papers are stamped C. of E.!' said one voice, irritably.

'Bilge!' said the other voice, 'he's mine. Look here – it says his father is Peruvian. That must mean he's a Catholic.'

Papers rustled, then the first voice continued.

'Then why the bloody hell did they put C. of E. on his documents?'

That did it. Obviously in the R.A.F. you couldn't even call your soul your own.

I struggled to speak and, noticing this, the two opposing padres leant over me.

'Yes, my son?' said the R.C. one in sepulchral tones.

'What is it, lad?' said the C. of E. one, in a sort of solicitous chant.

Finally, after a herculean effort, I managed to get the words out.

'Piss off – I'm alive!' I whispered, and promptly passed into a peaceful sleep.

The inoculation had given us both some obscure form of reaction poisoning that seethed through the muscles of our tortured young bodies and twisted them in knots.

The medical term is, I believe, myositis, which really only means – inflammation of the muscles. I don't recommend the experience to anybody.

The medical officers aside, had it not been for the care and devotion of the nursing staff we would never have made it. Day and night those lovely and splendid nurses tended us, cleaned us and slowly got us back on to our emaciated legs.

I weighed about ten stone when I arrived at A.C.R.C. After this little lot, I was down to under eight.

The poison slowly came out, in appalling abscesses, and left me as weak as a baby. It also affected my eyesight which wasn't absolutely 6/6 anyway and I could now only see dimly into the ward.

Those supper ladies fed us on anything decent that they could lay their lovely thieving hands on and, little by little, we got our strength back.

My partner in suffering, eventually sat on my bed with his small kit, ready to go on special leave. I don't think he was too sorry to be bowler hatted.

I lay there for a few weeks more and then was sent home – pending invaliding out of the service. This I flatly refused to do – I'd spent two years of my life getting in and I wasn't going to be pensioned off till I'd done something worthwhile. I was convinced my eyesight was only temporarily affected and no arguments or orders were going to get me out.

The powers that be knew there'd been a right 'balls up' and were only too glad to get rid of me but I stood, or rather lay, firm. This nonplussed them a bit and they went into an official huddle to try and find a way out.

First of all I, obviously, had to be given a full medical board. That, at least, would show me the folly of my ways.

Not so, however, because my body was so fit that apart from the healing abscesses there was no sign of the poison – except of course for my confounded eyesight.

The M.O. said, 'Read as far down those letters on the chart, as you can.

I replied, truthfully, 'What chart?'

Somehow I managed to convince the board that, although underweight, I could be passed as fit. Possibly mesmerised by my impassioned pleading, they agreed to put me down as A4B, which meant fit for service other than flying.

My plan was simple – if I could only stay on in the Service I could always remuster back to general duties, aircrew, when my eyes improved.

So while the 'brass' decided what to do with me, they posted me as supernumerary to A.C.R.C. pending posting for some other job. I hung around for weeks, passing my time by playing endless games of table tennis with the international squadron which was billeted upstairs in Abbey Lodge.

This collection of assorted aircrew volunteers came from strange places like the Falkland Islands, South America and even Fiji. Among them for some strange reason was Jack Watling, a young and successful actor of great charm. By night, he was playing the highly strung flight lieutenant in Terence Rattigan's *Flare Path* in the West End. By day, like me, he was an A.C. plonk aircrew cadet.

Jack reckons we played well over a thousand games of table tennis while we were at A.C.R.C. and I'm sure he's right.

The cricketing commanding officer now took a hand in the proceedings and I marched in to see him. He was a bit taken aback at my changed appearance and really made a special effort to sort me out.

'Why not go in for a commission?' he suggested, 'such as in Intelligence.'

I couldn't resist laughing, 'What's so funny, Bentin?' he asked sternly.

'Well, sir,' I said simply – my recent brush with death had left me little awe for senior officers – 'only a few months ago you had me in front of you as a possible deserter. Now you're inviting me to consider trying for a commission in British Intelligence.'

He saw the ridiculous side of this immediately. I left with his

87

smiling promise that he'd get me an interview with the commissioning board as soon as practicable. He managed this within a couple of weeks and once again, with the extraordinary confidence that my recent experiences had given me, I sailed through the whole thing buoyantly.

I improved physically as my morale rose, and two weeks later I was posted to Cosford, in the Midlands, where uncouth airmen like me were turned into officers and gentlemen. The Air Council had decided that four weeks' intensive training would be the minimum requirements for this difficult task though this only applied to 'Penguins', that is to say non-flying personnel – quite another procedure was used to commission aircrew.

These flying type non-commissioned officers were turned into the 'real' thing by being given their King's commissions while still on their operational squadrons or flying training centres. One day they were sergeants, flight sergeants or warrant officers and the next, by orders of the Air Council and gracious permission of His Majesty King George VI, they were in new uniforms with the narrow 'ring' of the acting pilot officer on their sleeves.

Our case was different. For four weeks we worked at an intensive training programme of lectures, about such vital subjects as supervising latrine siting and digging, the organisation of the Royal Air Force, correct procedures for putting lesser mortals on a charge, leadership and discipline and even the exact width of the braid ring on the sleeves of our hoped-for A.P.O. uniforms.

Never once did anyone officially mention that other subject – aeroplanes. I don't suppose many of our instructors had ever seen one close to.

Sessions on the firing range were the only constructive moments of the whole course as far as the actual war was concerned.

I happily shot out the centres of any target put in front of me with any weapon the armament section would let me handle – to the obvious delight of the armourers who usually spent quite a lot of their normal training sessions ducking.

Pop had indeed taught me well and for once I didn't let my old man down.

I also enjoyed route marching, swinging along with five hundred other cadets, rifles slung over our shoulders, happily singing all the old marching songs that young men will always joyfully sing, if you put them in uniform and march them. (I don't say that this is the right thing to do. I just state, as a fact, that it is so.)

That long month dragged to a close. As part of our training, we spent a good deal of it on the parade ground drilling squads, and eventually flights, of airmen by ourselves.

It was quite fun really trying to remember on which foot passing which you had to give the order to halt.

'One Pause Two' – Salute – 'One Pause Two. About turn! Quick march!' The gravelled and asphalted parade ground sang to our shouted commands, of which mine were perhaps not the most precise but, undoubtedly, the loudest.

'Like an organ, old son! Use your bloody diaphragm!'

Robert's advice gave me the clear ringing tones of a foghorn.

One panic-stricken cadet – a 'boffin', or scientist type in radar – panicked while drilling his squad and couldn't even remember the word 'halt'.

As his command of airmen slipped from him his squad marched, delightedly into the distance while one wag shouted out. 'For Gawd's sake say something, if it's only goodbye!'

Finally, I think in April, 1943, we took part in a large and impressive passing out parade and then dispersed to our various homes on our kitting out leave.

I handed over all of my £55 allowance in exchange for a service dress and cap, gloves, shirt and ties, etc., shoes and a useless and expensive piece of compulsory equipment known as a 'camp kit'. Anything less 'camp' I had never seen. It must have weighed a good 65 pounds and can only have been designed for use in the Crimean War.

Constructed solidly of wood and metal, with a heavy canvas stretcher on it, it also comprised a folding wash basin and a sort of child's paddling pool of canvas in which you were supposed to ablute yourself.

I paid for it in disgust and lugged it into a taxi. Once I'd got it home I never saw it again. The rest of the war I used a light metal 'safari' bed and washed in cut-off petrol tins warmed by 'Benghazi' fires.

Other pieces of equipment I had to sign for on a form called a 664B. Woe betide you if you lost any of it in battle – you would be called upon to pay for it yourself.

I asked the equipment officer if I had to get a receipt from the Germans for any ammunition that I might fire from the pathetic .38 calibre revolver and 12 rounds of Argentine ammunition which fitted into a webbing holster from which the weapon became almost undrawable. The holsters had obviously been designed to make us the slowest guns in the West.

I put my trusty weapon safely away in a drawer before going to Europe and carried instead a Colt .45 calibre revolver of impressive dimensions and heavy knockdown power, that a sympathetic American had swapped me for a bottle of Scotch. With it came a couple of hundred rounds of short, fat, powerful ammunition.

During this leave in my brand-spanking-new uniform, with the supporting cap wire illegally removed and the cap itself carefully steamed and shaped into a facsimile of aircrew's operational ones, I set off to pay a formal visit to Abbey Lodge and to thank those lovely nurses.

As I approached the building which had so nearly housed my corpse, I saw coming towards me, an equally brand-new cadet who could have been me those few months ago.

As we came level with each other on the narrow pavement we both smartly saluted at exactly the same time. With perfect timing, our arms neatly interlocked, as though we were performing an evolution in a square dance.

Still chuckling I went in to see my team of pretty saviours and to kiss them all, one by one.

While I was on leave, Pop called me up to tell me my beloved cousin John was missing – believed killed. The story of his passing is a strange one and one more piece of evidence of survival for me.

Joan, John's younger sister had grown up to become a nurse at a big London hospital. One night she had been on duty and was sitting down in the Sister's office at the end of the ward when she was shocked to see John in front of her, as solid as if he actually was in the room. He ran his hand over his thick hair to show Joan it was wet and then, with that tremendous smile of his, vanished.

Joan was so shaken she had to come off duty and the next morning rang Pop to ask what it all meant. Dad comforted her, but a feeling of dread came over him and that night he dreamt or had a vision, whichever you like.

He told me that he had seen a bay with cliffs – 'Not an English bay,' he said. The clouds were low over the sea and out of them came a German fighter followed by a British one.

The British plane shot the German one into the sea. While it was circling round, as if to see whether there was a survivor, a second German plane appeared and shot the British one down.

Pop was very clear on these points and told me one day we might check them out. But he was quite certain that John had 'passed over'.

This vision was borne out, in every detail, in the oddest way.

Alan Dawkins, my elder cousin and John's brother, was Cunningham's pilot in the Middle East. When Sicily was invaded the Imperial War Graves Commission contacted Alan, because they had found John's grave there. Alan got compassionate leave and flew over to see the grave which was in a cemetery near the cliff tops overlooking the sea.

While he was there he heard the story of John's death, through an interpreter, who got the details from a Sicilian who worked in the cemetery. They were exactly as Pop had described them months before.

The strange part of the story was that buried next to John's body was the German pilot he had shot down.

Many years later, Alan, who now lives in Africa, confirmed once again the details of John's death, that so closely followed Pop's vision.

When the Graves Commission asked Alan if he would like John's remains to be taken home, he said: 'No, I think it is better that the two of them lie side by side here.'

I don't believe either the German pilot or John are anywhere near their bodies. Knowing John, they are close friends in that parallel world along with many other people I love dearly.

Commissioning leave over, I was posted – like a letter – to the Initial Intelligence course. To my surprise, I found it was located at Highgate in an old walled Victorian gabled house guarded by R.A.F. Service policemen and huge Alsatian dogs.

In contrast to the Cosford course this one was worth every fascinating minute of its intensive run. Part of it was devoted to evasion and escape under the supervision of M.I.9, the highly secret organisation that controlled the M.I.6, the widespread network of Resistance fighters in Belgium, Holland and France.

Every day and night in Europe hundreds of these brave men and women risked their lives and the exquisite tortures of the Gestapo to run the escape routes like 'Comet' and 'O'Leary', along which thousands of soldiers, sailors and above all, airmen made their way to Spain.

When I hear some youngster today say, proudly, that he or she is a member of the Underground, I always ask politely, 'And which station platform do you clean?' It prevents me throwing up.

I have been asked to tread warily over my experiences in Intelligence so I will only give broad details of any courses or later operations that I was involved in.

Two veteran World War One escapers lectured us enthrallingly on their own escapes from Turkey and Holzminden in Germany and we learned how to make a tunnel, dispose of the earth, set up warning systems and the hundred and one tricks of the escaper. During a survival lecture one escaper actually taught us how to cook a hedgehog.

Some of the escape and evasion techniques have been dealt with at some length in various exciting books written by subsequent escapers, so I won't add to that information.

We were taken in a special sick-making, black-out but to the headquarters of M.I.9 to see at first hand some of the ingenious escape aids they devised and made there.

After driving round for what seemed like hours, presumably to confuse us as we sat imprisoned in the bus, we arrived at a tree-lined location, somewhere in the heart of the countryside. On being gratefully released from our bus, we said in unison: 'Ah, Beaconsfield.'

At about this time M.I.9 had a big 'flap' on because more than a hundred of their agents in France had been betrayed to the Abwehr, the German counter espionage outfit, and subsequently handed over to the Gestapo.

This was entirely due to the treachery of a British soldier who had deserted at Dunkirk taking the mess funds with him.

Hiding in France, he had started to run a small 'escape' route. Through this, word of his exploits, but not his deserter's background, got through to M.I.9, which had only then recently been set up.

He worked quite efficiently for the organisation till he got caught by the Abwehr and spilled the beans.

Having seen the results of Gestapo torture, I can understand anyone breaking down but I will never understand why M.I.9 used this doubtful character in the first place.

He was finally shot, I understand, by the Milice, the French Vichy police, while engaged in Black Market activities in Paris. This happened just before the liberation of the city, so he would have been shot anyway.

*　　*　　*

The best thing about this well thought out course was that it gave you a firm grasp of the German Air Force order of battle –

a broad idea of the Resistance movement without burdening you with detailed, and therefore dangerous, knowledge and, above all, the opportunity to meet your opposite number in Intelligence services such as the Free French, Poles, Czechs, Norwegians, Dutch and the Americans who had, by now, joined us. Some of these were ex-members of their own countries' clandestine organisations and they enthusiastically gave each other full co-operation.

At Highgate you could talk reasonably freely – in fact you were encouraged to – in direct contrast to your total security when you walked out of the gate.

Once they had got over the fact of my extreme youth and inexperience, these splendid colleagues undertook my briefing and I absorbed everything they taught me. We lapsed into various languages while discussing the intricacies of the trade, and the babel of voices rose to the roof as we endlessly argued out the problems of espionage and counter-espionage, in this 'safe' house.

As I spoke French, fluently but ungrammatically, I expected to be transferred to the Free French section. In their wisdom, the organisation thought otherwise and I found myself with the Polish squadron – while the Pole, who went in for the final interview after me, was posted to the French. I often wonder if the paperwork got muddled up somewhere along the line.

Anyway, there I found myself in 1943, the youngest Intelligence officer in the Royal Air Force and for all I knew, in the whole free world.

I was 21 years old.

10. My bleddy Poles

The Poles were a law unto themselves. When their homeland was raped, many of them had escaped to fight the Germans with a burning hatred that was difficult to understand if you hadn't experienced the same horrors yourself.

When I joined them in 1943 I had become totally confused by the shifting political scene. For example, early in the war, Finland was referred to as the country of the 'gallant little Finns', and their incredible bravery in beating back the invading Russian hordes, crossing the ice of Lake Ladoga, conjured up a picture of unsurpassed gallantry. That was pretty straight-forward.

The Russians, however, had been the savage aggressors and their costly mass attacks were described by eyewitnesses at 'the work of mindless robots'. So far, so good. The heroes and the villains were clearly drawn, like cowboys and Indians.

Then Hitler invaded Russia and set in motion his Apocalyptic 'Operation Barbarossa'.

My mind started to bend a bit as the Russians, overnight, became our trusted and gallant allies – co-workers in the world struggle against the Fascist Hyenas – while the Finns were now cast in the role of 'Treacherous Nazi running dogs' and given the labels of low cunning and animal ferocity.

Then there were the Americans to try and get into perspective. They had been long sneered at by the Press as isolationist warmongers, growing fat on the proceeds of European suffering – or as a nation of cowardly usurers who exchanged British territory for worn out First World War destroyers. Now suddenly they emerged as brave comrades in arms. treacherously wounded by the infamous Japanese attacks on Pearl Harbor and fighting back gloriously against these arch enemies of democracy, etc., etc.

For any well-balanced person these developments required the sort of political somersaulting that has become quite commonplace nowadays. But for my emotionally motivated mind, as they call it, it was totally unacceptable. So, along with millions of other young people, on both sides of the world struggle, I ignored it and got on with the job, as best I could. But it has always been a source of complete wonder to me that so many others made the 'supreme sacrifice' of their lives in the face of this insane situation where the propaganda machinery could go straight into reverse.

The Poles were a marvellous example of the sort of single-mindedness you needed to 'finish the job' with the 'tools' Churchill had given them. In the case of 300 Squadron, these were two flights of Wellington bombers.

The machines were one of Sir Barnes Wallis's pre-war designs, built with his revolutionary 'geodetic' construction – a sort of interlocking web of duralumin struts – fabric covered, on the fuselage, and now in its Mark X version, powered by the remarkable Hercules XI engines.

It wasn't a graceful looking aircraft and was referred to as the 'Ruptured Duck', but it was immensely strong and reliable. By 1943, however, it was too slow and vulnerable, even though it was armed with a twin gun turret, forward, and a quadruple gun turret at the rear.

All these guns, unfortunately, as per the current British policy, were only of .303 calibre and their effective range of about 600 yards was well below that of the Messerschmitt and Focke-Wulf fighters of the German Air Force, with their heavy cannon and machine-guns.

This meant that the poor old Wimpeys – as they were affectionately named after the Popeye cartoon hamburgerholic, J. Wellington Wimpey – were largely relegated to night operations, where the darkness acted as a protective cloak. They were used mainly in the short-range role of special operations, such as mining the enemy sea approaches.

When I arrived at Hemswell, as eager as a beaver on heat, this type of operation was in full swing.

The Poles who made up 300 Squadron were partly regular pre-war aircrew of uncertain, lied-about age and great flying experience and partly my contemporaries, but, in one way, they were all the same.

They had all escaped or evaded either the Germans or the Russians and made their way out of Europe through France and various other routes. They were also slightly mad, in the nicest possible way. They came from every part of Poland and had such contrasting names as Kucharski, Kuzian, Patchka and Stadtmuller – many of them typical high-cheeked-boned Slavs, while others were equally distinctively Teutonic, with fair hair and hard blue eyes.

Their names didn't come too easily to the tongue at first. *Punch* had a marvellous cartoon of a Polish pilot reading a medical eye chart, while the M.O. said, 'Just the individual letters. Please don't pronounce the whole bottom line.'

For some reason, best known to the official mind, the code name for airborne mine laying was 'Gardening'. The mines – each one 1,800 pounds of deadly ingenuity – were referred to as 'Vegetables'. What all this nonsense really concealed from the Germans is anybody's guess. There was nothing nonsensical, however, in the way the job itself was tackled.

Royal Navy specialists had been attached to Hemswell, to teach the R.A.F. armourers how to handle the intricacies of these weapons and to show the aircrews how, when and where to drop them. My job was to learn these techniques, as quickly as possible, and then, to pass this information on to the aircrews, as clearly and graphically as I could.

Put simply, mine laying by air, consisted of each aircraft carrying three of these deadly weapons and dropping them in the 'swept channels', between the enemy's own minefields, which guarded the approaches to such German submarine bases as Lorient and St Nazaire, or the E-boat bases, around the Texel, in north western Germany.

Easier said than done, when you consider some of the actual difficulties under which these operations were carried out. Firstly, the Wimpeys had to cross western France, at low level, to minimise their detection by enemy radar. Then, by expert navigation, the crews had to find a landmark, like the lighthouse on the Isle de Batz, off the coast of southern Brittany. Using this as a marking point, they then had to time their exact run-in on a fixed magnetic compass heading. Finally, they had to drop their mines, from exactly 1,000 feet altitude, squarely into the narrow entrance channels.

In daylight, with modern navigational aids, it would be about as easy as finding a whore in a cathedral. By night, pecked at by enemy anti-aircraft fire and sometimes half blinded by searchlights, it was a bloody miracle that my crews dropped their mines, so often, into the right place.

The 1,000-feet mandatory dropping height wasn't just some capricious order. Below that altitude, the parachutes that slowed down the mine wouldn't have time to open and the weapon would break up, uselessly, on the sea. Above 1,000 feet, the mine would tend to float down out of the 'swept channel' used by the enemy submarines, and merely reinforce the already enormous German minefields, protecting their U-boat bases.

The Poles, or as I now thought of them 'My Bleddy Poles', did this difficult and dangerous job with great efficiency and skill – but it did little to slake their thirst for vengeance. On the way back, the air-gunners invariably popped off at anything that remotely could be German. One of the gunners confided to me that he'd blown up a cow which was being milked – 'no bleddy milk for bleddy Boche' – as he put it.

Our casualties at this stage were non-existent. In the words of the official communiqués: 'All our aircraft returned safely.'

300 Squadron, outwardly, settled down to the 'Gardening' routine. Inwardly, it was fuming at the delay in the very personal all-out Polish war programme of bombing, bombing and more bombing.

Sometimes, however, things went up the wall. In this case, for one of my new found friends, Ozzie, they went wrong in a strange way.

This particular night I had briefed these crews to drop mines outside Lorient. As usual, I went out into the bleak Lincolnshire night to see them off.

Each Wellington stood on the runway, thundering and shaking against its brakes. In the subdued blue glow of the cockpit lighting, the pilot and navigator waited for the shaded green controller's light to flash, rechecking everything as they did so. As they were given the 'green', the pilot eased the throttles fully forward. With the propellers screaming in fine pitch, the lumbering black shape of the Wimpey slowly picked up flying speed till it hauled itself laboriously upward into the freezing darkness.

This time Ozzie was the last off and I watched the glow of the exhausts of his engines fade into the night. Suddenly his port engine blossomed into flame and the Wellington seemed to skid sideways in mid-air.

From numerous flights, familiarising the crews with 'Bullseye' procedures – that is to say practice bombing sorties – which I had flown with the Poles, I could picture the frenzied activity going on in the aircraft: the feathering of the port engine propeller to stop it turning and the simultaneous operation of the built-in fire extinguishers, while the pilot struggled to keep the asymmetrically-powered plane from plunging into the ground in a steep turn.

This he could do only by holding the controls right over, on the opposite side to the burning and useless engine, while he trimmed his aircraft to fly on the one source of power left.

His only hope of making it safely, in his now dangerously underpowered and overloaded aeroplane, was to jettison his load of mines down into the darkness below, knowing that the area was sparsely populated and the mines were quite safe from explosion until their safety plugs had melted in water.

Breathless with anxiety, we watched the Wimpey stagger back into the circuit. Along with everyone else who had rushed out to the end of the runway, we waited for the outcome.

As Ozzie brought his crippled plane to a rocky but safe landing, the fire engines and 'meat wagon' rushed alongside him. The foam extinguishers swamped his glowing port engine. The crew baled out of the escape hatches. Then Ozzie himself shouted out of the cockpit window.

'Bleddy mines,' he yelled, 'I drop bleddy mines.'

'Where?' I yelled back, idiotically.

'How bleddy hell I know bleddy where? Some bleddy place out bleddy there!' He gesticulated wildly into the darkness. Then, suddenly remembering his aircraft might still blow up, he hastily disappeared and almost fell out of the front hatch.

As duty Intelligence Officer, it was my job to find where the 'bleddy' mines had fallen, and the armament officers' job was to come along with me and render them safe and, if possible bring them back. They were, after all, highly secret. Our big concern was that these three great cylinders had possibly landed on someone and flattened him.

The armourer had already explained to me that the mines would be quite safe, as their soluble safety plugs would prevent them exploding. Either their parachutes had opened and they had drifted down, or they had broken up on impact. The point was – where?

Waiting for daylight would have seemed to be the obvious solution, but there was the remotest possibility that one of the mines could have fallen into water, somewhere, and become 'live'. So the sooner the armourers found them the better.

This seemed reasonable thinking. We set off, in two fifteen-hundredweight trucks, to find the weapons, followed by the armourers, in their five-ton lorry.

Ozzie, who, despite the medical officer's arguments, was determined to come with us, gave a running commentary on his near fatal flight.

'Bleddy sure mines drop five, six miles from field,' he muttered, consulting the pocket compass we had brought with us.

The night was pitch black and we didn't dare use the spotlights because of possible enemy intruder aircraft. So we woke up the few isolated farmers we could find, in the hope that they might have seen or heard something in their area – but we drew a blank.

At first light, two colossal explosions shook the air round us and rocked our vehicles violently. Over a thick clump of trees, to the east of us, a great double flash lit the sky and a heavy cloud of boiling smoke rose black against the red dawning.

'Jesus!' I swore.

'Bleddy Christ!' echoed Ozzie, as we sped in the general direction of the disaster area.

We turned the corner of the road and were met by a shambles of twisted trees and flame-scorched hedges.

By a million-to-one chance, two of Ozzie's mines had parachuted into a large pond. One of these weapons was acoustic and had been designed to be set off by a heavy mechanical clattering, such as would be made by a ship's engines. The other one was magnetic and could only be triggered by the proximity of a large mass of metal.

By falling into the water, both mines had eventually become 'live', This had taken about a couple of hours and there they had lain – partially submerged and quite hidden in the darkness.

At dawn, fate had decreed that a farmer would set out down the road with a large tractor – towing some hefty piece of farming machinery. The clatter of his tractor and tow and the nearness of their combined mass of metal set off both mines simultaneously. There was just one comforting thought; the poor farmer couldn't have known a thing about it.

*   *   *

Don't think for one moment that my Poles were all vengeance and hate the whole time. Quite the reverse – they played just as hard as they fought.

Parties were as wild and uninhibited as you would expect in any pilots' mess during wartime, but the Poles added their own particular flavour to them with a huge tea urn, filled with a sort of thin 'borsht' of beetroot juice, to help keep the alcoholic intake from paralysing the enjoyment centres.

Then – there's no two ways about it – they did have a very special way with women.

For a hung-up, tongue-tied and shy person like me, it was a perpetual revelation to see them at work on a girl. As Ozzie confided to me: 'If all else bleddy fails, bleddy put the bleddy thing in their bleddy hands and burst into bleddy tears.'

Whatever the technique was, it never seemed to fail. Even the most stony-hearted girl was not left unturned. My Poles played the whole thing like there was no tomorrow. For many of them, there wasn't.

They took pity on my 'penguin' longings for flight and I regularly flew with them, day and night, whenever I could get the chance.

With British squadrons the sheer weight of red tape made it extremely difficult to get airborne for much longer than a short air test. But with 300 Squadron, I was accepted as one of them and up we went, hour after hour – belting around northern England, with me, at the controls, revelling in it all. The pilot would stand by me giving helpful hints, or he would even go back aft and play cards; a sheer piece of bravado that was intended to give me confidence, which it certainly did.

Soon I was getting quite hot at instrument flying. Because of my dodgy eyesight, the instrument panel and I were close friends and I brought this ability up to a reasonable level of efficiency by spending hours, off duty, in the Link Trainer, a sort of miniature earthbound dummy plane, which was fitted with a full set of blind-flying instruments.

On two of these unofficial trips we very nearly 'bought it'. The first near brush with the 'grey man' was brought on by a series of tricky conditions which built up into a dangerous situation, within a matter of minutes – a combination of cumulus nimbus storm clouds and ground mist right down to the deck.

The navigator, who was not overly experienced, panicked a bit when he realised that he had lost himself and us, over the high ground of the Yorkshire moors.

The 'clag' closed in round us, chillingly, and our last visual pinpoint was a railway station of doubtful identity. The only and obvious course was to climb – to avoid running, head on, into the dreaded 'stuffed cloud', as it was so horribly aptly called.

This sudden deterioration in the weather, with a big shift in the wind, was really unexpected. We were obviously miles off course so the pilot called for a Q.D.M., which was a heading given to you by your home station or Group Radio to enable you to find your way back from your radar or D.F. detected position. We all strained our eyes, peering into the clammy darkness of the streaming clouds, while the rain ran off our windscreens in sheets.

As we finally broke out of the grey muck, we all simultaneously saw it. Dead in front of us, as we roared out of the mist, was a large flock of terrified sheep and an equally petrified shepherd.

The pilot hauled back on the control column and 'gunned' the throttles, to hurl us up and over the jagged crown of the moor, while the sheep scattered left and right, like an exploding woollen bomb, and the shepherd flattened himself among them.

A few nights later I was on a 'Bullseye' with another crew. This meant flying a dummy mission, with a load of practice bombs, but with an operational briefing and a carefully worked-out set of courses, right round Scotland and northern England.

We even had fighter affiliation, in which a local night fighter squadron would intercept us near our final target, the bombing range.

Off we went, and everything worked according to our flight plan. Below us lay the perimeter lights and flare paths of dozens of airfields. There lights would appear quite suddenly, as a flare path lit up to bring in a returning aircraft, and then winked out at the radar-detected approach of some other aeroplane which was not carrying a device known as I.F.F. – identification, friend, or foe. (Not to be confused with F.F.I., which stood for free from infection, and consisted of a hurried routine examination of your genitals by the medical officer of the station you were posted to.)

Sure enough, directly below us, a flare path blacked out, just about the time and position we were expecting the dummy attacks from the Mosquito night fighter.

'Bleddy Christ!' yelled the rear gunner, then lapsed into incoherent Polish as a huge shape shot past us, with guns blazing.

The aircraft shuddered, as we flung over into the corkscrew dive, which was the accepted manoeuvre to get you out of this situation. The Wellington dropped, vibrating madly, into the long darkness below.

I yelled with pain as we shot down in that mad curving dive.

My ears had failed to adjust, in the unpressurised aircraft, to the sudden loss of altitude.

The pilot's instinctive reaction to his rear-gunner's shouted warning, had certainly swung us out of that first over-eager burst of fire from the twin-engined German fighter, which had 'intruded' into our airspace, and our sudden descent had thrown us off his airborne radar screen.

The Polish gunners were cursing fluently because they hadn't fired back – but how the hell they would have had time to fire in that fraction of a frantic second is beyond me.

This sort of cat-and-mouse game went on, every night, on both sides. Many allied and German aircraft, alike, were lost to the stalking night fighters; so, if the German pilot hadn't been so eager he'd have had us cold.

At about this time an extraordinary story was circulating round Bomber Command. Apparently a British pilot, who was a keen 'press-on' type and a bit 'ropy' in his instrument flying, was practising this necessary craft in a Link Trainer, much as I had been doing, after hours with the Poles.

Seated in his small, stubby winged, mock-up aeroplane, with the blind flying hood clamped down over him, the pilot had been practising instrument approaches, which were indicated on the plotting table by the movements of the 'crab', a sort of three-wheeled ouija board that duplicated exactly, on a large-scale chart, the results of the movements of the controls in the Link. Sitting behind the plotting table was the Flight Sergeant 'Chiefie', Instructor, who gave directions, over the R.T. set, to the pupil pilot hidden beneath the hood.

This was early in the long winter evening and the Nissen hut, which housed the link, hadn't got its black-out curtain properly adjusted, leaving a bright ray of light spilling out of the window.

Suddenly, the flare path lighting of the airfield went off, as an 'intruder' zoomed into the circuit and, before you could say 'Hals und Beinbrücke', the German pilot of the night fighter had spotted the errant beam of light. Diving down, he gave it a liberal squirt of cannon and machine-gun fire.

The bust of shells 'walked' right across the Nissen hut. As the terrified 'Chiefie' made a dive for cover under the plotting table, the little aeroplane was blown clean off its operating pedestal and landed, upside down, with the badly wounded pilot, who had half his backside blown off, trapped underneath.

So naturally grim is the 'black' humour of airmen, that the rescuing team of pilots from a nearby dispersal hut yelled with laughter as they dragged the poor devil out from underneath and rushed him off to the Station Sick Quarters.

They just couldn't get over the fact that here was the only pilot ever to be shot down in a Link Trainer.

11. Bomber's Moon

The bleak autumn passed into a black freezing winter and, suddenly, we were switched over to bombing raids.

The heavy four-engined Lancasters, Halifaxes and Stirling bombers were, by then, taking over the main weight of the mounting fury of night attacks on Germany. At this stage of the war, however, the twin-engined Wellingtons and the few Whitleys, which flew in distinctive nose-down attitude, were occasionally used whenever a 'maximum' effort was required.

The target was the Ruhr, or, as the crews called it, the 'Happy Valley', a great sprawling industrial complex in western Germany, bristling with anti-aircraft flak guns and buzzing with German night fighters. It was hardly surprising that we started to suffer casualties.

These raids were followed by two heavy ones, on Munchen-Gladbach – described by the Group Intelligence Officer at our 'linked and scrambled' telephone briefing, as 'a dormitory town'.

'What's that?' I asked, innocently – identifying myself as the Ingham I.O.

'Use your bloody loaf!' snarled the Group I.O. 'Where the bloody women and children sleep, you clot!'

It was a sharp lesson for me, in the ethics or rather nonethics of war.

That night, and the following one, 10,000 women and children died in the blazing ruins of Munchen-Gladbach. Apparently it wasn't just the Germans who were 'only obeying orders'.

As the strain of night-bombing grew, the parties got wilder, though they were excuses more for noise and high spirits than for heavy drinking, mainly because hard liquor was hard to come by and the watery beer was only a strain on the bladder.

The Poles were still confirmed 'birdaholics', however, and went at the job 'balls out', as the American engineers used to say – an expression which, oddly enough, as a technical rather than a rude one!

The non-operational night, after one of these 'thrashes', I decided to walk back from Hemswell to Ingham, our satellite station, along the winding road, high on top of the wind-swept icy wolds. The full moon was appearing fitfully behind scattered clouds and the air had a sharp bite to it.

As I got about halfway between the two airfields, with the wind 'harping' the telephone wires and shaking the trees in their winter sleep, I felt as if I was the last man on Earth.

A chill ran through me, that wasn't just caused by the freezing night air.

In front of me, framed by a long line of swaying poplar trees, was a narrow crossroads, which carried a small lane into a winding drop down to the little cemetery at the foot of the hills.

My heart picked up a beat or two as I saw, quite clearly, an old-fashioned hearse, drawn by two black shrouded horses, with the hunched figure of the driver sitting on the 'box', seemingly waiting for me at the deserted crossroads.

The moon once again was covered by the scudding clouds but, for a moment, it gave me a clear glimpse of this terrifying sight.

From Pop's painstaking instruction in supernatural phenomena, I knew that to start running from this sort of vision was to give way totally to terror and that I would, very likely, go on running till my heart failed me.

With a tremendous effort of will, I continued to walk uncertainly forwards, praying inwardly – and, through some strange foolish defence mechanism – I started to whistle a tuneless sort of defiant dirge, as my reluctant feet carried me nearer to the gruseome tableau.

The whistling sounded so mournful that I stopped it and, in dead silence – except for the keening of the wind – I approached the macabre group at the crossroads.

I was really at the end of my tether and half turning to run, when, for an instant, the racing clouds broke up and, through the ragged gap, the moon shone, full and clear, like a great yellow-blue searchlight.

The hearse and cortège vanished and, in its place, was a farm wagon loaded with a great pile of dark mangel-wurzels and two ancient tarpaulin-covered bicycles, propped up in front of it, while the driver was just an old, tattered-coated, scarecrow.

In the midst of all the real dangers and terrors of war, I was more shaken by that ridiculous incident than by all the physical perils that beset me later.

* * *

The next night, we were operating again. This time on an extreme range target, requiring the fitting of large collapsible long-range tanks. The target was, I think, Posen. From this raid, Ozzie and his crew failed to return.

The following day I was posted to a nearby R.A.F. Bomber Wing, at Wickenby. I found myself flung head first into an all-out effort, which was building up into the great bomber offensive of the winter 1943–44.

I hadn't time to grieve for Ozzie and his 'bleddy crew'. The young form attachments quickly and the 'busy' young accept their passing, much more easily than do older people.

Wickenby itself was a whirr of activity. The Wing was made up of two squadrons, 626 and 12, equipped with Lancasters, most of them being of the Mark III type, powered by Packard Merlin supercharged engines and fitted with the top-secret H2S, a radar-scanning device that showed the shape of the target beneath, even though the area was completely obscured by cloud.

These planes were, then, possibly the finest bombers in the world.

Even though they were still armed with the short range .303 machine-guns, they at least carried quite a punch with two guns in the front turret, two in the mid-upper and a further four in the rear-gunner's position, between the two graceful 'surf-board' shaped fins.

Developed from an earlier unsuccessful twin-engined design, called the Manchester, the 'Lanc.' as it was genuinely, affectionately called, was Britain's most successful bombing plane.

My senior Intelligence Officer – Willy – was a delightful and highly strung First World War pilot, with a load of medal ribbons, including the Military Cross.

The station had two tip-top squadrons, staffed by first-class commanders and crews, and one of the best navigation leaders in the whole Group – an Australian, who had a natural instinct for plotting courses that weaved safely through the huge concentrations of enemy flak and fighter zones that covered half Europe.

If the crews could accurately fly those courses, their chances of finishing their full tour of 30 trips were high.

This Bomber Wing was made up of young men from all over

the British Empire, as it then was. The earthy tones of the Geordies from Newcastle mixed with the twangily dry accents of Australia and warm Scottish voices contrasted oddly with the guttural tones of South Africa.

They came from Canada, New Zealand, Rhodesia and every other part of the Commonwealth – all united, probably for the last time, in the same struggle for survival.

This was something I've never forgotten, even in these divided and confused times we live in.

Our targets were mainly located in the 'Happy Valley' but now, more regularly, Bomber Command started to plaster Berlin and Hanover, Hamburg and Bremerhaven, with an ever-increasing weight of bombs.

These assaults have been described as 'terror raids'.

'No possible justification for mass murder,' righteously protested another lot of 'experts', most of whom had been born after the event.

So it may well be. But, not being God, and having seen the exhausted and often terrified crews return, again and again, to the flak and fighter riven skies, above the blazing targets, I am not prepared to judge them, or their masters.

The Germans started these 'terror raids' and reaped the whirlwind.

The poor bloody lacerated aircrews, with their nerves stretched beyond endurance, were only the instrument – and that weapon, jagged from the savage casualty rate, never turned in the hands of those who wielded it.

Let the leaders bear any burden of guilt and not the young men, whose bodies and minds I saw broken, in that searing three-dimensional holocaust.

Such times bring out some outstanding characters and a few of these were really way out. For example, we had a commissioned air gunner called Roy who, as he delighted in telling us, had been in the chorus of the 'Desert Song' and who was as 'gay' as Caesar's Camp.

This tall, willowy, one-off was one of the bravest people I ever met and had won the Distinguished Flying Medal, when he was a sergeant air gunner, as opposed to the Distinguished Flying Cross he later won as an officer.

Apparently, even in war, there was a sharp line drawn between commissioned and non-commissioned gallantry, only traversed by the holders of the Victoria Cross, who could be of either rank.

Roy died – cut to pieces by a cannon shell in his rear turret – keeping up his 'gay' banter, according to the crew, for the whole of the long agonising return trip.

Stories about him were legion. For example, on being bracketed by searchlights: 'Jesus! Skipper! They want a bloody encore!' And again, as he squirted his four chattering guns down into the blue-white burning beams in a hopeless attempt to shoot them out: 'For Christ's sake give us a pink, duckie – this colour shows my bloody age!'

Willy, my S.I.O., had a blazing row with a senior officer over a snide remark that had been made about Roy.

'He's got more guts in his arsehole than you've got in your whole body! Christ, it must gall you to have men like him on your squadrons with D.S.Os, D.F.Cs and D.F.Ms while all you've got is a bloody little piece of lettuce leaf for shooting up the bleeding Arabs! Sir!'

Willy stuttered in rage, as he referred to the officer's pre-war green ribbon awarded to him for operations against tribesmen in Iraq or somewhere else East of Suez.

*   *   *

One disastrous night, during an all-out, maximum effort on Berlin, the route markers shifted badly.

These markers were like great candelabra of glowing fireworks that slowly descended on their parachutes and showed up the vital turning points running up to the target area.

The unexpected 'shift' of these cascading yellow lights, combined with a howling gale, played hell with the carefully planned raid.

The target indicators, which were a red and green version of the yellow route markers, were blown erratically over the great city area, and the whole raid was broken up into scattered individual aircraft: cut to pieces by the undamaged flak guns below.

The German night fighters were up in force as well. That night the Command lost nearly ninety aircraft, several of which were ours.

The following day we 'stood down', while we counted the damage and rested the battle-weary crews.

At about the same time we 'lost' our W.A.A.F. Intelligence Officer. This was a great relief to us all, because she really had been a dead loss, as far as the aircrews were concerned.

When the crews returned from a long raid, certain vital information had to be extracted from them, as quickly and effortlessly as possible. Then, half asleep with the effects of reaction, plus a steaming mug of cocoa and rum, they could get their heads down and try to sleep it off.

This particular 'bluebird', was so taken up in fascinating the crews that she really didn't do the job too well.

The main questions were: 'Did you see any lights in the sea?', referring to the possibility of spotting lights from rubber dinghies, loaded with their shivering survivors from ditched aircraft. A top priority question when survival in the wintry North Sea was, at most, a matter of hours, and one which our crews, knowing they could well be the next ones to ditch, willingly answered.

The other questions were partly technical and partly general target and route information, to be used for future raids – but the essential thing was to collect the facts and then get the crews off to bed.

This didn't seem to penetrate too deeply into the woolly thinking of this attractive girl. So, one night, the crews decided to teach her a lesson.

To her question, 'Did you see any lights in the sea?', their enthusiastic answer was: 'Not only lights, but the whole bloody German Navy. Wasn't that so, Mack?'

'Sure, Skipper. I saw the *Gneisenau* and the *Scharnhorst*.'

'And the *Prinz Eugen*. Clear as a bell.'

Now any hard-bitten I.O., who is a disbelieving animal anyway, would have said: 'And the bloody rest, mate! Pull the other one!' But not our prima donna.

Shaking her pretty blonde head excitedly she rapturously batted her long eyelashes.

'Where?' she breathed sexily!

The crews pointed to their charts and carefully spelled out a map reference.

Our heroine didn't even bother to check the longitude and latitude on the operations wall map, but, seeking sole and selfish glory, hurried off to phone the joyous news straight through to Command itself, by-passing Group Intelligence on the way.

By sheer luck she got through to an inexperienced I.O. at Command, who became a bit confused as she repeated her name several times in quick succession.

He became equally excited. As both of them were, by now, visualising the headlines in the newspapers, with appropriate pictures, his judgement became equally impaired. Without checking the vital map references, he got straight through to the Commander-in-Chief.

As the excited Command staff hurried into the Operations Room the fateful position of the German Navy was plotted.

On the top of Ben Nevis!

The W.A.A.F. officer left us, pronto, for parts unknown and, so rumour had it, the slightly less glamorous job of a catering officer.

After all, why not? She also probably knew damn-all about cooking!

While we waited for replacements the aircrews clambered aboard their 'floggers', old clapped-out cars of various vintages, and beat up the surrounding countryside.

Lincoln, that lovely old cathedral town, was a much-visited rendezvous for us all.

The *Turk's Head* at the bottom of the hill and the *White Hart* at the top were favourite. Here I would meet my Poles again and get all the latest gen.

One morning I stood goggle-eyed, in the bar of the *White Hart* at the sight of James Stewart and Clark Gable, respectively a colonel and a major in the U.S. 8th Army Air Force, swapping drinks and shooting lines with a mixed party of assorted airmen from many nations.

Finally our replacements arrived and among them was one crew so young I just couldn't believe it.

Having spent a lot of my boyhood clutching a bag of sweets and my big brother, while we absorbed the culture of the talkies, I was still impressionable enough to remember *Dawn Patrol*, a famous film about World War I fighter pilots – starring Douglas Fairbanks Junior.

One scene in the picture has the disillusioned, aged-before-his-time Squadron Commander inspecting the new batch of replacements who were so young and inexperienced that he was sickened by the useless waste of their young lives.

Here, before me, was exactly the same situation.

A crew of eight, normally, made up a Lancaster's operational requirements – pilot, navigator, bombardier, flight engineer, wireless operator and three gunners. There they were – all brand new sergeants, not one of them much over eighteen and some of them had probably lied about their age.

The old clichéd movie scene replayed itself as I, a grizzled 21, asked their pilot: 'How many flying hours?'

'A hundred and twenty-six, sir,' he replied brightly – he was so inexperienced he called me 'sir'!

That was his total flying time, including conversion to multi-engined aircraft.

'How many night cross-countries?'

'One,' he replied unbelievably.

'And you, sergeant?' I asked, switching to the navigator.

'Oh! That was my first night cross-country too, sir. We got a bit lost,' he giggled, nervously.

'Jesus Christ!' spluttered Willy, who had overheard this exchange from the Ops. office next door. A moment later he appeared, red in the face with fury.

'They're children! Bloody children!' he shouted.

Willy snatched up the phone to protest to the Station Commander, insisting that this crew must not be considered operational until they had completed at least another three night cross-country trips.

Incredible though it sounds, the Station Commander was adamant. Our next operation, after our enforced stand-down, was to be a maximum effort and that poor schoolboy crew was thrown into the melting pot with not the remotest chance of making it either to the target or back.

Where stupidity and crass inefficiency sometimes won out there was also, thank God, an abundance of basic humour, which itself was a blessed morale builder.

After the next raid on Berlin, the technical adjutant of one of the squadrons told me that he was worried.

'What about?' I asked innocently, knowing the answer.

'The Elsans,' he bleated plaintively. 'Every time we have a raid on the Big City I have to indent for more Elsans.'

The Elsans, a chemical toilet well known to campers and caravanners, was in short supply because, as they were a mandatory issue to aircraft on long trips, numbers of them were being dropped over the target area, fully loaded and enthusiastically 'topped-up' by generous contributions from the ground crews.

How it was that the aircrews concerned, bracketed by the flak and coned by the blinding searchlights could still find time for a schoolboy prank, I still can't fathom.

One thing I'm sure of – the Germans could never have done the same.

This sporting pastime was brought to an end, suddenly and officially. not due to a shortage of these vital pieces of equipment,

111

but by a top priority order, strictly forbidding these actions and threatening dire penalties to any offending crew.

The reason, amazingly enough, was that, on examination of what was left of these cylindrical tin commodes, after a straight, whistling fall from 20,000 feet, the Germans came to the conclusion that this constituted chemical warfare.

This was confirmed in their logical Teutonic minds by a post-mortem carried out on a flattened and excreta covered victim.

Apparently, the German Air Force officially complained to the Red Cross in Geneva and this unorthodox secret weapon was forthwith banned.

We were now involved in two successive raids directed against the mysterious complex of buildings at Peenemunde, on the shores of the Baltic.

I knew, from Intelligence summaries, and other carefully gleaned sources of information, that Peenemunde was a centre for secret research, probably involved in the development of Hitler's long-promised 'vengeance' weapons.

The raid was laid on, due to the bright-eyed perception of a young W.A.A.F. Intelligence Officer at Medmenham, which was the headquarters of the R.A.F. photographic interpretation unit.

Here high altitude mosaics and individual low-level pictures, taken from fast, unarmed, photo-reconaissance aircraft, were studied and examined, in minute detail, by a highly skilled and intensely imaginative team of hand-picked specialists.

Among them was a W.A.A.F. officer called Babington-Smith who spotted a strange diminutive aeroplane, almost invisible, even when viewed through a powerful magnifying glass.

The little plane was resting on some kind of ramp and this clever girl's guess was that it was a pilotless flying torpedo or bomb.

Intelligence agents working with the Polish underground were instructed to get more detailed information about this weapon and, through our Special Operations Executive, sent back the news that Doctor Wehrner von Braun and General Donner-berger, both known to be high-altitude rocket research experts, were now working at Peenemunde.

Then, through an incredible series of events, a flying bomb actually went off course and fell into the hands of the Polish team.

This was flown to England in a plane specially sent for the purpose, and a complete example of the V.1 flying bomb came into the hands of British Technical Intelligence experts before it had come into operational use.

Meanwhile these vital raids were laid on. Aircraft of our Group, and others, were integrated into a complicated attack pattern to guarantee the maximum weight of bombs falling into the comparatively small target area.

The route in to target skirted Denmark and then rain straight down to Peenemunde. The target photographs and material arrived by dispatch rider and I stuck them up all round the detailed briefing map of the area.

At least when our two squadrons went out that night, they knew everything we could find out about the target, its defences, and the reason for the raid.

The attack, mercifully, was an unqualified success, requiring only one other hammering to complete the job.

The snag of an attack on highly specialised targets like this or the Dortmund-Ems Canal was that, if you didn't really 'prang' them the first time in the surprise attack, new defences were poured in and subsequent raids met with terrific opposition from gunfire or massed attacks by fighters.

Hundreds of irreplaceable German technicians and highly trained staff were prominent among the casualties and, in the two raids, thousands of detailed plans and drawings went up in flames.

The whole attack delayed the launching of both the V.1 flying bomb and the unstoppable V.2 rocket bomb by at least six months and, virtually, saved thousands of civilian lives.

One strange incident, directly due to these concentrated operations, happened soon after the Peenemunde attacks.

A third and final raid had been called for, as we feared it might. Luckily, at the last moment, because of the weather, it was cancelled.

The cancellation came through minutes before Press-tit-time, the moment when the pilots and crews, already in their aircraft, would start their engines and taxi out round the perimeter tracks.

It was a particularly foul night by this time, with a howling wind cutting across the pitch black airfield. Rather than break radio silence, the news of cancellation went with the trucks sent out to collect the aircrews.

I was 'Duty-Joe' that night and had to go out 'beacon bashing', which meant bumping round the airfield, with a driver, checking the automatic navigational beacons, a sort of lighthouse for aeroplanes, to see if they were operating correctly.

As we crept round the perimeter track, the teeming rain swamped down on our truck and it was purely by luck that I caught a glimpse of something large and white, billowing fitfully against the fence.

I got out and found myself clutching an open and torn parachute, which, although caught on the fence was still trying to drag along the body of an airman harnessed to it.

By some miracle he was still alive and turned out to be a Scottish rear-gunner who alternatively muttered curses or moaned, understandably, in pain from one of his legs which was broken.

His story, told to us later by the M.O., really matches the Link Trainer casualty's experience.

As the aircrews had been taken out to their aircraft for the raid it had been obvious that their vitality, after the two previous attacks, was at a low ebb.

Settled snugly down into his rear turret, with the warmth of his furry 'teddy bear bum freezer' and fur trousers and boots, topping layers of sweaters and long underwear, the sergeant had dozed off. His last sleepy conscious thoughts were that, at any moment, the engines would burst into life.

As he slumped in the pitch blackness of his turret, lit only by a tiny glow, his 'intercom' plug must have slipped out of its connection.

When the truck came to collect the crew the skipper had called up his crew members, over the R.T., to tell them the raid was cancelled and then they had piled into the truck, which was already half filled with dimly seen airmen.

In his relief the skipper didn't count heads and the truck belted back to the Messes, leaving the lone rear-gunner – unseen and sleeping like a baby.

About two hours later the gunner woke up with a start, his battle-weary mind instantly aware that the engines weren't running.

'Skipper! Skipper! What's up?' he called into his oxygen mask microphone, over the swish and howl of the storm outside.

To his horror he now saw that his R.T. plug was disconnected and, in his confusion, he must have relived some part of the previous night's raids.

Whatever the reason, he thought that the silent engines had failed and that the racing whistling wind was caused by the Lanc. diving down to crash.

He took the crew's silence for their failure to contact him before they had all baled out.

Firmly grasping his parachute release ring, he spun his turret sideways and baled out backwards, as per his 'abandon aircraft' drill, through the double turret doors.

The rear turret of a Lancaster stands some three or four feet above the deck and the gunner knocked himself out cold, as his head hit the asphalt of the hard standing.

His last thought must have been to pull the release ring – which he did – and the pilot chute fell out, dragging the main canopy of the parachute with it, as the powerful wind gusts seized and filled it.

The unconscious sergeant was now swept rapidly across the deserted blacked-out airfield, bumping and banging against any obstacle that got in the way until he finally stopped where we had found him, jammed against the perimeter fence.

So persistent are the confused mistaken images of the human mind that, as we carried his semi-conscious form to the comfort of Station Sick Quarters he attempted to thank us in a mixture of Scots and broken German.

12. The ghost wore blue

Willy insisted that I got some leave, because I was sleeping badly. In those days, sleeping pills were frowned on, and consulting the medical officer was used almost as a last resort.

The question, 'What trade did you remuster from before you became our M.O.?' wasn't entirely an airman's joke.

Before I went off on a seven-day pass I was clearing up some papers in the Ops. room. There, browsing through some aircraft recognition manuals, was 'Pop', our oldest navigator, who was all of thirty-six.

He had just finished his 30-trip tour of operations and was hanging about waiting to be posted to a less 'hairy' instructor's job at the Central Flying School.

This warmhearted and canny Yorkshireman was one of my favourite people and I knew that he was inwardly deeply relieved to be going back to his wife and children.

I normally never talked over my deep convictions about survival with anyone, but with Pop I often opened my heart. As my transport arrived, we shook hands and he said to me: 'Have a reet good leave, lad. You've earned it!'

The seven days went past like magic and I returned to Wickenby, near midnight, to find it glistening with snow.

I notified the guard room that I had returned at 23.59 hours, and, with my small kit over my shoulder, trudged off to the hut that I shared with four other lads.

The moon was shining on a scene like a Christmas card, as I turned off the road, that led through the plantations of young fir trees, and the night was still, breathless and crystal clear.

Just as I came opposite our Nissen hut I saw Pop, a quite unmistakable tall figure, walking towards me in the moonlight.

'Hi, Pop,' I called, 'I had a great leave!'

He nodded and waved a hand at me, as he continued across

116

the path, and passed, out of sight, behind the opposite hut on the other side of the road.

I crept into the Nissen as quietly as possible, so as not to wake my aircrew friends and had soon joined them in the deep sleep of the young.

At six o'clock, our batman, Charlie, a marvellous worldly wise Cockney, who was a scrounger of great talent and indeterminate age, woke me.

' 'Ere's your tea, sir,' he said. 'Nice to 'ave you back. Beat up London all right?'

Then his puckish lined face tightened. 'Bloody shame about Mr W.,' he said simply.

My sleepiness vanished. 'Mr W.' was Pop.

'Bloody shame about what?' I asked, a feeling of dread chilling me.

' 'Course you wouldn't know, sir. He went into the wolds wiv a new crew.'

'When?' I gasped, unbelieving.

'Two nights ago,' replied Charlie sadly.

But I had seen Pop the night before, as clearly and distinctly as I now saw Charlie. The moonlight reflecting off the snow was too bright to allow any error in recognising someone I knew so well.

Then I remembered that 'Pop' hadn't replied to my greeting, other than by a nod and a wave and that he had moved in silence.

I remember one 'professional' intelligence agent telling me that you can disguise everything about you but the way you walk and your appearance from the back.

A number of times he had saved himself from being caught by known German Abwehr counter espionage operatives, by recognising them from their back view.

I have absolutely no doubt that I positively recognised Pop as he walked towards and away from me in the cold clarity of that previous midnight. Unlike the wold's 'hearse' incident, here was a genuine super-normal experience.

It was typical of this kindly and considerate man that he had volunteered to fly, as a replacement navigator, with a brand-new, inexperienced crew whose team-mate was down with flu. On an ordinary safe night cross-country trip they had ploughed into a 'stuffed cloud' and blown up.

The raids continued and mounted in fury – so much so that, after one particularly disastrous attack on the Ruhr, an infuriated flight commander, driven to distraction by the savage mauling he had received from enemy night fighters, strode into the Ops. room and straightway phoned through to Command.

He'd had more than enough and, quite rightly in this case, blamed them for the faulty organisation of that particular raid and, by God, he was going to let someone 'high-up' know it.

By a strange quirk of chance he somehow got connected straight through to Bomber Command Ops. room and a brisk, rather icy, voice answered the phone. The flight commander, who was beside himself with fury, really let fly.

'Tell the stupid bastards who laid on this bloody operation they're out of their bleeding minds,' he ranted. Then, f—ing and blinding, he went on to tell Command precisely what it could do to itself!

The cold voice broke in sharply, 'Do you know who you are talking to?' it asked.

'No! And I don't bloody well care!' shouted the flight commander.

'This is Air Chief Marshal Harris,' announced the voice crisply.

There was a distinct pause, then the shaken pilot asked hoarsely: 'Do you know who you're talking to, sir?'

'No,' came back the chilly reply.

'Thank Christ for that!' said the flight commander, and hung up.

At the height of these attacks I was, unexpectedly, posted to another station.

At Hemswell, the visiting Senior Officer commanding our Group, had favourably considered my application to join the Air Transport Auxiliary, the organisation that ferried aircraft from the factories to the operational airfields. They were much more liberal, as far as the required medical standards were concerned, and many of their pilots had disabilities which had precluded them from operational flying.

The A.O.C. had promised me that he would do his best to help me complete my training as a pilot under the aegis of the A.T.A. and, in my excitement, I thought this was the posting I had been waiting for.

Willy, reluctantly, agreed that he wouldn't protest against the posting, as he knew what it meant to me, and he even got the Equipment Section Officer to issue me with warm flying clothing, as a sort of parting gift from the Station.

But, apparently, once you are in Intelligence, the powers that be are loath to let you go. When I arrived at 9 Group Headquarters, I learned, to my dismay, that I was not listed for transfer to A.T.A. Ferry Command but had been assigned to a Fighter Control course.

This was sheer stupidity. With the corrected lenses in the goggles I had had wangled out of the Medical Officer at Rauceby, I was once again capable of flying. But hours of eyestrain, sitting in front of a dimly lit radar screen, could only result in a recurrence of the severe migraine that had dogged me for years.

Anyway it was obvious to anyone that this would eventually endanger the lives of the aircrew I was supposed to be controlling, so, after one trial run, I asked to see the Wing Commander in charge.

I explained the situation in what I supposed to be a reasonable manner, but this officer seemed to take the whole thing as a personal insult, and even threatened to have me courtmartialled for disobeying a direct order.

'Then why not send me back to the Bomber Wing, I've just left?' I suggested. 'I was doing a fair job there and they were happy enough with my efforts.'

That really made him blow his top.

I was banished to non-operational Intelligence duties, while this pompous officer decided what punishment could fit such a crime as I had, apparently, committed.

I think his trouble was symptomatic of this whole Group Headquarters, which, tucked away in a nice safe corner of north western England, hadn't been subjected to the pressures of the Groups at the heart of the operations.

Anyway I felt pretty depressed and drank heavily – only being saved from making a complete fool of myself by the cheerful friendship of Ray, a young fighter pilot who was on 'rest' from operational flying.

We both loathed the complacent atmosphere at this Group H.Q. and openly showed it. This called down even greater fury on my head and, as a punishment for some derogatory remark, I was made duty orderly officer for fourteen days.

Every night I made the rounds of the H.Q. building, which was an old country house, and scooped up literally piles of 'secret' and occasionally 'top-secret' documents, which had been left lying around the various unlocked offices.

Each night, I took these papers down to the Central Registry and solemnly got a receipt, witnessed by the Orderly Sergeant, for each and every one of them.

I wrote out a formal complaint, pointing out the appalling lack of basic security. This was pointedly ignored and, on the final night of my tour of duty, I noticed a thick file marked 'Top Secret', left quite openly on the top of a desk in a certain office.

I had never examined the documents, other than to make a note of their titles and numbers, if any, but the wording, on the thick cover of this particular file, stuck in my memory.

It was Operation Overlord* and I got a separate receipt for it. A few days later I was placed under close arrest, without any warning whatsoever.

Ray managed to get in to see me and tried to find out what it was all about, but everyone was as close as a church.

I really got angry then, and demanded to see the Senior Officer commanding the station or, if the powers that be preferred it, the Peruvian Ambassador. This seemed to cause quite a stir. The high brass of the Group hurriedly consulted my Record documents – which had been delayed, as usual – and found, to their dismay, that I had dual nationality. This upset any plans they may have had for railroading someone they didn't like.

I was immediately marched in to a grim-faced convening of a Board of Enquiry.

'Do you realise the seriousness of the charge?' I was asked sternly.

'What charge?' I countered cautiously.

'The loss of a highly secret document, as a direct result of your dereliction of duty,' I was told, in ringing tones.

'As Orderly Officer,' went on the President of the Board, a well-fed, wingless Wing Commander, 'you – and you alone must take full responsibility for the loss of any document in your care.'

Inspiration came to me.

'If you mean Operation Overlord,' I said, with great clarity, 'I've got a receipt for it.'

'Jesus Christ,' said the Senior Officer. 'Hand that receipt over immediately.'

'Not on your Nelly, sir,' I replied with some heat. 'By the way, I demand to see the Peruvian Ambassador.'

After that, things moved smartly. The Board of Inquiry hurriedly unconvened itself and I was placed under 'open' arrest, pending a hurried consultation about what the hell they were going to do now.

I returned to my billet and told Ray.

* *Operation Overlord* was the code name for the Allied invasion of Europe.

He got hysterical with laughter. 'Oh brother!' he choked. 'Now we'll see the shit hit the fan – you can't lose! You mad bloody Peruvian.'

Doubtless something hit a fan somewhere, because, the next day I was released from 'arrest' and whipped off to Blackpool by a staff car, chauffeured by a pretty W.A.A.F. driver.

Arriving at an imposing building in the famous seaside town, which the R.A.F. had virtually taken over, I was wheeled in to see a flight lieutenant who was wearing the lapel badges of a medical officer.

He was about 34 years old and had a nervous manner, as though he was worried about something.

'Ah yes! Bentin,' he muttered, 'I understand that you are not able to cope with the demands the Royal Air Force makes upon you and want to leave the Service. Well I don't think there will be too many problems with that . . .'

Inspiration seemed still to be with me.

'I see,' I said coldly, 'and who's been on the blower to you – mate!'

That shook him, as I'd obviously hit a raw nerve. I was being given the old heave-ho and he was obliging some senior chum of his by a lightning diagnosis of Extreme Anxiety Neurosis.

'What do you mean?' he asked uncomfortably, sensing things weren't going to be as smooth as he'd been led to believe.

'Well, I'll put it another way – presumably you want to practise psychiatry after this little lot's over,' I went on, making every word count. 'Because if you railroad me I'll go straight to the British Medical Association and have you struck off.'

'Gawd!' said the uniformed head-shrinker.

To my amazement, he actually apologised. As I left the office I heard him getting on the blower to my tormentors.

As we drove sedately back to 9 Group Headquarters, I thought, 'God bless my Guardian Angel – not forgetting, of course, the Peruvian Ambassador.'

A couple of days later I was posted to London, to the Central Medical Board – regraded A4B; which meant fit for operational service, other than flying and ordered to join the Belgian Squadron – 350 – *Escadrille des Chasseurs*.

On that leave, before joining my new station, I realised how shaken I had been, by the whole business at 9 Group. Suddenly it dawned on me that were I of pure European descent, as that snotty-nosed selection board had required, I would very possibly have been shot.

13. Belgians and buzz bombs

The Belgians were a very different lot from my previous posting.

In one way, they were very like my Poles, in that nearly all of them had escaped from the Germans and many of them had come over to Britain during the evacuation of Dunkirk. One or two of them had joined the R.A.F. later, from the Belgian Congo and even South America.

The names – Van de Veken, Vandenheuvel, Van der Meer and others like them indicated their Flemish origin, while names like Donnet, Meurice and Legrand, told of French ancestry. Fleming or Walloon, they were a joyful crowd of pilgrims – led by Michel, their Squadron Commander, who was a real eccentric and often flew in a bright red wig.

'The Boche won't recognise me, Spy,' he said to me with great conviction – completely forgetting that his helmet and goggles covered practically all of his hair.

But Michel had good reason to want not to be recognised by the Germans. As a brand-new aspirant, in the pre-war Belgian Air Force, he had only just won his wings when Belgium was overrun. He and a friend, who had also faded inconspicuously into the civilian landscape, plotted their joint escape.

They stole petrol, by siphoning it out of German staff cars and stored it in a garage, until they could fill up the tanks of an old T.K.I. which was a sort of small Tiger Moth. One day, just before dawn, they topped up the machine and nipped across the Channel to land in England and join the R.A.F.

The Germans would almost certainly have taken reprisals against his family, had they known that he was then commanding the Belgian fighter squadron, which was a real thorn in their side.

I had only been with the Belgians a matter of a few days, when we were flung into the Normandy beach-head battle.

Fighter Command tactics were totally different from the carefully planned and detailed Bomber operations. In the compilation of target and route information, I was a one man band. I had to work out the courses as soon as the target came through, and often raced out to the aircraft, still clutching the C.S.C. course computer to alter them, to allow for a sudden change in the wind.

It was all very exciting and I had no time to learn, beforehand, but had to pick up the job as I went along, because the 'Spy', I was replacing had left as I had arrived.

But Michel and his crews were patient men and soon showed me what they needed and at last all those hours flying with the Poles became worth every minute invested in air navigation.

To this happy, pleasant, squadron of brave men I was just another eccentric 'foreigner' like themselves – unorthodox and not too receptive to bullshit – so they accepted me, with warmth and understanding, and we got on just fine.

Then, overnight, we were pulled back from operating over the beach-head and targets of opportunity and shifted lock, stock and barrel to, of all places, Hawkinge – the airfield high above Folkestone which had been largely the central focus of my boyhood.

The pilots loaded everything they could into their Spitfire IXs and our ground crews were brought back and loaded into trucks. This left me to clear up all the Intelligence data we needed and, with a madcap pilot called Van, I flew up to Hawkinge in our old and venerable Tiger Moth, which had seen better days.

The reason for the sudden pull back from the beach-head was the increasing use by the enemy of the V.1 flying bombs. I had helped, in a small way, to delay their arrival with the attack on Peenemunde, but they were now crossing the Channel in droves and knocking hell out of London and the Home Counties.

The Spitfire IXs with which we were equipped were not fast enough for the job of catching these robot bombs, so the whole squadron had to convert almost overnight to the much faster Spitfire Mark 14 which was heavier and more powerful with its enormous new Griffon 65 engine. This excellent aeroplane didn't even start in the conventional way. The massive multi-bladed propeller was turned over by firing a sort of large shotgun blank cartridge, called a Koffman starter.

When Van and I flew up to Hawkinge we nearly got shot down by a trigger happy ack-ack gun crew. It seems incredible that a trained gunner could mistake a slow-moving biplane Tiger

Moth for the stubby, fiery monster of a V.1, racing along at 400 miles an hour plus, with the tailpipe of its pulse-jet engine spewing out a long flame.

Some poor devil of a Polish fighter pilot also nearly bought it around the same time. His frantic words heard on the W.T. were: 'Don't shoot! I'm a Pole with my bleddy tail on fire!'

As the stream of tracer shot up near us Van swore: 'Merde!' and dived for the deck and we flew the rest of the way, hedge-hopping over the tall trees and contour flying over the Downs. When we finally landed at Hawkinge we were both giggling like schoolboys.

I could hardly recognise the once familiar airfield. The great hangars, with their solid buttressed sides and corrugated iron roofs that had sheltered the huge bat-like Handley Page 0400s of my childhood were gone, blitzed in 1940, leaving only a grassy rubble to mark their remains.

Still without runways, the airfield was an undulating acreage of short grass. Once Hawker Furies and Harts had used it as their base. Now it served as an aerodrome for two squadrons of Spitfires, besides ourselves, plus an extraordinary collection of varied machines known as the Air Sea Rescue Flight.

This strange assortment of aircraft consisted of a Walrus, a slow, single-engined amphibian, that had done sterling work picking up ditched airmen, even entering German minefields to do so, plus a Spitfire Mark V referred to generally as 'clipped, cropped and clapped', as its shortened wings restricted its altitude. Finally there was an American Navy Grumman Avenger, the origin of which nobody could explain and which everyone firmly believed was stolen.

When the buzz bombs first came over us, at an average height of a thousand feet above the airfield, everything took off in all directions. As the attack increased in numbers, even the Walrus, which, flat out, could just do 80 knots, joined in with its single machine-gun. We cowered in slit trenches, not only from the V.1s, but also from the berserk Air Sea Rescue Flight.

The effect of the V.1 attack was chilling. They literally came over in hundreds, buzzing along with that loud two-stroke motor bike sound that you, selfishly, prayed would keep on going – because, when it stopped, down plummetted the robot bomb, to explode, with terrific force as we then thought.

The huge 'gun belt' of large and medium calibre anti-aircraft guns, that General Pyle had deployed from Sandwich to the end of the Romney Marsh, dealt reasonably well with these horrors – the great barrage filled the sky round the targets with masses of black smoke puffs as the proximity-fused shells burst. Then flowers of oily red flame would suddenly blossom like some obscene 'rose' and another V.1 would fail to reach London.

Our job was to keep up constant patrols over the Channel and intercept them, attacking on the dive and blasting them into the sea. Other patrols circled further inland and caught the flying bombs as they racketed over the sleepy countryside. But sometimes thick fog would clamp down on the Kent coast and you felt a peculiar helpless frustration as the gyro-controlled V.1s, still stuttering loudly, passed quite low over our Down-top airfield. Then, only the radar controlled heavy gun batteries had any hope of blowing them out of the soupy sky.

Wing Commander Vic Beamond, from the Fighter Wing at Manston, developed and adopted a revolutionary method of dealing with the buzz bomb. One day he came over to show us combat films taken from his camera gun. He was approaching a V.1 with his ammunition exhausted. We saw the bomb pass out of sight as he flew alongside it.

'Then,' as he explained simply, 'I put my wing under it and tipped it up so that its gyros tumbled and it fell out of control.'

Naturally he did this over as open a part of the countryside as possible and, what's more, he did it time and again. For sheer, cold-blooded bravery that takes a lot of beating.

Normally we ate, on duty, at the Officer's Mess, a typical old brick building of pre-war design. Off duty, we were billeted in a charming country house, called *White Ladies*, where our superb Belgian chef, who was, theoretically anyway, a clerk, prepared Lucullan meals of great size and variety.

The method of obtaining the necessary meat is worth mentioning. A bargain would be struck with one of the neighbouring farmers, who then tethered a suitable cow in a large open field. As soon as he was safely under cover, a Spitfire would appear and, making a low pass over the field, would 'trip' its guns.

The cow's 'passing', though a bit messy, was perfectly humane as the burst of fire killed it instantly. I won't argue the ethics, but the deed kept my pilots in the protein they needed and, of course, they shared it out generously with their allies.

One morning, I was shaving leisurely in the bedroom I shared with three Belgian pilots, when the roar of a Spitfire pursuing a buzz bomb thundered over the Downs towards us. The guns chattered and the V.1's motor stopped almost overhead, as it turned on its back and dived into our small orchard.

The next thing I remember was picking myself up from a pile of debris and glass at the end of the room. I had literally been blown under the bed. Apart from bruises and a few cuts I was unhurt, though grey from head to foot with dust. I was also deaf for about three days.

Another time I was walking around the perimeter of the grassy airfield, gazing out reminiscently at the misty outlines of Folkestone, which lay in the sunshine way below me, when I was puzzled to hear the sound of an approaching express train. It foxed me, because the nearest railway line bisected the town itself and was a good three miles away as the crows flew.

The roar of the explosion and the blast that, though screened by the crest of the hills, nevertheless threw me several feet backwards, confirmed my suspicions that this wasn't an express train.

By the size of the crater, it must have been a large cross-Channel shell, fired from the huge guns on Gris-Nez. Again, due to my Guardian Angel's diligence, I escaped with a temporary deafness and a few bruises.

I wrote my family about this, because it struck me as not too alarming an example of my seeming immortality. My brother sent me a delightful drawing of my Guardian Angel, with his eyes crossed and halo twisted, being borne off on a stretcher, by two cherubim.

'Poor bastard,' one is saying, 'he's had Bentin for almost six months.'

About this time I was called upon to attend a court martial.

This was not for my benefit – I was asked by Michel to act as 'prisoner's friend', for a young sergeant pilot of ours, who had been charged with being in illegal possession of four gallons of petrol.

An impressive judge advocate's representative arrived, a full Squadron Leader in rank, who, with another two officers, formed the court. The prosecuting officer was a Fight Lieutenant, who also had probably never seen an aeroplane, either.

The heinous crime was solemnly read out, in the formal shape of the charge, and the court martial began.

I have no doubt that the sergeant had nicked petrol from the bowser tanker – and so had practically everyone else. It so just happened that my friend got caught doing it.

After the prosecution had finished his detached and professional approach to the job, I rose nervously to my feet and addressed the court. I was the only amateur in this grave matter

126

of the administration of justice, King's Regulations and Air Council instructions.

In the best style of Lionel Barrymore, in one of his impressive court scenes, I launched forth into a description of the young pilot's harrowing escape from the Germans, and his subsequent unblemished record of brave service with the R.A.F.

By now, overcome with emotion, I enlarged on the dangers of his career as a successful fighter pilot.

'Who are we to judge,' I croaked, nearly overcome with my own eloquence, 'we who are not called upon to risk death daily.'

I went on, in the same vein, finishing up, almost in tears, at the prospect of this saintly youth, who, incidentally, had pinched a damn sight more than four gallons, now standing pitifully before the court.

As I reached the climax of my plea for mercy, the Belgian sergeant somewhat took the edge off my speech by bursting out with: 'Give it to 'em, Spy.'

He was sternly warned to remain silent and his words were stricken from the record. I sat down, sweating, amid an amused silence and, in my own mind, a thunderous roar of applause.

Now, either the judge advocate was influenced by the extremely good lunch we had thoughtfully provided, through the enthusiastic skill of our great Belgian chef, or he was just thoroughly delighted by this display of amateur histrionics.

Anyway, probably due to a combination of both, the case was terminated abruptly and only a reprimand was administered to appear on the good sergeant's records.

Tho show there was no ill feeling, the sergeant even gave the judge advocate a lift back to the Mess – his staff car having failed to start because another Belgian pilot had siphoned all the petrol out of it, for his own use.

One day we were taken off the V.1 patrol and I was ordered to brief a long-range sortie for the complete Wing. This trip was to be a fighter sweep far into Belgium. For this reason, long-range tanks had to be fitted to the Spitfires. These consisted of two wing tanks or a belly tank, whichever was needed, or even a combination of both.

Off they went, to hammer German installations outside Brussels, and shoot up anything military, moving on the roads. In a much shorter time than a bomber Wing would have taken, back they came, breaking off formation to come into the circuit.

As I stood outside our dispersal hut, at the far end of the airfield, I could count our aircraft, as they came in. Thankfully, it looked as though they were undamaged.

Not so one Spitfire of the other Squadron. It had been badly shot up by flak and was coming in to a belly landing with its wheels and flaps up – its hydraulic system shot to pieces.

Skidding crazily across the grass on the collapsing belly tank, which acted as a sort of skid, the Spitfire careered over the airfield, shedding various portions of itself as it hurtled straight towards me.

First the wings broke off and then the engine wrenched itself sideways, as though on a hinge, leaving the terrified pilot totally exposed in his seat, with his legs raised, still clutching the useless control column. I stood as though I had melted into the asphalt of the hard-standing, my leg muscles refusing to obey the urgent need for flight.

Twenty yards from me the plane slithered to a rasping, smoking halt, the pilot staring straight at me, with a dazed look on his chalk-white face.

I moved groggily towards him and then broke into a run, hoping to get him out, before the tank went up but, as I reached him, he fainted and I damn nearly followed his example. By this time, a couple of other pilots had rushed up and, together, we got him out, or rather got him away, because he was practically out of what was left of his aircraft anyway.

Examining the plane afterwards, I figured out that had it not broken up in that exact sequence, we would both have ended up plastered against the side of the bombproof shelter behind me.

The next day we each went on a 48-hour pass, which Michel had ordered me to take.

On the platform at Folkestone Central station where, years before, I had helped deliver a baby, I had the happy experience of being reunited with Kit, my boyhood chum.

Kit was flying, with the Fleet Air Arm of the Royal Navy, in those wickedly obsolete Swordfish torpedo planes, that should have been 'junked' before the war. His nerves had been stretched unbearably and that cheerful open face of his was lined and drawn.

We talked at each other nineteen to the dozen – falling about, laughing, all the way up to London in that hard-arsed Southern Railway carriage.

He'd had a pretty rotten time altogether, pathfinding over Tobruk, but you'd never have known it from his racy conversation and affectionately blasphemous references to the 'old stringbag of a plane' in which he, somehow, had managed to stay alive.

In London I dropped in at the OGNISKO POLSKI, the 'Polish Hearth', a club for Polish forces and their associates, which then had its premises in Exhibition Road, Kensington. There, to my delight, I heard news of Ozzie and his navigator Stinger. Their story really deserves a book to itself for it is, indeed, a saga worth recording for doubting posterity.

On that raid over Poland these two had been the sole survivors of their Wellington, when it was coned by searchlights and shot to bits.

Ozzie had managed to bale out, after Stinger – a difficult thing to do for the pilot of a badly damaged plane, with half a dead crew aboard because, as soon as he left the controls, the aircraft would go into the sort of contortion that. 'George', the automatic pilot, couldn't cope with.

But Ozzie had got away with it and they both dangled down on their chutes, till they landed, unhurt, somewhere in Poland.

They were young, well set up and extremely fit specimens of Polish manhood, and the two of them could speak Polish, German and French. Immediately after landing, they set out to walk back, or rather to 'screw' their way back to England home and beauty.

Perhaps a good title for their story would be 'F – as in Freedom' because, without ever once contacting any member of the elaborate network of willing helpers, that made up the Resistance escape routes, like O'Leary or Comet, these two inexhaustible young men made their amorous way across half Europe.

As the Polish squadron leader who was graphically describing their exploits said, 'They both went through a helluva lot.'

Even allowing for the universal man-shortage that was plaguing the European women, I do feel that their achievements rank with those of Don Juan. What's more, it was all done by personal recommendation – bouche à bouche, as it were.

When they were finally smuggled over the Spanish frontier, by the 'contrabandistos', who made a regular living out of that kind of thing, they were literally at the end of their strength.

Once again, in the words of my Polish friend, 'Michael, they were both bleddy clapped out.'

9

14. I enter a monastery

From time to time I was pulled out of squadron operations of these various units to attend special courses or to carry out other odd duties, on attachment. What these were is not relevant, but I should mention some of the experiences that happened to me while engaged on some of them.

For example, a battle course or 'combat' course was available to Intelligence officers who would have a closer contact with the enemy. The specialised weapons programmes were done largely under the blanket of S.O.E., the special operations executive.

Two of the top combat instructors were ex-Shanghai policemen. They were gristle-hard men, light on their feet and fast as snakes. Their job was to teach the handgun, the knife and other less conventional methods of murder. They even demonstrated the garotte – a piece of piano wire with wooden handles exactly like the ones used to cut cheese in pre-war Sainsbury's shops.

Their methods were so efficient as far as the handgun was concerned that by using them I can still fire my 'double-tap' – to you, two shots – off in under one second.

They preached the revolver as the most reliable weapon, and the Browning 9M/M Hi-power automatic or the Sten and German Schmeisser sub-machine-guns for fire power.

Their arguments are, even today, still valid though please God, we will never have to use them in anger again.

One incident illustrates what hard men they were and, indeed, had to be.

To the question: 'How many men have you killed?', the terse reply from one ex-Shanghai policeman was: 'Fifty-four, sir. Not counting Chinks.'

* * *

At the end of the long summer I found that the Belgians had

been told that they would go into Brussels which had recently been liberated. I had then been immediately posted to another job and lost track of 350 squadron, till I finally got back into Europe as an operational I.O.

Obviously my main use to British Intelligence, other than for straightforward 'ops', came to an end with the fall of Belgium and the subsequent release of all personnel attached to M.I.9, or used by them for teaching aircrew evasion and escape procedures.

From now on, unless they were shot down in Holland, they would fall directly into German hands. The Italian side of it came under another department of M.I.9 in the Middle East and so didn't concern me.

Some facets of escape were still applicable but the war looked as though it would soon be over now.

The main thing was to make the crews aware that they must be especially careful in their behaviour in Dulag Luft, the transit camp in Germany where they would start their captivity. This specialised interrogation camp was riddled with hidden microphones, and staffed by skilled Abwehr experts, often posing as shot-down allied airmen themselves.

For about three months I was shuttled from one short posting to another, such as a few weeks with the Czechs at North Weald, and then with a mixed bag of trainees at an O.T.U., that is an Operational Training Unit, for Spitfire pilots at Kirton-in-Lindsey.

My only memory of North Weald was being put on a fizzer and sternly warned about passing a dud cheque – unknowingly – in the mess.

This amounted to the monumental sum of £4 10s. and was due, as the accounts section then found out, to their failure to pay in my allowances for some twelve weeks. This had left me with my pay of about £5 a week to meet my mess bill – only I didn't happen to know the accounts had stopped paying me.

The upshot of it was that I wasn't cashiered or drummed out in disgrace, but again got an official apology. For once I didn't have to call for help from the long-suffering Peruvian Ambassador.

A short attachment of 10 Group in the West Country wasted more time and there I, once again, met the pompous Wing Commander who was so upset when I refused to carry out fighter control duties at 9 Group. He was surprisingly friendly, or should I say wary, since my Board of Enquiry at 9 Group had marked me as tricky to deal with in a summary fashion.

One job I did during this boring interlude was marking a map with pins to show the increasing number of V.2 rockets falling on the Metropolitan area of London. This was highly alarming because several of them fell near my family, one near my parents at Barnes, blowing in their windows yet again and covering everything with soot and dust. Both Pop and Mama were unhurt and I was more than grateful for that.

At about this time Pop told me a strange story, while I was on a 48-hour pass.

Our family in South America was universally concerned about us and sent my parents regular food parcels which Mother shared, typically, with her neighbours. One cousin also wrote Pop asking for any information he might pick up, psychically, about certain investments and various personal family matters.

Pop replied in an airmail letter, giving certain dates in red. Not long after, two M.I.5 counter-espionage operatives came to see him.

Had Pop written this letter, they asked and what was the significance of the dates?

Pop told them why and what the information meant and they both looked at him in disbelief, till Dad said to one of them, 'By the way, your mother's name is Elizabeth and she passed over about ten years ago.'

He then rattled off another string of names and descriptions, everyone of them 'dead' accurate, if you will forgive the unintended pun. The two M.I.5 men left a bit hurriedly. I, for one, would love to have read their report.

It turned out that Pop's dates had, quite by chance, coincided with large troop convoy sailings from the States.

At last I got my sailing orders. Literally in this case, because I went across to Belgium in a troop transport.

As we arrived at Zeebrugge another ship, which had come over in convoy with us, blew up on a mine. Among the casualties were a number of A.T.S. girls, some of the first women's auxiliaries to arrive.

Why they couldn't have flown such a small number over to Belgium is beyond me. I suppose in war, women take their chances with men, but it always seemed so much more horrible when it was women who were the victims.

At Brussels I got orders to proceed – strange how you always have to 'proceed' – to Eindhoven, on the Dutch border. There to my joy, the Belgians were stationed. Their losses had been rough, however, and some of their old spirit had been dampened.

Sadly, my job wasn't with them, and I trucked up to Helmond to join a Typhoon wing equipped with rockets and specialising in ground strafing and forward troop support.

At this time the preparations for crossing the Rhine were well ahead and it was a matter of a few weeks before Eisenhower would make the fateful decision.

The wing was billeted in and around a monastery, of all the unlikely places, and I remember the Father Abbot asking me if it would be possible to remove the Varga girls, pretty pin-ups of cheeky busty birds from the *Esquire* magazine calendars which a squadron artist had copied. The 'blow-ups' of these sexy ladies were painted on the bar we had built in the mess and apparently were upsetting the monks badly.

The Intelligence section of the wing was run by an unsympathetic and grumpy middle-aged industrialist. His second in command wasn't much cop either.

The aircrews weren't mad about either of them. As both of them tried to lumber me with their superior knowledge, I braced myself and prepared for trouble – which, strangely, never came.

The situation was made considerably brighter because, firstly, we were busy and, secondly, the Intelligence section Clerk Corporal Harold Taylor became a firm and good friend. With Harold that means for life.

I count Harold and Mary as two very close friends today. He is one of the few people I know who really shared some of my experiences and can vouch for their truth.

Harold and his wife both wrote to each other every day and he restored a lot of faith I had lost in ever finding a relationship as close as these two obviously had.

The aircrews themselves were, as usual, ready to accept anyone who was really interested in them and this more than made up for the offhand discourtesy of my two 'brother' officers.

The Typhoon was an amazing plane, originally designed as a fighter and the forerunner of the splendid Tempest. The 'Tiffie', after teething troubles which once threatened to 'ground' it, had found its best place in the scheme of things when it was converted into a rocket carrying platform.

These weapons, of which it could carry up to eight, or less with the wing tanks fitted, were capable of delivering the same knockout punch as a six-inch gunned cruiser. They even sank large ships in the Baltic, as we moved up in the final attack.

Their main targets were tanks and trains, both of which they could destroy with just one direct hit, and the technique developed by the pilots was a simple one.

They got their reflector sights on to the target as they dived down and then as the 20 mm. tracer shells from their four wing canons walked up to the target, they fired their rockets.

These shot down along the lines of fiery shells and often succeeded in blowing a locomotive clean off the lines, or a tank turret high into the air.

My crews were as formidable as their planes and two incidents illustrate this well.

The first involved a pilot who flew his plane with a broken back and both legs paralysed and, using only the stick and 'trim' controls, succeeded in landing safely on our short strip.

The second was when a squadron commander on our wing returned from a sortie with a third of his starboard wing shot clean off. This had the effect of making his Typhoon go into a roll as soon as his speed dropped below 200 knots. It made landing impossible, with wheels either up or down, as the speed was far to high.

The only answer was to bale out and this the C.O. did with a display of cool courage which, to me, has had few equals.

Not that he was 'grandstanding'. He just considered that this was a good opportunity to demonstrate to his pilots the best way to get out of his badly damaged aircraft.

As he approached the airfield he was in contact with flying control and asked them to relay his instructions over the open tannoy broadcast system.

Flying control duly 'patched' him in and we all clearly heard his voice, just like those pre-war flying displays where they relayed the formation stunt-flying team orders.

His words still come across that long bridge of years.

'I'm going to trim the aircraft fully forward and hold the stick right back between my knees. This will keep me straight and level till I release it – then we'll go into a steep dive and I will be shot out well clear of the tailplane.

'I'm unclipping my oxygen hose now but I'm disconnecting my R.T. plug, at the last moment, so you can hear what I say right up to bale out.

'Here goes the canopy.'

The glittering bubble of Perspex blew off the Typhoon as it approached us at a height of about 1,500 feet.

That cool voice continued: 'I'm unclipping my Sutton Harness and getting the straps clear, in case I get hung up on it.

'Now a quick check! Yes! that seems all right. See you in a minute – over and out.'

As the last words echoed from the tannoy, the Typhoon which by now was roaring overhead to one side of us, but opposite our farmhouse control tower, dramatically flipped over into a vertical dive, throwing the C.O. well clear of his aircraft.

His pilot chute streamed out and pulled his main canopy open almost immediately. As his machine whined down to explode with ground-shaking violence a safe distance away from us, he floated down to a perfect landing. Ten minutes later he was downing a beer with us in the mess.

This happened long before ejector seats came into service and was the nearest thing to one I have ever seen.

*   *   *

We had Army Liaison Officers with us to make certain that we attacked the right targets and didn't clobber our own army as it moved forwards behind the Bomb Line.

This was an invisible wall, which was represented on our battle map operations as a series of yellow and black dashes drawn in grease pencil on the talc which covered the chart.

One of these A.L.O.s was called Barry and we became close friends. He 'genned' me up quickly on the right procedures and taught me the elements of the techniques that I needed to know, without once adopting the rather superior air that my senior Intelligence officer treated me with.

Fair haired and moustached with a very British sense of fair play and humour, Barry shared a lot of his thoughts with me and I got to know and like him a lot.

Then, overnight, he left us to join a special glider regiment that was getting ready to cross the Rhine as part of the big airborne operation – his last words to me being a promise to bring me back a Luger pistol.

Three days later the long stalemate ended and the actual Rhine crossing started. In the pale darkness before dawn the giant air operation thundered overhead.

Parachute troops were also being dropped to seize and save the vital Rhine bridges from being blown up as the opening Allied barrage opened up on targets on the opposite banks.

The previous night American forces had poured into our airfield with massive bulldozers, which were now lined up on either side of the runway. As the transport Dakotas that had carried the paratroops and towed the gliders over the dropping zones roared overhead, the use for these bulldozers became plain.

The aircraft were at the limit of their fuel range and many of them were badly damaged by flak. The full 250-plus of them wheeled in a great circuit of our landing strip.

Under American flying control officers they were guided in to land in a long stream and touched down at 20-second intervals. A precision operation requiring great flying discipline.

The dozers' job was to clear the runway when inevitably one or other of these Daks pranged on the runway itself. As the damaged plane skidded to a halt, a dozer rumbled out on to the runway and, even while the crew were scrambling out, pushed the crashed plane sideways off the strip. It was the most efficient operation I had ever seen, and had these drastic measures not been adopted, the rest of the transport planes would never have made it down safely.

American thinking, unlike ours, was never parsimonious or mean-minded as far as equipment was concerned.

Whereas our high ups seemed to wage war as though they were paying for it themselves – the Americans got the job done as quickly as possible, never counting the cost of equipment for a moment.

In this spectacular display of good old American 'get up and go', every one of those crews walked away from their landings.

That night we had a tremendous 'thrash' in the mess, of which my only clear memory is waking up in the morning fully dressed from head to toe in the uniform of an American Air Force captain, right down to the flight jacket.

Our Wing Commander whose Christian name was Kit and who was affectionately known as 'Shit', went missing as the attacks mounted in ferocity. Seventy-two hours later he returned, leading some 200 German prisoners.

His replacement – a Group Captain who had been flying Hurricane cannon fighters in the Western Desert before converting to Typhoons – lasted exactly one day before he 'bought it' by diving into a narrow railway cutting and losing his wings on the steep sides. He may well have misjudged the Typhoon's massive wing span in comparison to the smaller Hurricane that he had spent so many hours flying.

John Derry, later to become a famous test pilot and be killed at a post-war Farnborough Air Display, turned up with a Spitfire fighter-bomber wing that specialised in slinging 500-pound bombs at enemy targets.

News also came that Barry was dead, killed in that first

murderous glider assault on the dropping zones. His manner of death was typical of this splendid young man.

The Horsa glider that carried him, his wireless equipped 'jeep' and his batman, had crash-landed safely as dawn broke.

Barry got out all right but a concealed 88 mm. dual purpose gun had smashed the glider as it lay there at the end of its skidding landing run.

The shell wounded Barry's batman and, characteristically, Barry went back for him. As he was carrying him out of the wreck a second shell from the high velocity gun killed them both instantly.

*   *   *

Back came our Wing Co., at the head of his prisoners whom he handed over to the 'brown jobs'.

Immediately he set up a massive wing sortie to clobber enemy transport moving up to the beach-head.

The whole wing raced off and this time one of the 'fluid six' flights left their R.T. transmitters open.

I was up in control following their progress and heard the whole thing. The voice of one of our Canadian pilots crackled over our W.T. loudspeakers.

'Hell!' he yelled. 'That bloody hospital is shooting at us.'

'Watch out, Number Two!' chimed in the flight commander's voice. 'Don't blast the Red Cross.'

But his warning was too late.

We distinctly heard the throaty crackly of the four 20 mm. cannon, followed by that excited Canadian voice.

'Jesus Christ,' it said, simply. 'The whole bloody hospital's blown up.'

The Germans had, apparently, disguised one of their ammunition dumps by painting huge Red Crosses on the roofs.

The same night there was a massive raid, by hundreds of heavy bombers, on the Ruhr.

I went up into the bell tower of the monastery and watched the markers go down on to the target area which, although quite a long way away, was brightly lit and clearly visible with great fires burning.

The candelabras of burning red and green markers hung over the centre of the fires, slowly dropping, on their parachutes, right into the blazing centre of the industrial complex below.

It was a weird feeling to see the end result of those bomber briefings so many months before, and actually to see the receiving end of the great bomber attacks.

Those action packed days and nights passed in a kind of semi-detached dream as though you were next door to reality.

Ambulances, heavily laden with battle casualties, rumbled down the road that flanked the airfield, while massive reinforcements of men and material clattered and lurched their way up to the beach-head across the Rhine.

Never once did the Luftwaffe show itself and the barrels of the 40 mm. Bofors guns of our R.A.F. Regiment stayed silent.

Once a badly mauled B24 Liberator appeared high overhead and, as the whole crew baled out, it circled and swooped with no hand at the controls like some aerial Flying Dutchman.

We were just about to scramble a section to shoot it down when it finally reared up and, with its remaining two engines shrieking in protest, it plunged down to explode in a huge sheet of flame, just clear of our airstrip.

Next morning we got our final orders to pack up and move forwards to cross the river at Wesel.

As we rumbled across the bridge it struck me, as it must have done so many others, how far we had all come since those grim despairing days of 1940 when the island people stood alone against the seemingly unstoppable Nazis.

Yet here we were, five years later, creaking over a badly damaged bridge, across the Rhine so long associated with the German legend of invincibility.

Outside Wesel we set up our tents. In the warm sunshine it was a pleasant feeling to be under canvas.

There I left my Typhoon Wing to join another one which had lost its Intelligence officer. This one was a mirror copy of the previous wing and I settled down quickly and easily.

Harold Taylor had seen me off when I left, thoughtfully handing me a flask of tea and a packet of sandwiches.

'Don't make a bloody fool of yourself, sir,' he advised in that quiet Yorkshire voice of his. 'See you in Huddersfield when it's all over.'

And, do you know, he did.

15. The ultimate blasphemy

Our convoy of trucks bumped slowly towards the little town of Goch, or rather what little remained of the little town of Goch. More than 350 'heavies' had bombed it into a charred shambles over which hung the sickly stench of death.

One wall remained standing and across it, in white paint, someone had daubed the words: 'This was Goch!'

It was 1945 and the smiles of the farming folk of Holland had been replaced by the hate-filled half-glances of the stunned Germans. I felt deeply compassionate towards them – but not for long. The airfield we were making for was a fighter base at Achmer Husted, on the banks of Dortmund-Ems Canal, a costly target that Bomber Command had tried so hard to knock out.

Within an hour of getting the ground crews into this airfield we were under sniper fire. Men started to fall and my new Wing Co. – a South African – told me to take an R.A.F. Regiment scout car and winkle the snipers out. I had a sergeant and a driver with me. We were armed with a BESA heavy machine-gun and our own sidearms.

We cautiously felt our way across a deserted bridge spanning the oily waters of the canal and passed signs of a recent firefight. Seventh Armoured had gone through earlier and the reeking air told of a sharp engagement at close quarters. Multiple flak guns lay abandoned behind their cover – otherwise we would have bought Achmer-Husted at a far higher price.

A spatter of bullets spanged off the side of our small steel fortress. It sounded too light to be of military calibre – more like some last Volksturm scrape-of-the-barrel reservist armed with a light hunting rifle.

The mind works very clearly under fire and this analysis of the bullets flying round me seemed quite normal at the time.

The fire could have come from a farmhouse about a hundred yards to the side of us. Smokeless powder is the devil to locate but we'd spotted movement at an upper window.

The driver turned us to face it and the sergeant gave the farmhouse a hosing with the BESA. The heavy ball ammunition chopped into the fabric of the building tearing out great chunks of its flaking plaster. There was a still, fume-laden silence as the gun ceased firing. Then a cry came from the farmhouse.

While the driver covered us with the heavy machine-gun we jumped out and, right and left, spread out and approached the building, both ready to blast with our Schmeissers, those efficient German sub-machine-guns.

From behind the building came stumbling three small scare-crows of soldiers, throwing their light rifles before them.

Their teeth chattering with terror, three 12-year-old boys stood shivering and weeping in front of us.

I felt sick, but as one of them made a sudden move I automatically raised the Schmeisser and my finger started to squeeze the trigger.

'Nay, lad,' the sergeant's hand fell urgently on my gun. 'They're nowt but bloody kids.'

I gulped, realising how instinctive combat training had nearly made me commit infanticide.

'What the hell do we do with them?' I asked, completely at a loss.

The sergeant, a bulky, sticky ex-miner, grinned.

'Start the little buggers off right.'

He undid his webbing belt. Taking each unprotesting Hitler Jugend in turn he sat down, put them across his knee and belted them across the buttocks.

Their quivering paralysis of terror changed to boyish howls of anguish but somehow, when their short chastisement was over, we all felt cleansed.

Ever since Eton I have hated beating and I have never touched my own children but here, for once, it was a good thing. This tough Yorkshire miner, with his paternal instinct, had saved all our sanities.

Incredibly, with that outlandish touch of family normality, the three murderous snipers turned back into three naughty boys. I wonder if they ever appreciated what he had done for them and how near their death they had been.

As we drove them back to hand them over to a prisoner-of-war cage, they were as excited as kids on an outing.

So illogical is war that as we passed the airfield, where their victims were already stiff in death, these perverted children excitedly pointed out the aeroplanes. But who is to say that these little horrors were any less brave than Boy Jack Cornwall, who won the Victoria Cross at Jutland, in the First World War?

When I got back to the airfield two Sherman tanks were standing there. Their crews came from Seventh Armoured and had an odd request – could they have some of our rockets please?

They actually welded the rocket rails on to the gawky, high silhouetted tanks and later fired the 60 lb, rockets, two a side, in anger against the enemy. Whether they hit anything I'll never know.

David Niven, who later became a good friend, told me that we must have been in this same battle together because he was with Phantom, a freelance European development of the Long Range Desert Group and they had been the force that passed through the sniper area an hour or so before.

The Typhoons had settled in and re-armed and off they went to badger the panzers of the Gross Deutschland Division.

This formidable, highly trained and experienced German group had been blasting the Shermans to pieces with their heavy Tiger tanks and hunting Jadg-Panthers.

Soon the crews returned with good results and the Gross Deutschland retired hastily into the covering woods.

The Wing Co. approached me. 'See any hunting rifles, Spy?' he inquired.

'I was a bit too busy, sir,' I countered cautiously.

'I can always use a good hunting rifle,' he said slowly. 'Christ man, go and find me some.'

I can never resist the opportunity to lay my hands on a fine piece of craftsmanship, be it a hunting rifle or a well-made door lock. So I piled into a jeep with my corporal, a long-suffering, bespectacled Geordie who kept muttering, 'Mad bugger,' between his teeth, and we set off into the 'cleared' area across the bridge.

About ten miles up the road, through the dense but orderly pine forests, we found a small village. I got out and, covered by my muttering corporal, I routed out the head man.

'Haben sie die waffen?' I asked in my halting German.

'Ja, ja, naturlich,' nodded the nervous burgher – and, from that small village, produced more than a hundred assorted arms.

The villagers kept dropping this pile of weaponry at my feet till I looked like some martial Joan of Arc being surrounded by metal faggots.

The summer air was hazy and strangely silent except for the rattle and clunk of the weapons as they fell in the growing pile. I felt tense and kept my Schmeisser ready.

'Alles in ordnung,' said the burgo-meister, with a stainless steel grimace which passed for a smile.

I withdrew the bolts from the rifles and shoved them down a well, selecting two shotguns and a fine telescopic weapon for the Wing Co. Then, still wordlessly, I swung back into the jeep, never ceasing to cover the villagers, and roared off back the way we had come.

About a mile down the cobbled stretch of road there was a sharp corner. Cautiously edging its way round, was a buttoned-up armoured car. The gun swung to cover us as we skidded to a halt. Then the hatch opened and a Phantom lieutenant leant out.

'Where the bloody hell have you come from?' he inquired, holding his .38 on us.

'Up the road about a mile there's a village.'

'I should bloody well think it its,' replied the Phantom warrior, 'and we haven't bloody liberated it yet!'

'Christ,' I said hoarsely. My driver muttered, 'Mad Peruvian bugger,' and roared off, nearly jerking me out of the jeep.

Later a Phantom captain grinningly told me.

'You had the whole Gross Deutschland lot watching you, mate. Their 88s must have followed your every move in that village.

'We got one of their captains to talk and he said, "Ve knew it vas a trap so ve didn't open fire und give our positions avay." '

My poor long-suffering guardian angel must have had celestial kittens.

Within 48 hours we were off again, belting up the autobahn where it hadn't been blown up or rocketed. Where it had been cut we made a detour and on one of these diversions I met my match. I shall always think of this incident as the 'Shoot Out at the OK Sty'.

For most of our progress through Germany we had subsisted on an unrelieved diet of 'K' rations, bully beef and 'M and V', a tinned mixture of meat and veg that lacked any taste whatsoever.

Not having met any hedgehogs to bake, I felt that my section might profit gastronomically by a real meat meal. As we passed a farmhouse and stopped for the inevitable brew-up and a piss, I spotted a fine pig standing warily in the farmyard.

I hate killing anything, but an untended animal in the middle of a running battle is like captured weapons – part of the legitimate spoils of war.

Egged on by my faithful team, I drew my trusty .45 Colt and approached the pig, confident of my ability to kill it painlessly with one shot. But I reckoned without the battle conditioning of that remarkable swine.

Its head went up and it poised itself tensely on its trotters. I swear that pig knew about guns because, as my revolver came up and the hammer clicked back, it was off like greased lightning.

My first shot blasted low over its racing back. My second missed its rump by inches as it shot behind the barn.

Surprised, and to a rousing supporting cheer, I sped after it fully expecting to settle its hash with my next shots.

The pig had other ideas and, as I rounded the barn, it charged me, knocking me clean into the midden. It then belted round the other side of the barn.

In a mad parody of western shoot-out we stalked each other, as my airmen whistled and yelled encouragement.

The pig stood still for a moment and I squeezed off my remaining two shots. As I did so it suddenly rolled over and I thought I'd won. But it just completed the roll and came up on its feet turning again and rushing straight at me.

By this time I was laughing so much I couldn't reload and I had to scoot out of its path, helpless with mirth. It stopped about 30 feet away and pawed the ground like a Spanish bull.

That finished it for me. Drawing my manure-covered self upright I whacked up a grave salute to this Prince among pigs and, with my last vestiges of sportsmanship, I let it go in peace.

As we bounced off up the road, we cheered my gallant opponent. As it passed out of sight I couldn't help feeling that here was the true embodiment of Teutonic courage.

We were headed for an airstrip outside Celle, a small town, just north of Hanover.

We had barely cranked to a halt and started to set up the 'ops' tent, when the Typhoons thundered into the circuit and broke formation for their approach.

As they landed on the hastily repaired strip – a 'Jock' doctor raced up to us in his jeep.

'Got any medical orderlies?' he shouted above the roar of the aircraft engines. 'Any K rations or vitaminised chocolate?'

'What's up?' I asked for I could see his face was grey with shock.

'Concentration camp up the road,' he said shakily, lighting a cigarette. 'It's dreadful – just dreadful.'

He threw the cigarette away untouched.

'I've never seen anything so awful in my life. You just won't believe it till you see it – for God's sake come and help them!'

'What's it called?' I asked, reaching for the operations map to mark the concentration camp safely out of the danger area near the bomb line.

'Belsen,' he said, simply.

Millions of words have been written about these horror camps, many of them by inmates of those unbelievable places.

I've tried, without success, to describe it from my own point of view, but the words won't come.

To me Belsen was the ultimate blasphemy.

* * *

After V.E. Day I flew up to Denmark with Kelly, a West Indian pilot who was a close friend.

As we climbed over Belsen, we saw the flame-throwing Bren carriers trundling through the camp – burning it to the ground.

Our light M.E. 108 rocked in the superheated air, as we sped above the curling smoke, and Kelly had the last words on it.

'Thank Christ for that,' he said, fervently.

And his words sounded like a benediction.

16. The day peace
broke out

The end of the war in Europe came for us after a night of alarms and preparations for a massive assault on shipping in the Baltic.

At one o'clock, I was in the control truck when the orders to stand down came through.

This was confirmed an hour later and a full Cease Fire was in operation.

'Well, that's it,' said the flying control officer flatly, 'I thought I'd say something historic and that's it.'

An all pervading feeling of anti-climax settled over us.

But then I realised something. 'I'm alive!' I yelled, upsetting my mug of tea, with its four lumps and no bromide. I stumbled out of the truck and ran to the nearest tent.

'Wake up,' I shouted. 'It's all over – the bloody war's over!'

'Do you know what bloody time it is?' grumbled a sleepy voice. 'It's two o' bloody clock.'

I ran to my tent and, picking up my Schmeisser from underneath my sleeping mate's bed where I had put it for safety, I rushed outside and let off a full magazine into the air.

With a shout the wing came tumbling out of their tents, holding various weaponry in front of them.

'It's over – fini – terminado – kaput!' I yelled at them.

The noise of excited reaction burst into a great clamour and a few more shots were fired into the air.

Then the Wing Co. arrived.

His quiet presence sobered us down.

'All aircraft to be fully armed and fitted with long range tanks and four rockets each!' he snapped out. 'Christ man, I trust these bastards about as far as I can throw a Tiffie.'

But although when dawn broke the armourers were still busy loading up, the Cease Fire continued in an unnatural quiet.

The same silence seemed to grip all of us and we moved about somehow at a loss.

This hang fire of action only lasted a day or two. It may seem strange that we didn't have a party to celebrate – but then only those few kilometres up the road lay the stench of Belsen.

At last our orders were to clear out and we moved en masse, up to Schleswigland – a large air base near the Schleswig Meer, a huge series of lakes that stretched into the Baltic.

Our route lay across Hamburg. As we passed through the mind bending destruction of that tortured city, I realised again that compassion was still the greatest gift we have.

The sight of the first R.A.F. uniforms brought a strange reaction from the few scarecrow people left in the ruins.

There were no children, I remember, and no old people – just a handful of automation-like men and women who were past caring about anything but basic survival.

Underneath those undulating heaps of brick and concrete were the hovels they lived in, along with the 140,000 estimated unburied dead if, by burial, you mean a conventional grave.

Hamburg was one gigantic grave.

From that chaos we trucked far up into the summer-blessed countryside of north Germany's Schleswig-Holstein.

This was almost completely untouched by war and the neat farms and villages we passed through bore little evidence of the ferocity of the past weeks.

B.164 Schleswigland as the R.A.F. called our new and final base was also unmarked. But littered along the great perimeter of this important airbase were hundreds of German aircraft, some like the great four-engined transport JU.290s, in full operational order, while others were dismantled or sabotaged – but on the whole the Germans had left it too hurriedly to do much damage.

'The 'Non-Fraternisation' order, which forbade any form of communication with the German population, other than essential orders, settled over everything like an invisible grey blanket.

This mass sending of the German people to Coventry seems a little childish now, but I suppose someone had good reasons for ordering it.

I kept myself busy with various projects – some semi-official and others out of plain curiosity.

I suggested to my C.O. that I found out as much as I could about German research aeroplanes and, blessed by the Wing C.O. whose desire for hunting rifles I had at last been able to satisfy, Kelly and I set out to scout round the area.

We mainly used the little Messerschmitt 108 which by an odd coincidence was named the Taifun. This nippy light sports plane was Professor Willi Messerschmitt's forerunner of his formidable ME.109, but it was a four-seater.

With two up she handled like a fighter and Kelly was a first-class pilot. I learned a lot in that lovely little plane.

We also picked up some more legitimate spoils of war – in this case hundreds of German air force radio valves, which we used to get back into service the many radio sets stacked at Schleswig.

Having provided the whole wing with communications for home listening, we then flogged the rest of the valves in Brussels when we eventually went on leave.

Really my job was over. Apart from making out a report on the mass of German experimental work on jet aircraft I had little officially to do but wait for demobilisation.

One morning I was in the ops office doing my duty stint when a Fieseler Storch landed outside – this was a high wing, short take off aircraft, like the one used by the Germans to rescue Mussolini.

This aeroplane could land on a sixpence and dropped down neatly on the grass outside the office. An immaculate Flight Lieutenant got out and came over to me.

'You the duty officer?' he inquired.

'What can I do for you?' I asked politely.

He produced a double copy document.

'Sign this manifest,' he said brusquely. I started to read it.

'What exactly is the manifest for?' I asked slowly, as that warning bell started to ring at the back of my head.

'Never mind that – just sign it,' said the Flight Looie in an aggressive tone. 'It's for that Junkers 290 over on the other side of the airfield. It's got to go to Farnborough immediately.'

'I'm not signing a blank manifest,' I said flatly.

'Well, bugger you mate!' said the angry pilot. 'You'll hear about this, chum.'

He turned angrily on his heel and piled into his Storch, taking off in a spectacular climb.

I got on to my bike and took off as fast as I could pedalling like a racing champion round the perimeter track.

As I suspected, the JU 290 transport plane was loaded to busting with loot. Carpets, refrigerators, radiograms and even a small yacht chocked up neatly in the middle.

I made a quick mental inventory and pedalled slowly back to the ops office.

Within minutes of my return the Storch dropped neatly down, once more, on to the grass outside.

This time its pilot was a VIP – his broad ring denoting his elevated rank.

'Where's the stupid bastard that won't sign this manifest?' he shouted, waving the documents in front of me.

'I'm sorry sir,' I said calmly. 'The manifests are incomplete.'

'What do you mean you clot?' stormed the red-faced VIP.

'They don't show details of the cargo,' I went on, 'and if my name is going to appear on both copies, I will only sign under protest.'

'Right,' he rapped out, 'then I order you to sign right now.'

'Shall I add the yacht, carpets and refrigerators now or later?' I asked, making every syllable clear.

He stood speechless, for a moment, and then stormed out and took off in a dangerous and unnecessary display of filthy temper. I still don't think those particular items were the legitimate spoils of war, but I was learning fast.

I spent a lot of time hunting for the pot with my lovely Alsatian dog Sally, who was my constant companion wherever I went.

We had found her on the way up, still guarding a dead German officer who had been lying there for days. Our dog handler had finally lured her away and, after getting her half starved frame back into condition, had given her to me. We were inseparable and she had an amazing instinct for finding game.

When I left Schleswig I had to leave Sally – but England and a six month quarantine wouldn't have been right for her. The great forests and plains of Schleswig-Holstein were her happy hunting grounds.

* * *

The senior A.L.O., a stocky redhead called Dennis or Desmond had a bright suggestion one morning.

'Any yachtsmen here?' he inquired brightly. 'They've got some beautiful sailing jobs down in the harbour. Anyone care to give me a hand?'

We knew he was a keen yachtsman, as he seldom talked about anything else. As I had had a bit of experience with dinghies in Dover harbour and the waters off Folkestone, I volunteered. So

148

did two other lads, one an A.L.O. called George and the other a pilot whose name I can't remember.

Happily we set off for the harbour, with Desmond pointing out some of the beautiful yachts that the Germans had gathered there after looting half Europe. These magnificent little ships were still tended by a faithful team of German sailors, now prisoners of war but usefully employed looking after near enough a million pounds worth of yachts.

The one Desmond had picked out for us was a 5.5 metre class sailing boat and her lovely lines gave promise of great power and speed.

I only knew the bare essentials of sailing from the Sharpies and K class dinghies of my youth and little enough about these, so I naturally imagined that the other two lads were experts.

Unfortunately as it turned out, they thought exactly the same about me. Desmond then was the only one who really knew what he was doing, a fact that he quickly demonstrated by getting us organised in record time.

We gladly followed the stream of explicit orders that rattled from his excited lips and we all knew just enough to recognise what pieces of rigging or equipment he was referring to, but we watched each other like hawks, hoping to learn from the other's expert example.

In no time at all, helped by the willing hands of the professional Germans, we were under way. With a stiff following breeze on that perfect sailing day we were soon belting out into the vast Schleswig Meer.

Those great lakes are a superb sailing ground and the Germans naturally had supplied us with first-class charts. We were able to stand out into the channel with confidence and swoop easily into the open water.

We made a brave sight as we sailed speedily down the long stretch of shining lake and at first everything went like clockwork. You would have thought we were blue-water sailors of the highest calibre as we sprang athletically to execute the shouted orders of our skipper.

We didn't, however, always do things quite his way and he would become restless as we fumbled with some part of the gear while coming about.

As he yelled 'Lee oh!', the traditional cry of sailing men as the boom came over in this manoeuvre, we were a little slow in hauling in the slack sheets that controlled the expanse of white sails. He started to have real doubts as the wind increased in

149

strength and things began to happen more quickly.

The boat was impeccable. A living thing in the water, she sailed beautifully and responded instantly to every movement of her helm or retrim of her sails.

Then it happened.

In coming about, on the opposite tack, Desmond had seen one of us doing something he shouldn't. In leaping up to correct the mistake he momentarily forgot the main boom. At that moment the wind caught us unexpectedly from a different quarter.

The boom swung over. In ducking out of the way, Desmond lost the helm and we went aground.

As we juddered to a halt he leapt overboard and started to push us off, standing up to his shoulders in the shallow water of the shoal and rocking the ship while we scrambled from side to side at his shouted commands.

He succeeded brilliantly. With a sudden swoop, the 5.5 metre yacht freed herself and slid off the side of the mud bank, leaving Desmond swearing in her wake as he tumbled backwards under water.

'Man overboard!' I shouted, rather proud of remembering the drill. Regrettably, that's where my knowledge of the correct procedures ended.

I fully expected a whirl of frenzied and professional activity to galvanise my skilled companions. Nothing happened. They just stood there, stunned.

With the wind filling the sails, off we shot, leaving Desmond far behind struggling in the water. Through his own foresight we were all wearing lifejackets, so he was in no immediate danger of drowning.

As he shook the water from his eyes he saw us disappearing at high speed towards the horizon.

I hurled myself at the helm and grabbed the wheel as we careered along, leaving our skipper a fast diminishing orange speck on the surface of the lake.

Then it dawned on all of us – Desmond was the only one that really knew what he was doing. However, we weren't battle hardened for nothing and somehow we got the racing ship around on a new course while one of us kept an eye out for our captain. Sure enough, there he was – a tiny head and shoulders waving frantically.

The ship wore round and, gybing brutally, we raced towards him with our lee side well down in the rushing white foam. As I nervously steered straight for him at a good eight knots, it suddenly dawned on me that if I kept the same course we would run him down.

It also dawned on Desmond, who frantically paddled himself out of the way as we swept past. Our razor-sharp bow missed him by inches and left him bobbing and cursing in our wake.

Round we came again, with the gear protesting loudly at our harsh and inexperienced treatment.

Then back we came on the opposite tack – swooping once again on a collision course with our frantic skipper.

This time, as we swept dangerously close past him, George managed to ring him with a lifebelt on a long line. Desmond grabbed it, and found himself being towed through the water, like a human torpedo. He'd have drowned for sure but he had the presence of mind to turn on his back.

Even then, being dragged through the racing wake at eight knots was an exhausting business. Had we not been stopped – all standing – by another shoal, he would have either drowned or been forced to let go.

We felt the shoal shiver through the rigging and gear as though we had been hit by a mine but, by some miracle, we were still afloat and in sailing order.

We got the half-drowned Desmond aboard and he spat out waterweeds and curses in about equal amounts. Then we set about getting us off the 'putty' which luckily we had only struck a glancing blow. Eventually we refloated the yacht and much chastened and well cursed by the irate Desmond, we set off for the harbour. By the time we approached it, everything was running smoothly again and we once more batted along, speedily and efficiently.

Desmond's pride had been somewhat ruffled by his experience. So he decided that, as our strange manoeuvres had probably been witnessed by the interested German professionals, we would show them how to berth in style and with British efficiency.

We made our final approach at some speed, because the wind had shifted quite a bit. It now lay dead astern, sending us along at a stiff clip.

The plan, of course, was to down mainsail at the appropriate time and coast into the inner harbour, to be fended off by two Germans who were waiting for us on the wooden catwalk that divided the harbour in two. They stood there, holding a long bamboo boat hook as though it were a lance; ready to catch us and help swing us parallel to the quay.

We entered the harbour at a good seven knots and Desmond rapped out: 'Down Mainsail!'

Would that we could have!

Despite our frenzied efforts the mainsail stoutly refused to budge an inch. The Bermudan track of the mainsail had jammed tight, probably with all the savage gybing that we had subjected it to. This meant that we still proceeded at seven knots, straight for the catwalk. Desmond was beside himself.

The Germans stood fast and pointed their bamboo lance at us bravely. The hook on the end caught just abaft the bowsprit and the long bamboo pole bent like a bow.

Then, as we turned, down came the mainsail with a rush, completely covering Desmond at the helm. The ship veered wildly and the bamboo lance hurtled back, sending the first German into the inner harbour.

The second one started to run but the yacht, still at full speed and now completely unguided, crashed into the catwalk and cut it clean in half, hurling him, after his comrade, into the water behind him.

The watching Germans must have wondered how we had managed to win the war!

*   *   *

Kelly and I now swanned around north Germany, collecting as much data as I could find on German jet and rocket aircraft.

Technical Intelligence was obviously mainly concerned with this, but the Germans had been carting the stuff off, piecemeal, and I felt I could grab quite a bit of it before the official teams turned up.

The Russians were also after everything they could lay their hands on and had got hold of a good chunk of Peenemunde, and some of the German rocket scientists, before our lot arrived.

It was a glorious game of tag, with all sorts of technical advances as the prizes. I just missed some valuable plans I'd heard of by a matter of a few hours.

Meanwhile my conception of what constituted the lawful spoils of war had undergone a radical change since the episode of the JU 290 at Schleswig.

Kelly and I heard of half a million sewing machine needles hidden somewhere near Lubeck and, as I knew there were some more interesting aeroplanes in that area, we scooted down there.

An American, French and Belgian team were all ostensibly after the research aircraft. Oddly enough, we kept bumping into each other near the possible sites of the hidden needles. In the end we got quite hysterical, and Kelly and I cheered the embarrassed official teams everytime we sped past each other.

The aircraft were fascinating however. Henschel, Arado, Messerschmitt and Lippisch – in fact every German designer – had built special machines to take the new jet engines.

Even the V.1 flying bomb turned up in a new disguise. The designers had fitted it with controls and a blind flying panel of a sort, lengthened the wings and gulled them at the ends. They had also fitted a jettisonable undercarriage and called the whole mess the *Volksjaeger*.

The intention was that suicidally-minded members of the Hitler Jugend, Baldur von Shirach's youth organisation, would fly these extremely unstable and tricky machines. Some were fitted with cannon and others with just explosive warheads. If this was the only other choice, no wonder my three Hitler Jugend had volunteered to be snipers instead.

The real machines, like the ME 262, had done great execution among the Flying Fortresses and Liberators and the ME 163, a little rocket-powered tailless plane, had knocked down even high-flying Mosquitoes. Had Hitler not been such a raving lunatic, all these ME 262s would have seen operational service long before they did, but he saw them in the role of fast fighter bombers and lost a golden opportunity – for which we were all sincerely grateful.

The aircraft were hidden all over the place and I was able to direct the attention of the technical boys to quite a few sites, before the parts had all got spirited away.

The Russians had also arrived, as a goodwill mission, of which they seemed to have an unending supply and heated bargaining of the schoolboy swap variety went on.

'I'll give you two ME 262 tails for one ME 163 wing – all right, make it three 262s and I'll throw in an Arado nose cone.'

Exhausted by these efforts, Kelly and I got some leave to go to Brussels. This lovely city had not been badly knocked about by war and was teeming with armed forces from every nation.

The trains were still running then and were jammed, both inside and out, with every sort and size of warriors on leave. The W.A.C., A.T.S., W.A.A.F. and W.R.N.S. had also added their feminine charms to the city's already ample attractions, and there certainly was no shortage of willing partners.

Kelly had that arrow-straight smouldering handsomeness of his Creole ancestors and his deep Oxford-graduate tones trembled the eager wombs around us. As the poor girl's version of Kelly, I slowly lost my shyness and fell in love deeply and repeatedly.

To finance our leave we had also liberated one or two things that helped us through the week, but in all fairness we shared the resulting francs with many airmen who were not so well supplied.

I had got hold of a movie camera taken from a German combat cameraman who obviously wasn't going to need it again and I asked around to see if anyone wanted this highly sophisticated piece of cinema gear. Yes, indeed, there was a small film unit on the outskirts of Brussels that would gladly take it off my hands. Naturally I was keen to see them at work and duly asked to watch the filming.

'Mais certainement, mon vieux!' said my civilian informant and the next morning I was taken by car to see this artistic team of enthusiasts in action.

The studio was in a small converted barn, not too far from the airfield at Melsbroek, and the passing aircraft must have presented a problem, or so I thought. I remarked on this and was told that the films were silent anyway – being more visual than an ordinary talkie. I visualised a return to the golden age of silent comedy of Buster Keaton and was even more delighted at the opportunity to see it all.

Seeing it all was a good description – I entered the studio to the delighted cries of two girls who were lying stark naked on a bed.

You could certainly say the films they made were visual – dialogue, unless it was short and Anglo-Saxon in content, would have been superfluous. Bright red with embarrassment I completed the deal and got away as soon as I could.

Afterwards Kelly told me I was being a prude and suggested himself for a screen test.

We got back three days late and the Wing Co. only crimed me with orderly officer for ten days. This was quite fair, as it was entirely my fault anyway.

This chore finished, we set off for Lubeck and another meeting with the inevitable Russian goodwill missions. But that area had been picked clean of anything remotely connected with research. While we were there a young Guards major asked me if I could help him out.

'Delighted,' I said, 'always willing to co-operate with the Pongos!'

154

'You see,' he said getting slightly nervous, 'It's this camp I'm in charge of – it's not really an ordinary P.O.W. camp but – well – rather a special one – frankly, putting it bluntly old man – it's a baby farm!'

'A what?' I gasped.

'A baby-farm – you know for breeding Hitler's master race.'

'We've got a large collection of big blonde birds there and, well, they were only put there for one purpose, and now the S.S. have gone – they're well – you're a man of the world – so, can you help us out?'

His twenty-four years looked earnestly at my twenty-three years.

'Nothing doing,' I said. 'I'm not bringing truckloads of my airmen down to service your bloody Boche blondes.'

'Funny thing,' he muttered. 'They all say that.'

Had I not recently been on leave in Brussels I wonder if my duty would have been so clear to me.

I was never to complete my technical report on German research aircraft because fate stepped in again with a quick body blow.

I'd been out hunting with Sally and I felt feverish. This feeling increased when I found myself some miles from the airfield, after a long chase, tracking a wounded deer someone had clipped earlier. Eventually I finished off the poor beast and started for home, by now shaking badly in the grip of some virus.

By the time I'd managed to get back to the mess I was in a bad way with my teeth chattering as though I had the ague. The M.O. who was a bright character, got me to bed. Within hours I was in the first stages of double pneumonia. This started up the old trouble from A.C.R.C. and I really thought I was for it.

They rushed me off to the base hospital, at Schleswig. I don't remember too much of the next few days until I came round and lay like a washed out towel in the care of the R.A.F. nurses. Again I owe a big debt to those marvellous girls and, within a fortnight, they'd got me up and were exercising my cramped and wasted muscles back into action.

The whole thing had been a bit much though. An odd side effect was that I couldn't stop crying. Not weeping – just crying – pints of water from my tear ducts, quite happily. The medics were as puzzled as I was and shifted me down to 8th General base hospital near Bad Oeynhausen, the B.A.F.O. headquarters.

It was obvious I was still weak and the M.O. there put me in a ward with some other types who had also had a basinful. One of these was a holder of the conspicuous gallantry medal who had baled out once too often.

Every half hour or so he would yell, 'Abandon aircraft! Bale out! Bale out!' and jump out of bed.

Heavy sedation only helped when he was clean out for the count. They couldn't give him much more or he would have probably become addicted.

Another character took a fiendish delight in chucking bottles of urine at the nurses and had to be restrained. Occasionally however some inexperienced young nurse would respond to his sly plea for a bottle and narrowly escape injury as he flung the half full glass container at her pretty head. Eventually he cracked and was carried away, wailing loudly.

One chum who had been cured of whatever it was that had got him down, was sitting on his bed ready for transport to take him to the base airfield and home.

The Red Cross girl, a lovely but dim redhead, came round with some games and hobbies. As usual we all said no thank you, politely, except our urine bottle marksman who glowered threateningly at her. But the cured one sat on his bed and thought he'd better show willing. She was so excited that she'd finally found a customer for her wares that she, thoughtlessly, gave him a box of Chinese puzzles to play with.

An hour later, they took him away, muttering to himself as he tried, as though his life depended on it, to undo two tightly interwoven bent nails.

The malfunction of my tear ducts continued, ridiculously, and I had to drink pints of fluid and take sodium chloride pills to make up for the salt loss. The high medical brass decided to ship me back to England to see if they could stop me leaking there.

Off I went, in a Dakota, along with a load of the wounded and the sick. These weren't war wounded, but various accidents in the air and with carelessly handled weapons, plus a sprinkling of car crashes had taken quite a toll. The sick were just sick.

Sea fog, which Kent is great at generating in minutes, clamped down on the coastal airfield as we crept through the overcast and coming into land at Manston in Kent we nearly rammed the cliffs. Manston, thank God, was equipped with ground controlled approach and was one of the very few stations with this splendid new landing aid.

I went up front with the crew, because if I was going to buy it, I'd much prefer to be with the chums in the front office. The dispassionate voice of the controller slowly guided us down through the mucky grey-out and we literally felt our wheels touch, as we got our final visual on the runway. Nowadays, they would have diverted us in those conditions, but we were low on fuel anyway.

So back home I came for a short term in Wroughton Hospital, and a long leave to compensate. There was obviously no real job for me left to do and the R.A.F. medical board even offered me a pension when they advised invaliding out as the simplest solution. I was mug enough to refuse the pension and wise enough to accept their suggestion.

When I got back home, things took some time to sort out. I used to go for long solitary walks to try and find my way back from that long scramble through the war.

I found I couldn't remember faces at all. I could remember dates, technical data, secret information and other things by the brainload – but all the faces of those young people I'd known and cared about and lost just couldn't get into focus.

And then, one day, they all seemed to merge into one face.

It was the smiling one of my much-missed cousin John.

I knew then that for me too, the war was, at last over.

17. My first loves

Just to keep the record straight. Anyone who thinks they are going to get the true confessions of an Anglo-Peruvian sex-maniac are in for a bit of a let down. This is not the book for you! Try the Ethno-pornography section at your local library.

However, this doesn't mean I haven't fallen in love – the first time was a deeply consecrated affair with an American film star who for me epitomised all that I desired in womanhood – or rather girlhood – because Deanna Durbin was never aware of the passions she had aroused in my eager young body, nor the swirl of romantic daydreams that washed over my soul.

I never had the good fortune to enjoy a night dream involving this plump, bun-faced, teenage opera singer or I might have got some relief for the yearnings. Instead I used to spend my pocket money on seeing her schmaltzy pictures or, to be fair to the lady, the saccharine-sweet films in which this healthy specimen of talented American girlhood appeared.

When I was broke, which was normally by the Tuesday, I used to cycle slowly past the back wall of the local movie theatre where I knew the image of my love was being projected.

I remained faithful to her memory until I fell even more deeply in love with our local dentist's daughter.

She was the antithesis of her rival – being slim and leggy, with short cut blonde hair, and practically no chest at all. But one summer's day, when she walked past me like a young gazelle, my heart leaped in me and I was involuntarily squeezed off an air gun pellet, narrowly missing her exquisite derrière by milli-metres.

This doesn't mean I was a teenage sniper – it was just that I was overwhelmed and for a moment careless.

Our love was apparently mutual. On my part it was under-standable but on hers not quite so much as, at about this time,

I had a complexion rather like a nutmeg grater – probably due to my unrequited passion for the lovely Deanna.

Eventually I summoned up enough courage to speak to this vision who, amazingly, spoke back to me. As our families had no suspicion of our budding Romeo and Juliet relationship, we were allowed out for long healthy walks together.

Our first kiss was, as kisses go, unskilled, but we made up for our lack of experience by sheer power – nearly driving each other's teeth through the backs of our necks. This must have shown in her next dental examination and we were separated.

Not literally with a crowbar, but by her family moving to the West Country. Had they not done so we would probably have run away and got ourselves married by any shortsighted registrar who would accept two shillings down and regular weekly payments.

*　　*　　*

In 1941 I fell head over heels into marriage. I was just nineteen and it would be ungallant of me to say more than that my bride was older than I was.

I was about as equipped to deal with this situation as a Bedouin Arab on skis. Inevitably, during the course of the war with the long separations and tensions, the marriage foundered.

In 1942 a lovely daughter was born to us and my deepest regret on our parting in 1946 was that this delightful child was taken from me to France.

I didn't see her again till she was 18 and had grown into an equally lovely woman.

It says a great deal for her character and upbringing in France that even today we have an affectionate, if somewhat intermittent, relationship.

As I never believe in dwelling on mistakes and misfortune once I have learned their lesson that is all I am going to say about my first marriage.

18. Picking up the pieces

February 1946 found me back in England, lean, shaky, with a demob suit for best, my uniform for living in, and my stammer back in full force, while the bottom had dropped out of my life.

I was so nervous that, one day, when I was walking along the bank of the Thames, three swans came flying up behind me – and I dropped flat on the deck.

Pop and Ma had taken me in and helped me but I couldn't sleep. Not because of the nightmares but for the simple reason that a cricket had lodged in the brickwork and tkk'd all night.

Eventually I was shivering as though I'd got malaria, and Ma called in the Pest Exterminator. He arrived with, believe it or not, a three-ton truck and two assistants, a load of pump-like equipment and a stethoscope. Solemnly he put this last instrument in his ears and crept round my parents' flat in Barnes, listening for that bloody cricket.

At last, clear as a bell – *tkk*, *tkk*. I could hear it without the stethoscope and the exterminator nodded his head sagely and got to work with the pump. This machine injected an evil smelling powder into a hole in the wall, which his assistant had drilled out, at approximately the point where the cricket had last cricked. The second assistant pumped away, while the head exterminator kept listening with his stethoscope.

From the flat below came heavy coughing and a gasping, retching sound, followed by a loud thump, and I remembered, with horror, that the owner was an elderly lady, who suffered from asthma.

The powder, which was designed to be lethal to crickets, was very nearly being so to our downstairs neighbour. We rushed down and got her round, as First Aid was hurriedly administered, while upstairs the extermination brigade left after a celebratory beer.

Almost as soon as that three-ton lorry had rumbled out of sight over the bridge – Tkk! Tkk! that seemingly indestructible insect was back. Its clicks were weaker however and, around midnight, they ceased for ever.

I was delighted to hear that my friend Tony Sherwood had returned intact from the wars and he and I with that cheerful and hospitable family of his, had a joyous reunion.

During the early part of my wartime stay in London, I had met Tony in a night club, where he was playing piano and I was standing in for the drummer. We played well together and instantly got on as happily off the bandstand. In fact we had teamed up first before I went on the boards, and I had played a short season as part of a three-piece resident hotel band in Exeter. Tony and I loved jazz and he was especially good at playing boogie.

During the war, our paths separated, only to recross in 1946.

In the R.A.F. Tony had chummed up with a talented youngster, called Eddie d'Arville, who looked the living image of Gene Kelly and came from a showbiz family. For a time, we thought of doing a threesome act, possibly because Eddie could have doubled for Kelly's d'Artagnan in *The Three Musketeers*. But Eddie fell in love with, and eventually married, Tony's delightful sister Pat and settled down to work with a multiple store in which he did exceedingly well.

So Tony and I decided to do a double act and we called it Sherwood and Forrest.

The act consisted of the two of us, in very tall and narrow black top hats and ancient frock coats, reciting an imaginary Russian fairy story exactly together and finishing with a frenetic rendering of *Black Eyes* in boogie tempo.

My brother gave us the idea for the fairy story, which he had done in amateur camp concerts, when he was serving as a gunner during the war.

We did a few auditions and got laughs from the other pros, but no nibbles from the various managements, who were looking for concert party acts. Ours was more like a cabaret. It certainly wasn't music hall as one disastrous audition at Collin's Music Hall in Islington, since pulled down, soon proved.

We nearly got a booking for a summer season but failed the crucial question: 'Can you sing *On the Road to Mandalay*?'

My decision to try and make a living as a comedian was prompted by my disgust at the wholesale slaughter of the war and the misuse of Science to achieve it.

I naturally shared Pop's belief that Science ought to be used for the benefit of Mankind. The dropping of the atom bomb finally disillusioned me completely when I realised that a scientist would have no free choice in the post-war world.

Obviously, if your field of research could even remotely be applied to war, it would be so. My own fascination with the rocket or, as it was then called, the unrotated projectile, required a knowledge of ballistics. Whereas I dreamed of space flight, it was clear to me what use the rocket was being put to.

M'Tutor, Uncle Billy, had become involved in the Society of Friends between the wars. I remembered that most chocolate firms in Britain were owned by the pacifist Quakers. Because I didn't know anything about the chocolate-making business, I searched around for an equally peaceful way of making my living without hurting anyone, and comedy seemed a fair choice. After all, I didn't know anything about that either.

To judge by some critics' later denunciations of my efforts at making comedy, even this method of getting my living is deeply traumatic to mankind. Having made the decision, I stuck to it, and my future career was set.

To quote a dictionary definition of a career, it is: *A headlong rush, usually downhill.*

Not a bad description, really.

Eventually we gravitated towards the Nuffield Centre, which was a Forces' canteen in London and a show place for the young eager artists who had just been demobbed from the Forces. This was run by a lovely person called Mary Cook who was talented, clever and motherly and herself a fine pianist. We got paid in sandwiches and coffee and the wholehearted appreciation of an uninhibited audience of young people who were still in the Services.

Originally the Centre was in the old Café de Paris, in Piccadilly. This famous pre-war night club had been hit by a bomb during the Blitz, instantly killing Ken 'Snake-Hips' Johnson, the well-known bandleader and another musician on the bandstand, and killing and badly wounding several other people.

There was no psychic trace of this event left in this circular night club, with its upstairs surrounding balcony and two sweeping staircases, flanking the small stage and dance floor. The atmosphere was marvellous.

Encouraged by our success and fortified in body and spirit by Mary's splendid sandwiches, in January, 1947, we tried another audition, this time at the Windmill Theatre. This tiny theatre

162

had been managed, since the thirties, by a clever showman called Vivian Van Damm, for its owner, a Mrs Henderson.

Van Damm – or, as he was known, V.D. – had turned the Windmill into a very respectable and tasteful nude show, with a sprinkling of entertainers. He had helped to create a new breed of comedians, who were both original and tough enough to face an all-male audience with ultra-clean material.

The second of these requirements was enforced by a Lord Chamberlain, who would have closed the entire operation if one word of smut had been used in any act at this unique theatre.

When Tony and I turned up for the audition, a young Welsh comic had just finished his act and was vigorously drying himself on a towel, and the auditioning management were just recovering from laughing too much.

He stayed to watch our efforts and fell about enjoying it, as we also corpsed the watching V.D. and his staff.

The result was that we all three got booked to work the Windmill, and a lifetime friendship started for me, with the small, slim, wire-haired terrier of a Welshman.

'Name's Secombe,' he said, 'Harry Secombe,' extending a soapy hand.

'Tony Sherwood,' said my partner, grabbing it.

'Michael Forrest nèe Bentin,' I added as we shook hands all round.

Tony had to rush off to a music lesson and that left Harry and I together. We looked at each other warily.

'Army,' he said chuckling. 'Bloody gunner – blind as a bat.'

'R.A.F.,' I countered. 'Had to fly with a braille instrument panel.'

'Sounds like between us we lengthened the war by at least three months,' he laughed, that marvellous total explosion of joy that put me, instantly, on the same wavelength.

We worked out that we had about three shillings between us – and the next question from him held our friendship in the balance.

'Well! Do we eat or shall we see the cartoon show?'

'The cartoon show,' I said unhesitatingly. From that moment the rapport was complete.

We both put comedy first. Mind you, since then we've eaten as well, as a quick glance at our shapes instantly confirms, but in those days comedy was almost a religion with us – a ridiculous soul-shaking laughter-filled mind-boggling religion – which effectively countered our empty stomachs.

The next day Harry introduced me to some wartime mates of his, who were part of a very funny musical act, called the Bill Hall Trio. This consisted of a violin player, thin and emaciated, with a woebegone expression of blank suffering, named Bill Hall.

A short, quiet, Keatonesque, bass-playing Glaswegian, called Johnny Mulgrew, and a wild Irishman named Spike Milligan, who played guitar and trumpet and talked comedy like a recently released Trappist making up for six years silence.

Bill was a football addict and a fine musician. As I had no music to speak of in me and no knowledge of football, he found me wanting.

Johnny's quiet visual comedy and understated pawky Scottish humour got straight through to me and I felt a strong contact there.

But it was the Irish streak of lightning that rang the bell the loudest.

In those days these young people had just been demobbed after gravitating from their various units in the Army into the central pool of Service artists.

We had all been through battle experience and every one of us had been shaken rigid by it. They had all been in the North African and Italian campaigns and only latterly, after ending up in various psycho wards – had been seconded to the C.S.E., Combined Services Entertainment Section. These lads had also actually worked in front of Service audiences as performers, while I had no solo performance stage experience, other than one appearance in an R.A.F. pantomime.

So we each had another bond between us. At some time we had all officially been 'round the bend' and spent long or short periods in a 'happy' ward.

The whole lot of us were deeply suspicious of authority and thoroughly sickened by what we had seen and been through, and we found our release in laughter. For one thing it didn't cost anything – and our total finances, after living off the 'generous' gratuities we had received, which in my case lasted almost a month, came to about a fiver between the entire bunch.

The Windmill audience didn't exactly receive us with open arms, but we got by all right to complete our six weeks, at the rate of six shows a day, with, in Tony's and my case £25 a week between us.

My share worked out at around three times my Service pay – a fortune!

Those weeks in that small theatre taught me a lot. The same

audience, in essence, came in for the first show, at ten o'clock in the morning and, allowing for casualties due to exhaustion from mental and sometimes physical masturbation, lasted through till the final curtain at around eleven o'clock at night.

The scramble for front seats, which were separated from the back seats by only a few rows, was something to see. Steeple-chasing had nothing on it. I once saw an elderly bishop make his classic chess move, to gain three rows clear forward advantage, in under two seconds.

The girls were lovely, and charmingly co-operative, if the eagle-eyed staff let you have half a chance to get to know them.

Even in our state of physical fitness and lean energy-filled alertness, these six appearances a day took their toll and we crawled off to our various digs in a state bordering on exhaustion.

The minute canteen at the top of the theatre was the focus of our life at the 'Mill', apart from that slippery glass-paved stage, with the dimly seen duo of pianists, Kurt and Ron, in the pit, which acted as a sort of anti-tank ditch against the constant threat of attack from the raincoated audience seething out front.

If one of the girls saw any strange phenomena taking place, as she remained rigidly posed according to the laws at the time, she reported it to the stage staff on her exit. The curtain fell momentarily, and the over-enthusiastic, sex-starved member of the great British public would be whisked bodily from the stalls, protesting feebly as he tried to adjust his dress, and deposited outside firmly, courteously and finally.

Harry, Spike, Johnny and Bill never played the 'Mill' at the same time as Tony and I, but followed each other on as the six week seasons changed. We usually congregated across the road at Allen's Club, a one-room bar above a sleazy café, where 'Pop' Allen invariably and cheerfully marked our score up on a slate.

The one-room club became a centre of the new comedy movement and here I met the towering duo of six-feet-four-plus Dennis Norden and Frank Muir, both ex-R.A.F., who had teamed up together as writers.

Then there was Jimmy Edwards – the fire-scarred, heavily moustached R.A.F. Dakota pilot, who had deservedly won his D.F.C. at Arnhem, flying his troop transport plane through that murderous flak, till the parachute troops had got clear and, finally, crash landing in flames, to survive and become one of our close bunch of disillusioned but determined-to-forget-it comics.

Alfred Marks, the talented Cockney Jewish character comedian, also won his spurs here with us. Alf and I often played chess in the canteen while we waited to go on for the next ordeal, before that hardened, comedy-resistant audience of repressed humanity, some six floors below.

Keith, the wittily bitchy, middle-aged, but amazingly well preserved, ballet choreographer and chief dancer couldn't help kibitzing at our chess games.

He would sweep in, wearing a floral kimono, and as he passed our table, would pause and say things like: 'The knight, dear – watch his bloody knight, you headstrong boy!'

Alf and I got so fed up with this, that we decided to fix him once and for all.

When I got paid, I bought another chess set and board and spent a whole weekend constructing an enlarged game, with extra squares all round and some added pieces, made up of combined castles, with knights' heads stuck on top, and two-headed bishops.

I hurriedly explained the idea to Alf and we laid out our unorthodox pieces, and waited for Keith's appearance.

He made his usual entrance and, as he passed the table, he did a beautiful double-take as he saw us engrossed in a far more complicated game than he had ever seen.

Being intellectual and immodest with it, he wouldn't admit he didn't know what was going on, as Alf and I made outrageous moves, in silence, with the new pieces on that unfamiliarly enlarged board.

'Ah!' said Alf wisely, 'beautiful move, Mike!' – as I combined a knight and a bishop's moves with one of the doctored pieces.

'Peruvian crossed grand-rook defence,' I said modestly. 'Santiago Cohone's favourite!'

'I thought it looked familiar,' remarked Alf, with whom I would never play poker. Then apparently noticing the dumbstruck Keith for the first time, he continued: 'Hello mate! Join us?'

'Later,' muttered Keith. From his table near the tea bar, he watched us like a hawk as he tried to figure out this mind-bending game.

We kept up the 'Pshess', or Peruvian chess, as we idly referred to it, for a whole week, while Keith followed our lunatic moves in silent absorption and never said a word.

The one mid-morning he swept by, in a flurry of kimono, and

stopped for a moment beside us, as we sat engrossed in our idiotic manoeuvres.

'Watch his double bishop darling!' he said silkily. 'Or it's mate in three!'

That did it – scattering the pieces in all directions, Alf and I exploded into helpless table-thumping roars of joy.

To this day I can still corpse Alf with one word – 'Pshess!'

Tony Sherwood and I also did a radio audition for Joy Russell Smith, a B.B.C. producer of a variety programme, who gave chances to unknowns who had something different to offer the listeners.

We presented ourselves at the Aeolian Hall, Bond Street, where the audition was held, and actually got a booking for the show, which was called *Variety Bandbox*. No sooner had we sat down in the studio, after our successful audition, when a long spaniel-faced individual in an ill-fitting demob suit, exactly like ours but even more so, nervously got up on to the stage and proceeded to convulse the entire lot of us, both management and waiting victims.

This strange and completely original comedian introduced himself as 'Francis Howerd, spinster of this parish', and his whole act consisted of veiled remarks and allusions to his somewhat prim and proper accompanist.

'Poor thing, she can't help it! Well! I mean all those hours sitting side saddle on a piano stool . . .'

The whole line of patter was so completely different and the delivery, once F. Howerd, Esq., got over his preliminary nerves, was impeccable. We applauded him to the echo.

It was obvious to me that here was a star in the making – not in the accepted sense of a song-and-dance man, or even a deliverer of slick one-line gags and comic wheezes, but the real McCoy – a one-off with a personality that owed nothing to anyone else.

Most of us young comedians, had modelled ourselves on some well-known personality and many junior Bob Hopes, Max Millers and Tommy Trinders, then at the height of their fame, turned up at these auditions. But you couldn't say that about Frankie Howerd – or for that matter, to a far lesser degree, about Sherwood and Forrest.

Frankie was a smash hit with that first *Variety Bandbox* broadcast and became a semi-permanent fixture on it – a springboard to his well deserved stardom.

We did reasonably well on the same programme, but couldn't

come up with another act in time for a second showing, and so we faded out of that brief radio limelight.

Tony and I also did a couple of television appearances on Christmas Day, 1946, at the old Alexandra Palace. Repeating the same act, our Russian one, twice in the one day – once in the afternoon and again in the evening. Such was the brief television career of Sherwood and Forrest.

After the Windmill booking, we did some sporadic concerts at Butlin's Holiday Camps and, finally, packed it in.

We parted professionally, without any ill will, because Tony had an offer he could hardly resist – of two years' free tuition at the Guildhall School of Music – and I wanted to do a single.

So Michael Forrest reverted to the original Michael Bentin, but I added an 'e' on the end, to balance the name on theatrical bills.

Several agents tried to persuade me to change my name to something snappier and easier to remember, like Mike Pike or Mick Park. Once I even got the suggestion of Mack Tuck. But I was adamant – Michael Bentine or nothing.

Nothing seemed the apparent alternative. I was so out of work I felt like a national recession. But I resolved never to go on the dole, because hunger seemed the only way to really overcome that damned stammer and desperation became the mother of invention.

I was still searching for a style and Mary Cook, bless her, let me try out any new acts I had thought up, at the Nuffield Centre, which, by this time, had moved to a street behind St Martin-in-the-Fields.

These semi-auditions inspired me to try out a crop of comedy vicars and stump speeches – a stump speech being a comedy form of address, in which you lecture the audience, rather than just tell them stories.

The results were encouraging and I started to incorporate 'props' into the act, that is to say things to hang the routines on, like pictures on a blackboard. I lectured on the human body, complete with a green fig leaf, which fell off in the autumn to disclose a brown one underneath.

Slowly and hesitatingly I developed an original type of comedy, drawing heavily on my rocky scientific background and trying out and shedding various accents and characters, till I eventually came back to the best thing a comedian can find – a comedy projection of his own innate personality.

I was by now a weekly regular at the Nuffield Centre, and the audience had become accustomed to the idea that, when I came on, at least I wouldn't just tell them stories. Good or bad, I was different.

Other comedians were emerging there as well. Benny Hill did a marvellously cruel German act, which obviously had possibilities. And one night a huge man, with a wildly off beat approach to magic, fumbled his hilarious way through disastrously funny tricks that all went wrong – and the audience would hardly let him leave the stage. His name was Tommy Cooper.

Jimmy Edwards, who was now a rising radio name, was also a regular favourite at the Nuffield Centre, and tried out all sorts of new routines on our captive audience.

Mary encouraged our frenzied efforts to find our own original lines of comedy while she fed us with sandwiches. For many of us, including me, they were the largest sources of protein of the week. They also made me a breadaholic. Ever since then, a sandwich is as great a temptation to me as a fix to some poor devil of a drug-addict.

Incidentally there was no desperate seeking after new experiences via drugs for our lot. We could go on a trip with one laugh from a responsive audience.

But I still hadn't found my next act yet. Not one that I could really call my own – until, one afternoon, I was having a much-needed meal at my brother and sister-in-law's flat in Barnes, which was located over a funeral furnishers and a small privately-owned french letter factory!

During a demonstration of yet another new act, before my kindly disposed and long-suffering relations, I stood on an old second-hand chair and accidentally broke the back off it.

The chairback had broken in a peculiarly distinctive way, leaving an odd shape in my hands.

Somehow it looked like a submachine gun and, as I held it, I said, 'I suppose you'll shoot me for breaking this.' Suddenly, like the literal bolt from the blue, the act hit me between the eyes.

If the chairback could look like a tommy gun, what other shapes could it make? Then and there, between us, each vying in excited competition to outdo the other, the chairback in our hands became a plough, a comb, a flag, a wood saw and a whole host of other things.

It was great fun and we thoroughly enjoyed ourselves – Bro sweeping aside my apologies by telling me the whole chair had only cost him five bob, anyway.

That night, as I walked home along the riverside road, to my parents' flat in Castelnau Mansions, I carried the chairback. In the moonlight, I tried out all those exciting shapes again. When I got back to their apartment and let myself in, I knew I had the act that I had been looking for – and dashed into their bedroom to wake my parents and show them what I had found.

It says a lot for my beloved Ma and Pa that, at three o'clock in the morning, they listened, half asleep but fully involved, and didn't call the doctor to have me put away.

Later in the morning, directly I woke up, I was back at the shapes, working them up into a logical routine, so that one movement and shape flowed into another, easily and logically. Then I shut myself up, in my small back room, and rehearsed, until I got a four-minute routine that worked.

When I finally showed my parents the strange original act that I had devised, Ma put it into words. 'That's it!' she said simply – and we knew she was right.

A week later, by constant rehearsal, I had developed the whole sequence into a flowing pattern of shapes, that seemed to appear in my hands, as if by magic. Then I took my courage in both hands, along with my broken chairback, and went to try it at the Nuffield Centre.

It was a riot – the affect on the audience being every bit as great as Tommy Cooper's marvellous nonsense.

After the act, which, although it was so ridiculously short brought the house down, I was having a well deserved sandwich, when, in mid-munch, two men introduced themselves to me.

They were agents, and quite unlike the usual run of these necessary parts of show business. Both of them were extremely intelligent and as straight as a die. Their names were Monty Lyon, the elder of the duo, and Dennis Sellinger the younger. Both were Jewish, and related, and two of the nicest people I have ever met, in show business or out of it.

Among the congratulatory clamour of my friends, Monty Lyon gave me his card and asked me to come and see him. Then, for the first time I realised – both of them had actually been crying with laughter.

The next morning I went to see them at their offices in Jermyn Street. They sat me in a chair and told me that I really had got something a hundred per cent different and, if I would place myself in their hands, they would help me to develop into a professional comedian.

I instantly liked the way that they didn't go for airy promises or wild claims as to what they could do for me.

Monty said, 'You've got something and it's going to take you a long way, but you've got a lot to learn and it isn't going to be easy. But I'm going to get you an audition with Val Parnell and I think he'll like you and your act.'

Parnell's name was co-billed with the Almighty in the eyes of show business, and I really felt my new agent had gone a bit far. But sure enough, within 24 hours Monty had fixed me an audition with that exalted being. Not the Almighty, but his stand in – Val Parnell.

This took place at the Prince of Wales Theatre, just after a session of publicity photographs which were being taken of Sid Field, who was the, deservedly, top British comedian of that period.

As he walked off the stage I walked on to it, and Sid Field, who didn't know me from a tuppenny stamp, but had heard I was auditioning for God, smiled encouragingly at me and said: 'Good luck son. Remember they're nearly human!'

The Iron Curtain, which was down at the moment, was raised, with a whirr of machinery, and I peered out into the darkness of the unlit theatre.

A crisp voice came from its dark emptiness: 'Mr Bentine. Take your time! Whenever you are ready.'

Hardened by so many auditions, in so many sleazy rehearsal rooms, I took one deep breath and I was away!

'N'Ladies and gentlemen, etc.' As the chairback routine gathered momentum I could hear chuckling and then – glory be – laughter.

At the end of the routine I bowed and the Iron Curtain slowly descended.

Outside the stage door, Monty met me, grinning all over his shrewdly cheerful face.

'Well Mike – you've done it!' he said. I opened in the West End, at the Old Hippodrome Theatre near Leicester Square, three weeks later. It was September, 1947.

The show was called *Starlight Roof* and starred Vic Oliver, Pat Kirkwood, Fred Emney, and sundry others. There were two tiny names, right down at the bottom of the bill – Julie Andrews and Michael Bentine.

19. Birth of the Goons – with forceps

Starlight Roof opened to rave notices. Most of them were for the unknown girl of eleven, Julie Andrews, who stopped the show cold on the opening night, by singing the aria *Je suis Titania*, accompanied by Vic Oliver.

Leggy and quaintly serious, this wise-eyed child stormed the audience every night of the run. Off the stage, she was as normal and unaffected as only an eleven-year-old can be.

We both suffered acutely from nerves, especially on that momentous first night, and sought mutual comfort in laughing about it together.

When the notices came out I was delighted to find that several of them gave me a warm welcome as an original newcomer but, as one critic pointed out, how can you expect a comedian to capture the audience in three minutes?

Strangely, the act, or me, or both, did just that. Mind you the strain was tremendous, as I had to pack everything into those few fleeting minutes. If I didn't 'get' the audience in the first 20 seconds, it was a struggle to get them at all.

Most comedians build up their act as they go along, adding small touches and new gags – but I had just the three minutes and no changes, except in my position on the bill, which the management altered about once a week. The only place I didn't go on was in front of the fire curtain.

Why? I don't know. Maybe Val Parnell wanted to see if I could hold any spot on a bill, because this can be vital to a comedian. Follow an animal act or, for that matter, a child and you're dead. Luckily Julie closed the first half with Vic, just before the 'Wild West End' finale, and so I never found out, but I'd say she was pretty hard to follow.

Monty was delighted with the reception I got and encouraged me to build up my act into a proper twelve-minute variety spot.

For this break into the West End I received £30 a week, which kept body and soul and respect together as well as providing me with a much needed wardrobe.

During the show, I spent a lot of time in Pat Kirkwood's dressing room, where this gorgeous, uninhibited, outgoing Northern lass and her mother Norah kept a sort of open house of interesting visitors throughout the whole run.

Pat and I had that odd rapport that makes you start smiling as soon as you see each other and chuckling even before you say hello. It helped greatly to counteract the nervous tension, which I built up every night in order to project my three-minute mayhem on the unsuspecting public.

Another good friend, Wally Boag, an American dancer of rubber-legged agility, brought the first balloon-sculpture act to Britain and fascinated them out front with his inflated giraffes and poodles and horses. Many people have stolen Wally's original act, but no one has ever been able to blow up the balloons in those marvellous trick ways he has. Forwards, backwards, half and half, any way – Wally could do a four-minute routine on just the blowing up bit alone.

Vic Oliver, who was a reserved and shy man, of great Mittel-European charm, kept himself more apart, but the huge friendly bulk of Fred Emney was a frequent visitor to Pat's dressing room. So was Jere McMahon, the American modern-ballet dancer whose languid elegance carried a wicked sting of wit.

Julie was having growing problems, shooting up like bamboo. When she said 'Eleven' in reply to Vic's 'How old are you?' it was only just believable.

As she came off one night, Jere grinned at her. 'O.K. honey! Back in the vice!'

That dressing room also contained, at different times, such diverse personalities as Baron, the top fashion photographer, whose assistant was a young man called Tony Armstrong-Jones, a naval lieutenant who was a sucker audience for good jokes and who was introduced to me as Philip Mountbatten, and a young Irish physiotherapist named Stephen Ward.

Baron died tragically, soon afterwards. His assistant became Lord Snowdon. The friendly lieutenant married the Queen-to-be and became an overnight Admiral. Stephen Ward helped to destroy a British Government. I became a twelve-minute variety act.

I also fell deeply in love, without realising it, and married a lovely girl of deceptive gentleness with a will like iron.

Clementina was a fine dancer whose technique stood out a mile from the rest of the *corps de ballet*. We seemed to drift towards each other over innumerable cups of coffee and a lot of laughs and, although both of us were well supplied with friends, we started to spend more and more time together.

As Clementina's own family was in Africa, I took her to meet mine. She took me to meet her 'adopted' one, which consisted of Madame Legat, the famous Russian ballet teacher and her entire, very Russian, family.

The contrast between cool Clementina and this gloriously unconventional and dramatically different ballet family is hard to describe. Madame Legat, who was deeply suspicious of any young man's motives, where her favourite pupil was concerned, gave me the sort of searching interrogation practised today by the K.G.B. I passed the test and became an 'adopted' son in that wonderful, unique family group whose affection I still treasure.

Neither Clementina nor I know at which point enjoyable friendship became love, but that is quite simply what happened.

I should have been totally happy with all these exciting blessings pouring down on me, but the banana skin was waiting and one day I learned that my mother was dying.

She hadn't been well for some time after a road accident in Yorkshire. But when she was taken into hospital for an exploratory operation, and I went to see her, Matron took me aside and told me bluntly that it was a matter of months.

To do the show that night and in the following weeks required even more effort, because death is one thing and suffering is quite another.

Cheerful and thoughtful for others as ever, Ma brightened that hospital like a giant Nightingale lamp.

One night when I was particularly down, though, of course, I never showed this on my visits to her, one of the Cockney stage hands asked me.

'What's the matter Mike? You're not your usual self tonight.' I told him.

Cockneys, for all their apparent toughness, are probably the kindest and most considerate people on the Earth.

'Anyfink we can do mate?' he asked gently.

'Can you help me get some oranges for her?' I asked, remembering my mother's favourite fruit.

At that time, oranges – even two years after the war – were virtually unobtainable in Britain and cost a fortune on the black market.

'Corst,' chuckled my friend, one of a family of cheerful compact Cockneys – all of whom, by tradition, were Covent Garden porters.

'Meet me in the Garden at three o'clock,' he continued. Grandad'll fix you up!'

I went to Covent Garden, which had fascinated me since my Fleet Street days, and was met by Grandad and two of his stalwart yeoman sons.

Then and there, at three o'clock of a bitter winter's morning, they had apparently nicked six dozen oranges, which they stuffed inside my trench coat till I looked like a pregnant spy.

As I staggered past a copper on his Garden beat, two of the oranges fell out. He stooped and picked them up for me, then with a straight face he said:

'Give your Mum our love,' and walked majestically on, leaving me gaping in the early morning lamp light.

Apparently everyone in the market knew and had helped out, but to save me the embarrassment of trying to pay for them, had pretended that the oranges were nicked.

Ma cried when I told her and, knowing her, no one in the hospital went short of an orange, especially in the children's ward.

Thirteen months after it started *Starlight Roof* had finished, Clementina and I were married and I was out of work. Ma was enchanted with her new daughter-in-law and somehow hung on till our first child was born.

This was Marylla or, as Pop called her 'Fastidio', which in Spanish means 'nuisance', referring to the wildly uncomfortable time Clementina had while she was pregnant.

Anything less of a nuisance than 'Fusty', as she became known, would be hard to find. She was an adorable baby and Ma was thrilled with her.

Two weeks later Mother slipped quietly away, while we were on a weekend down in Somerset.

From that moment onwards, just as though Ma was now arranging it, my 'career' took an abrupt upward turn.

Down to our last couple of pounds and with the rent due, I found myself playing a week's variety at a London suburban theatre – the Kingston Empire – on a show with Billy Cotton, the big genial Cockney band leader.

This down-to-earth genuine Londoner roared with laughter every night at my new act and wanted to book me for a variety tour of Britain. But Monty had brought Val Parnell down to see me work and, unknown to me, he was in on the Friday night.

Monty rang me later to say that I was to open at the London Palladium on the following Monday. Partly from shock, but mainly from hunger, I fainted.

Things had been very tough for Clementina and me and only the week before we had joyfully received a huge ham, from her family in Africa.

The postman looked a bit lugubrious about its smelly delivery and I rushed it down to the local butcher, to see if he could save some of it after its long, hot journey through the Red Sea.

When I went to collect the remains, that evening, the butcher, who knew us well, said cheerfully: 'I managed to save a couple of pounds of best ham off the bone.' And handed me a welcome parcel.

That night we feasted off it. Then it suddenly struck me that we were eating shoulder ham and the parcel had contained a leg, which must have been rotten right through.

People's kindness never ceases to amaze me. That butcher had given us our first decent meal for a week, rather than see young people disappointed and hungry even while meat was still so meanly rationed.

The Palladium opening night was like a dream. Bearded and long haired with the year of intermittent work I now did the act, in character, as a mad Professor.

The Palladium audience on the first night was mainly Jewish and probably the best audience in the variety world. For twelve minutes I 'tore them up' as they used to say and walked off the stage in a daze to a solid wall of applause and encores.

The next morning the papers gave rave notices to the unknown new comedy star and within one month I opened in the Folies Bergères back at the old familiar Hippodrome. To my complete surprise, with exactly the same act, I stopped the show as cold as Julie had two years before.

From near penury, which I can only describe as a show business disaster area, with a beautiful and brave wife and a brand-new baby, I was suddenly the current toast of the West End, at the enormous salary of £75 a week.

During this period of comparative plenty, plans for the first Goon show had at last materialised.

The nucleus of this explosion of post-war comedy had been at the Grafton Arms, a Victorian pub owned by the Grafton family and run by Jimmy Grafton or, as we called this urbane and clever man, 'The Major'.

Demobbed at the same time as the rest of us, Major James Grafton, M.C., had been one of the two brave men who had swum the Meuse River, to bring news of the rescue operation to the beleaguered paratroops at Arnhem.

Harry and I met him when Jimmy was writing for *Variety Bandbox* and our styles of comedy, which I was creating with Harry, had clashed. Liking and mutual respect were instantaneous and we had soon brought Spike along to meet him.

Having our operations room in a lovely old pub had its advantages. We were soon joined by the youthful and then plump Peter Sellers, and the idea of welding ourselves together in a radically different comedy format slowly emerged.

Peter had come into our orbit through the Windmill, and at first had only seemed to be an excellent impressionist with a great talent for character voices.

As our mutual friendship ripened, we all began to see the possibilities which could arise from becoming a close knit team. As Harry put it: 'You can't get closer-knit nits than us.'

Pushed by the intensely practical Jimmy, we met a scholarly and intelligently humorous B.B.C. producer named Pat Dixon. Pat was a bit older and more show-wise than any of us, and as radical in his approach to comedy as we were.

Tall and academic, Pat slightly overawed us at first but his sheer enthusiasm, as he recognised our raw potential, won us all over to his logical way of thinking.

I don't think any of us would ever have won the B.B.C. popularity prize, least of all Pat, who waged a never-ceasing guerrilla war with the administration. But, somehow, he persuaded that august body to let us have a trial recording and – *The Goon Show* was born.

My son was also, as they say, on the way – though neither Clementina nor I realised it at the time. In fact our local doctor diagnosed acute appendicitis and rushed her off to Putney Hospital.

Clementina had been energetically spring-cleaning the flat and washing everything in sight and virtually had collapsed.

When the ambulance came the only dry garment that she had was an old pair of my brother-in-law George's pyjamas and those my beloved had been intending to turn into dusters. Wearing this odd ensemble, Clementina was whipped off to the hospital. I promised to dash in later with some new nightwear.

This I bought at Jaegers in Regent Street and sped over to

Putney, to give a new nightie and dressing gown to my wretchedly dressed wife.

As Clementina, being a true Scot, never wastes anything, she put the old pyjamas in the smart Jaeger box and I left it in the back of my car outside the Hippodrome.

Halfway through the performance a detective from the C.I.D. asked to see me, and showed me the box, which some unfortunate criminal had nicked out of my old Wolseley. I identified the box and its contents and told the policeman that the pyjamas were worthless.

'Nevertheless,' said the copper, 'Chummy is a third-time loser and is well known to us for car-thieving.'

This meant that I had to appear in court at Lambeth, to identify the goods which the old lag had been caught with.

The judge, who was a dry and sarcastic man, took full advantage of the situation.

When I had been sworn in, counsel asked me: 'Mr Bentine, this box – does it look familiar to you?'

'Well,' I said, 'It looks like the box I had in my car.'

'Precisely,' he went on triumphantly. 'And this is the contents? Do you recognise the garment?' he continued, extracting the dreadful old striped flannel pyjamas.

'Yes, I do,' I said firmly.

'Are they your pyjamas?' he asked pointedly.

'No. They're my wife's!'

There was a silence and then the judge took over.

'Your wife's, Mr Bentine?' he quizzed me.

'Well. When I say my wife's, I don't mean my wife's actual pyjamas but my brother-in-law's old ones,' I floundered.

'Is your wife normally in the habit of wearing your brother-in-law's old pyjamas,' went on the old bastard, now thoroughly enjoying himself.

'Not usually,' I said, 'but it was all she had at the time – '

The eyes of the court fixed themselves on this obviously cruelly mean husband, and the women present probably thought I should be in the dock.

I explained the situation and the atmosphere cleared a bit, but I shall never forget the look on the face of that poor devil of a sneak thief, when he realised that he was going down for about two years for George's old pyjamas. I really think he felt that crime didn't pay.

Amid crime and punishment my son Gus was on the way.

When the *Folies Bergères* show closed, after an eighteen

months' run, I started touring in variety.

Monty Lyon had decided to retire and raise pigs in Ireland which, as he pointed out, was an unusual occupation for a Jewish man. In reality, he went there because he loved fishing, at which he was an expert.

Dennis Sellinger took me over and I joined forces with Lew and Leslie Grade who, with their brother Bernard Delfont, had arrived as children on Britain's hospitable shores, penniless and homeless, many years before, to emerge through their own hard working efforts as Britain's top theatrical agency. This they had accomplished by total application, and the determination of their remarkable mother.

Lew was the salesman of the family, Leslie the planner and Berny the showman.

I speak as I find, and Lew, especially, always encouraged me and helped me build up my act into a commercial success.

Tough as they come, he has the gift of enthusiasm and the courage to play his hunches. With Leslie's lightning mind, and Bernard's flair for picking shows, they made a formidable trio.

Off I went round the music halls for two years, dashing home between bookings to be with my family as often as possible.

By now, every Sunday, I was also rushing back to do a Goon Show recording and my weeks were full.

At my first visit to the Ardwick Hippodrome, Manchester, I met Eddie Gray, that original and funny juggler, who was an escaper from the Crazy Gang.

During the run of 'Folies', Dickie Henderson had told me that Eddie was an inveterate practical joker and had instanced wild stories about him. Meeting him in the flesh, I found Eddie to be the mildest and most ordinary-seeming of men, which was probably why his practical joking was so successful.

A perfect example of the strange offstage humour of Eddie Gray was revealed to me as, one rainy night, we waited for a taxi, while we sheltered round the front of the Ardwick Hippodrome.

Standing beside us was a small plump middle-aged Jewish lady, cradling a Pekinese dog in her arms.

Eddie turned to her: 'Excuse me, madam,' he said politely. 'But unless I am mistaken that is a Pekinese dog of fine breeding that you have in your arms?'

The little lady smiled nervously and agreed, reassured by Eddie's obviously sober respectability.

'I thought so, madam,' went on Eddie. 'How fortunate for the

179

little fellow – Professor Hibernitz (here he indicated me, wild-haired and bearded beside him) is probably the world's greatest living expert on the Pekinese dog.'

The lady beamed upon me: 'Pleased to meet you,' she said, obviously meaning it.

Before I could reply, Eddie continued ruthlessly: 'The Professor doesn't speak a word of English – I'll translate for you, madam.'

He turned to me and spoke a stream of gibberish. Taking up my cue, I replied in the same vein, finishing with the only recognisable words, 'pekinese dog'.

Eddie smiled and translated for the benefit of the dog-lover.

'The Professor is asking what you feed the little chap on?' he said.

'Well,' replied the little lady, 'a bit of chicken, maybe a bit of liver – mine dog is ver' fond of chicken liver.'

Although I naturally understood what she had said, Eddie now translated this into more gibberish.

I replied, shortly, finishing again with the words: 'Pekinese dog.'

Eddie looked grave, then said sadly: 'The Professor says you're killing it.'

'What should I feed it on?' asked the alarmed Pekinese fancier. Off went Eddie again into gibberish-land, while I answered in the same weird language, leaving it up to this strange man to make what he wanted of it all.

'Ah yes,' said Eddie. 'The Professor strongly recommends charcoal and celery – chopped fine – there's nothing like it for Pekinese dogs, the Professor says.'

The dear little lady thanked us and kissed me, and even made the Pekinese do so as well. As a taxi had now drawn up, in the teeming rain, we helped her into it and she drove off, still thanking us gratefully.

'What the hell was the point of all that?' I asked. 'You don't even see the end of your practical joke.'

'Ah,' said Eddie chuckling to himself, 'but I can imagine it. That Pekinese sniffling happily to itself, is going to waddle up to its food bowl – expecting its usual feast of chicken liver – only to find itself confronted by a brimming bowlful of charcoal and celery, chopped fine.

'It's going to look up at its mistress who, undoubtedly, will say firmly: "Eat it – It's good for you!" '

*   *   *

By now I'd begun to really get the feel of a variety audience and the act hummed along merrily, while I toured Britain from one end to the other.

During these years I met and enjoyed many of the old stars, like G. H. Elliott, the immaculate music-hall artist, billed in those days as 'the chocolate coloured coon', a description that would hardly go over big today with the Race Relations Board. Ella Shields – the ageing, but still wonderful artiste of *Burlington Bertie* fame – and many top liners.

There was Max Miller, that marvellous cheeky chappie and doyen of all Cockney humour and Ted Ray, with his suave yet broad delivery, and the larger than life, much-loved Jimmy Wheeler, of the hoarse staccato one-liners. I found them all to be kind and talented solo performers, who took the trouble to help and advise my budding efforts.

Then there were the new comedians like Eric Morecambe and Ernie Wise – in those days looking ridiculously young for such impeccable timing, and knocking themselves out to get a laugh.

With Eric and Ernie, I would often sit up in our theatrical digs, till the small hours of the morning, devising new and original routines, only to go out on to the stage, the same night, and do our standards acts, because Miss Cissie Williams, the iron-willed woman who booked the Moss Empire's circuit, would allow no deviation from the act 'as seen'.

Peter Sellers, David Lodge and I once slipped in a new and very well received Goon-type routine, about an Olympic judo expert, played by Peter, and Miss Williams had the whole thing cut out by the second house at Finsbury Empire. You were booked on your standard act and that's what you did – or else!

My mad Professor act, of the chairback, sink plunger and vacuum pipes, worked well nearly everywhere, and slowly I improved and broadened my performance.

Then one day Gus arrived – while Clementina was down in the country in Dorset. His life hung in the balance for several weeks as, for some reason, he couldn't keep anything down. We rushed him up to London.

Here the specialists didn't offer much hope for our rapidly weakening baby, and one of them recommended that we should find a first-class qualified children's nurse to ease his imminent passing.

And so Nursie came into our lives.

Nurse Frances Forbes, as she was formally introduced to us, packs more calm commonsense and sheer love into her small active frame than a whole regiment of women. The simile is deliberate, for Nursie served in a heavy anti-aircraft battery during the war, and Fus and Gus later used to say proudly: 'Our Nursie was a gunner!'

Trained at Luton Hospital, this efficient and lively lady arrived, ostensibly to help our son through the last stages of his tiny life, but when she examined him she clucked thoughtfully and said: 'There is nothing wrong with this beautiful baby!'

Nursie then brewed up some wonder mixture from her ample medical bag and, from that moment, poor Gus's feeding problems were over and he started to swell up like a pink prune.

If it hadn't been for Nursie we would have lost him at the age of six weeks – whereas she gave us 21 years of his wonderful happy life.

We thought that we had nearly lost Nursie though, within the first three days of her arrival. I had been kept out of her way and told to lay low, in case the sight of my long-haired bearded weirdo self might scare her off. While she was feeding the now gurgling and contented Gus, I had slipped down for a quick bath. Clementina, in a moment of busy preoccupation, had taken my dressing gown away.

Stark naked, I made a dash for my bedroom – only to be confronted by Nurse Frances Forbes, looking completely composed:

'Good morning,' she said. 'You must be the father.'

After that extraordinary encounter, which Nursie says didn't strike her as too odd because after all we were theatricals, it seemed reasonable to suppose that she would stay, as she happily has.

Fusty was having great difficulty in starting to walk. Not being too baby-wise, Clementina and I thought this was normal – but by fifteen months she was still not toddling.

Nursie was very concerned about this and went, with Clementina, to consult a specialist, at Great Ormond Street Children's Hospital.

He examined Fusty and pronounced serious brain damage.

'Nonsense,' snorted Nursie, and swept out, seething, with a deeply disturbed Clementina following in her wake.

Another specialist diagnosed a possible mild case of polio, and Nursie insisted on Fusty having remedial exercises, with a wonderful physiotherapist called 'Mitchy', who worked on those reluctant small legs of hers until, one day, off she waddled.

Thank God, since then Fusty has grown up into a madly

active and completely whole person, fully justifying Nursie's loving efforts and confounding that idiot of a specialist who condemned her so glibly.

Two other people, who have had a great effect on our lives, we met in the South of France when, with Nursie firmly installed and Fus and Gus so completely happy with her, Clementina and I stole ten days for our much delayed honeymoon.

At Juan-les-Pins were Sam and Marty Kershen, who had also dashed away for a quick holiday with their small son Lawrence.

From the moment we met them we all started laughing – because compact Sam and statuesque Marty are imbued with the sheer love of life that is all too rare a gift.

I remember we went for a drive, winding up the Moyenne Corniche to the Château de Madrid, a very ritzy restaurant, perilously perched on a solitary crag, overlooking a sheer drop, hundreds of feet down to the Mediterranean below.

Sam had warned us not to order anything other than coffee or tea, because our holiday allowance in those days was £50 per person, for everything.

However, when we were seated at the table, Clementina spotted one of her few real weaknesses. Sam, out of politeness, asked her what she would like. Without thinking, my beloved blurted out, 'Strawberries, please!'

At that moment Sam and I, as near as dammit, would have cheerfully pushed her off the cliff, but we just had enough money between us to make sure we didn't do the washing up, so my love got her strawberries.

Friendship is a marvellous thing and something I have fortunately never lived without. I don't mean the cheerful acquaintance of the many people one meets, but the mysteriously happy bond that carries unrelated people together through life. Such is our relationship with Sam and Marty.

Back again we flew to the family and for me, a new round of the music halls and a growing success for the Goon Show.

Pat Dixon had handed us over to Dennis Main-Wilson, an intense, bespectacled young producer of extreme enthusiasm, who took on the weekly wrestling match with our Sunday recordings.

At first the anarchic humour that we specialised in drew only a small but devoted audience of aficionados and a trickle of somewhat weird fan mail.

The progress of the early Goon Show has been told over and

over again and I don't want to bore anyone with my own impressions, except to say I enjoyed every moment of it.

Once we found ourselves confronted by six rows of visiting nuns, whom some lunatic in the B.B.C. ticket section had sent, probably thinking the words 'Aeolian Hall' sounded harp-like and appropriate for such a coachload of innocent visitors.

God alone knows what the nuns thought of the Goon Show but, at the end of the recording I'm sure the floor of the studio was covered in beads.

A great friend and helper at this time was an unfailing, cheerful and intelligent man called John Carlsen. I originally met him when I was rehearsing for the *Starlight Roof* and he introduced himself to me as the Press Officer for Moss Empires. Any publicity I got on that opening night I am sure I owe to John and when I finally made a real impact later at the Palladium, it was John who led David Lewin of the *Express* backstage to see me and to give me that all important write-up.

All through the rest of my up-and-down career, until John's recent passing, he handled my press relations work.

He was a brave man, a lifelong sufferer from asthma, which he made light of and possessed of an impish sense of humour. A perfect example of this happened during an ill-fated effort by Lew and Leslie Grade to present the world's biggest whale on the South Bank Festival of Britain site.

The great whale, called Jonah, was a genuine one and they had brought it, I believe, from the Continent at vast expense. The public didn't seem to be overly drawn to this splendid marine specimen and for some reason its preserving mechanism went wrong when the refrigeration failed.

Anyway, the Council demanded the removal of its rapidly developing decomposition, pronto.

Lew phoned me and asked me to mention the whale during my act at the Palladium where I was appearing at the time. I was opposed to this as I didn't really see how it would fit into my routine which was rigidly controlled for time by the management.

The whale was also rigidly controlled by the time factor of its now accelerating chemical breakdown and its presence was becoming an acute embarrassment.

As Lew and Leslie were somewhat dejectedly standing outside their Regent Street office, waiting for a taxi to take them to the site of their monstrous and odoriferous exhibit, John Carlsen

184

passed them. He couldn't resist it and, with that disarming smile of his he suggested, 'Frying tonight?'

* * *

Back at the Palladium, I was now part of yet another Variety Bill – this time starring Donald O'Connor, the young American film star and dancer.

This delightful entertainer didn't hit the Palladium audience with the impact of a Danny Kaye and was deeply depressed by this but, as I explained to him, it was only because he had been badly advised in the choice of his material. All the audience wanted him to do was to dance and sing, just as they knew and enjoyed him in his movies.

We got on great and it was Donald who encouraged me to take up the offer of Ed Sullivan, the American sportswriter-turned-showman, and go to the States.

Which is exactly what I did.

20. F.B.I. and Scar

The first time Clementina and I flew across the Atlantic it took sixteen hours.

'Mind you,' said the pilot, 'we had a tail wind.'

The plane was a Strato-cruiser, a commercial version of the B.29 bomber, with a double-bubble pressurised hull and a bar lounge approached by a short staircase. It was comfortable, if a bit noisy, and we got to New York in easy stages, first landing at Shannon Airport, in Ireland, and then at Gander, in Newfoundland.

Now, I am undoubtedly the worst dressed comedian in the world and once won an anti-award for precisely that reason. The Editor of the *Tailor and Cutter* was determined that he could do something about this and, as he was in charge of a series of advertisements for a man-made fibre, he approached me with the offer of a large fee if I would wear a suit properly made up in this material by a first-class tailor.

The advertisement was to appear in a daily paper and I duly went along to a tailor who counted the Duke of Edinburgh among his customers.

I was measured and fitted for the suit over a period of about four weeks but I suppose I am just not the right shape, apart from the fact that my erratic dietary habits make me go in and out like the tide. Anyway the finished suit looked as if it had been made for the Duke rather than for me.

There was no time for alterations as the photographer had arrived to take the pictures so I had to adopt various rather tortured positions to make it look as though the suit fitted.

It was exactly like the tag line of a famous old Jewish joke: 'That's the finest suit I ever saw on a cripple.'

This explains why on my arrival in the States I was wearing a black belted leather coat which I thought went dramatically well with my long hair and moustache and beard.

I certainly impressed the U.S. Immigration officials, who regarded us both with undisguised suspicion.

Not only had I landed, in 1952, at the most controversial moment in the Senator McCarthy anti-Communist trials, but there was also a barber's strike.

We were the only two non-American citizens on the plane when we landed at Idlewild Airport, as it was then called. Therefore, we were left till the last.

Finally I approached the desk where a fair haired Immigration Officer looked at me, in candid wonder. I suppose all I needed, to complete the picture of what the badly dressed anarchist was wearing, was a bomb, which is perhaps why they handled my brief case with such care.

'What are your political opinions?' asked the officer, without preamble.

'I haven't really got any,' I replied happily.

'You're an anarchist?' exclaimed the fair haired, all-American guardian of liberty.

'Actually,' I said cheerfully, 'I'm a comic.'

'A what?' cried the official, then, turning to his equally dumbfounded companion, 'Christ, Harry,' he whispered hoarsely, 'he admits it.'

Obviously things were getting a bit out of hand and I naturally attempted to smooth them over.

'Look,' I said, 'Ed Sullivan will vouch for me – I don't see why being a comedian should upset you, anyway. I mean, I've got both our air fares back.' And I fumbled with the tickets, to show him we wouldn't be a charge on the State.

The official looked even more surprised, but struggled to keep his cool.

'Friend,' he said, 'you have just admitted you are a Communist! Right?'

'Wrong,' I replied indignantly. Then it dawned on me. 'Comic' does not mean the same thing in America – where the word is used to describe a cartoon strip in the newspaper.

'Comedian! I meant I was a comedian, and I'm over here to work on the Ed Sullivan Show.'

'For Chrissake,' he smiled. 'Man you really had me goin' there, for a while.'

Throughout this exchange of pleasantries, Clementina had remained quite unmoved, possibly because she still felt sick from the bumpy flight.

Twelve years later, on my return to the U.S. in 1964 – the time interval indicates how much of a smash hit I was on my first trip – by a strange coincidence, the same Immigration Officer met me at the same airport, by now called Kennedy Airport.

Again I was with Clementina, but this time I was clean shaven. I can only think that the name Bentine is so unusual that it clicked some memory pattern in the official's mind.

His fair hair was thinner and the waist line was no longer young, but a great grin spread across his face.

'Mr Bentine,' he said, slowly, 'you changed your act.'

* * *

Hans Holzer, an American journalist friend of mine, met us at the airport, on the first trip to the United States. With his warmth and efficiency, he sped us through to New York, which was giving its usual well-known impression of a movie-set against the westering sun.

Hans had booked us in at the Beeckman Towers. We were so busy chatting that I didn't notice how high the lift was taking us. When the bellboy ushered us into the room we naturally went over to the window to see the view.

Both of us suffer from vertigo but, in those days, I really had it badly.

Our eyes zoomed down into the great canyon of streets below . . . and we backed slowly away from the window, clinging on to each other like children.

I think we would have tied ourselves to the bed, but Hans, who was a showbiz reporter as well, had other plans.

'Lindy's!' he enthused. 'Sardi's! Reuben's! Broadway! You've got to see them right now!'

He shepherded us out, feebly protesting, straight down into the heart of New York.

As we taxied back and forth across the city, in spite of Hans's happy optimism, my spirits fell to a new low. How could I possibly add to this already overflowing mass of show business talent that filled the theatres and night clubs, on and off Broadway.

Even the Sixth Avenue delicatessen, with its quick-witted waiters, was a fund of repartee which I knew I could never match. The names of international stars blinked glaringly from the canopies of the theatres and blazed out from the night club entrance marquees. In fact there were so many bright lights that nobody seemed to notice them. In fact, a large crowd had gathered round a shop front where the lights had fused – all trying to make out what was in the window.

When I finally, hesitantly, entered the portals of Lindy's famous restaurant my confidence was non-existent.

A bearded weirdo in a leather coat was then not a common sight in New York and curious eyes swivelled to follow us as I stumbled through the doors, tripping with nerves. I felt exactly like the gunfighter in a western when he enters the saloon and it all goes quiet. Then suddenly – 'Mike!' yelled a high-pitched voice.

Every eye switched to the sound. 'Mike Bentine! You mad bastard!'

Judy Garland, bless her, rushed up and flung her arms round me.

With her was my old friend Max Bygraves. Both due to open in a couple of days' time at the Palace Theatre, where Judy made her great American comeback.

At that moment, when I would have cheerfully legged it back to Idlewild and hopped on to the first plane, her brimming good nature turned the tide.

I had worked with Judy during her tour of Britain following her phenomenal success at the Palladium where she won the hearts of the British public and critics alike.

Highly strung and problem ridden, this superb artist was a joy to watch as she sang *Over the Rainbow* to an audience so entranced it was almost breathless. As the applause broke deafeningly into that emotion-filled silence she walked off into the wings, where I was standing, and said: 'Some bastard was coughing out front!' Then she downed a large gin and walked straight on again to acknowledge the almost hysterical ovation.

Offstage I found her friendly, and a sucker audience for 'Pro' stories, which she loved.

I had known Max Bygraves for years and we had toured together as well, so that meeting in Lindy's turned into an informal party and we were joined by other pros as we had a ball of a re-union.

For me it broke that awful gloomy spell and made me determined to break into American show business.

A few days later we booked into an apartment on East 54th Street. The 'Beaux Arts Apartments' was, in Hans's words, 'a good address' and overlooked the new United Nations building. The apartment itself boasted a sitting room and bedroom and had a television set with a round screen.

We catered for ourselves and bought most of the groceries at a small delicatessen on Second Avenue. It was managed by a large Irishman, who hadn't lost his brogue or his sense of humour. He also had the natural dignity of the Irish countryman and one day he gave me a lesson in humanity.

The delicatessen was as clean and hygienic inside, as the streets were dirty and littered outside. While I was shopping for the weekend, a tramp lurched into the shop. He was filthy, ragged, and stank of cheap drink and methylated spirits.

The Irishman cheerfully greeted him as though he was a much valued customer. Somehow interpreting his mumbled reply, he made him up a large sandwich, which he cut in half. Wrapping one portion in paper, he handed them both to the tramp.

Full of chatty banter, the manager led the unfortunate drunk to the door and waved him off with humour and dignity.

New York is a hard commercial city which, like all cities, can be callous, cruel and unfriendly, but that simple example of how to treat someone down on their luck, without selfconsciousness of charity, shines for me as a perfect jewel.

Just how alarming New York could be came home to both of us on this first trip with a sudden shock when, early one morning, the apartment door bell rang and I answered it wearing the long top half of my pyjamas and half asleep.

As I opened the door two enormous men in greatcoats slammed it back and forced me up against the wall, while they frisked me.

Clementina was still asleep in the bedroom and I kept my voice down in order not to alarm her.

'I've got nothing mate.' I gasped, as the two large men held me, feeling as if I was in some nightmare version of a paperback thriller. They released me and stepped back, one of them producing his identity card, in a flat folder.

They were F.B.I. agents.

By this time Clementina had joined us. Her obvious respectability and nervous indignation turned the tide.

Once again, my unusual appearance at that politically difficult time, had swayed the better judgement of these two quick-moving men.

Ed Sullivan was soon on the phone, at my urgent request, explaining my bona fides. That changed the whole atmosphere instantly. The F.B.I. men became extremely apologetic and explained the situation more fully.

Apparently the whole thing had started through my own naïvete in sending a letter to my idol, Professor Einstein. Completely forgetting his top position in national security, I had written asking for an interview, to discuss Pop's work with him. The letter was intercepted and, of course, I had quite openly put my address on it.

The F.B.I. at that time were excessively sensitive, what with the Fuchs affair and the Rosenberg trial. So they sent two operatives to bring me in.

After all, the Korean war was in full swing and the atomic bomb and nuclear physics were top security items. My letter had been very much concerned with the new revolutionary unified field theory and certain aspects of parallelism, neither of which, I felt, were remotely concerned with weaponry of any kind. Quite rightly, from American security's point of view, any communication concerning Professor Einstein had to be immediately investigated.

It was my being a comedian that stumped the two F.B.I. men. They had never heard of that 'cover' before and they couldn't reconcile my two interests in life – science and comedy – until Ed Sullivan put them firmly in the picture.

The interview, which had started so alarmingly, turned into an informal Mad Hatter's breakfast party. Both the F.B.I. agents were Ed Sullivan fans so, then and there, such was my relief at not being murdered and Clementina raped, that I did the entire act for them.

As they applauded my efforts the whole thing reminded me irresistibly of Pop's encounter with M.I.5, and as I closed the door after them I realised I was still wearing only the top half of my pyjamas.

At least for once I hadn't had to call in the Peruvian Consul.

That night we went out with Hans to a celebration dinner at a fashionable New York Restaurant, where the menu read: 'Traditional English dinner – Roast beef and Motza balls.'

We had only been in New York about a week when I got a telegram from Pop – his second wife, Wyne, had died quite suddenly from a cardiac arrest, during an asthma attack.

Bro rang me and told me that Pop had decided, wisely, to fly to Peru and see the family and would stop over in New York on the way.

We hurriedly moved into a bigger apartment and had just settled in when my first Sullivan show, of which there were to be three, went on the air.

In those days television was 'live' and the only recording method used was the Kinescope, that is to say, recording by filming directly from the tube.

At the dress rehearsal I was encouraged by the reaction of the large orchestra, and I felt that I had a fair chance of making an impact with my act, which was even more revolutionary in comedy for the States than it had been in Britain.

I should have guessed that, where the 'hip' musicians found humour, the public would not necessarily follow. Although there was good audience reaction in the studio, my wild appearance and unorthodox props and comedy puzzled the viewers. I will always admire Sullivan for keeping to his bargain and continuing with my other two appearances.

In the middle of it all Pop arrived, looking tired and confused. Almost within hours he had developed a wicked case of bronchitis and was well on the way to giving up the ghost.

Clementina wasn't having that, and made it quite clear that Pop must try to get to Peru. Once there, as she rightly said, the warm climate and total change of atmosphere would snatch Pop back from the dangerous apathy he had, understandably, slipped into. (New York had, by then, passed from the muggy humidity of autumn into the freezing cold and sudden snows of winter.) Pop was equally determined to 'pass' in New York and their battle of wills did more than anything to pull him round.

By some happy knack I could always make my father laugh, just as Ma had throughout their marriage. I knew the danger signs of his reminiscences too well to let him fall back into a drifting sentimentality.

It sounds cruel, but it was the only chance he had. We had to get him on the plane to a warmer climate, even if one of us went with him. Pop refused to allow that and, quite suddenly, cottoned on to the whole idea again and, as cheerful as a cricket, set off for Lima.

Forty-eight hours of nail biting waiting followed and then, at last, we got a telegram from him that all was well.

The family Bentin, in Peru, enfolded Pop to their ample bosoms and gave him a hero's welcome which lasted for eleven months. Pop returned to us in Britain a man reborn.

Jenny Grossinger, who had seen me work at the Palladium in London, now invited me to give a show at her huge holiday resort up in the Catskill mountains.

New York had always had an unhealthy anti-Semitic attitude and notices in hotels had often, unbelievably, read 'No dogs or

Jews allowed'. This idiotic and offensive nonsense had been modified, by law, to a slightly more polite 'Restricted Personnel', equally stupid and evil though it still was.

The notices eventually disappeared but the attitude remained, even surviving the war and the Nazi persecution.

In the Thirties, to combat this unendurable state of affairs, various Jewish communities had taken their vacations in specially built holiday camps in the Catskills and, for their entertainment, had developed a whole new branch of cabaret. This was called the 'Borsht Circuit' and became a cradle of new show business talent, developing such great stars as Danny Kaye, Jerry Lewis and innumerable others.

Zero Mostel, whom I had met during his Palladium stint, had also played the Borsht Circuit. Zero is one of the funniest men I have ever encountered, and his anarchic humour exactly fits his crumpled sad-eyed image, so like a half-deflated Jewish balloon.

My admiration for him has been unbounded since our meeting in his dressing room where I had rushed after seeing him play a matinee to an almost all-professional audience which he fractured with his impersonation of a reluctant coffee percolator and a glorious impression of a lost airliner.

I still have a valued photograph taken of us together with Zero's caption:

'To Michael Bentine, Britain's Zero Mostel, from Zero Mostel, America's Michael Bentine.'

Zero told me that the whole business in the Catskills had developed into a keen rivalry, each camp trying to outdo each other, in the facilities they offered to their clientele.

In Zero's words: 'Jenny Grossinger is thinking of building an indoor mountain.'

No question about it, the camps were really luxury resorts and had got just about everything – some of them twice over, including a 36-hole golf course. They also brimmed over with Jewish ebullience and high spirits and reminded me of nothing more than gigantic family parties.

Jenny had us driven up, through the breathtakingly beautiful country that lined the State highway, in that cold clear fall of the year. Those maple leaves, in their infinite variety of reds and golds, have to be seen to be believed.

With us, in the huge limousine, was a small party of musicians, wrapped up in lumberjackets and hunting caps, regaling us with tall stories of their prowess in war and the hunting season.

Way out, in the middle of nowhere, a deer ran across the dirt road and we hit it, badly injuring the poor beast. The musicians huddled together and refused to help me despatch the animal, so I naturally jumped out and killed it, quickly and painlessly as I had been trained to do, with one blow.

The rest of the journey was driven in awed silence – for in those days, Karate and Judo were not as universally known as they are today.

Our arrival at Grossingers was equally interesting. As I got out of the car and helped Clementina after me, we seemed to generate great interest. Dressed in a dark overcoat and trilby hat, with my beard, moustache and long hair, I looked exactly like a visiting Rabbi come to read Kaddish. That Clementina was non-Jewish seemed fairly obvious too and there was a low murmur of: 'Who's the shikzer with the Rov?'

Grossingers was everything Zero told me and more, with its own airport and just about every possible gimmick that man's ingenuity could conceive.

The show was fixed for that night and two other comedians were on the bill, Jack Pearl and Jackie Leonard. The one, a stand up one-liner of great experience and the other, a wonderful jolly fat man who was quite remarkably light on his feet, pirouetting so that his large stomach shot round slightly behind his hips in an arresting manner. Both were genuinely nice people and watched from the wings as I went into my act.

The reaction from a packed audience was disconcerting to say the least. They never laughed once, but enthusiastically applauded everything I said and did, while both the other comedians were convulsed.

The whole show was also broken up by various announcements, and even a dress show put on by Haddashah from Israel. With my outré appearance and the fact that my English was so alien to the New York ear, the audience believed I was a visiting Rabbi from Israel and was speaking Hebrew!

*   *   *

When we returned to the city, the incident of the unfortunate deer reminded me that the hunting season was soon to open in New York State so, shortly after our return to the apartment, I went to have a look at the famous sports store, Abercrombie and Fitch. This store was totally devoted to sport in every form. Being interested in firearms, I gravitated towards that section.

A huge phalanx of weapons and hunting accessories met my eyes as I walked out of the elevator. There were enough arms in the store to start a revolution, but my attention was attracted by a display of garishly coloured costumes in vivid colours.

'What are these for?' I inquired of a rather languid looking salesman.

'Various pursuits,' he replied without interest. 'What is your pleasure?'

'Well! That bright yellow one for example. What's that for?'

'Duck,' he said crisply.

'And the glaring red one?'

'Deer,' he told me warming to his task. 'We strongly recommend that one for deer. Believe me, sir! Red is the best deer colour!'

'But surely you'd be visible a mile off in that outfit?' I objected.

'What else,' he said triumphantly. 'That is the whole idea, after all!'

'I'm sorry. I don't follow you – '

'Look sir, by your accent you're British.'

I nodded in agreement.

'So what do you wear normally when you go hunting?' he continued.

'Usually I wear an old pair of grey flannel trousers – I mean pants, a pullover and a waterproof jacket.'

'God,' he said in awe. 'You'd remain alive for an hour here, no more.'

He led me over to a section of his department where a large number of peculiar objects were on display.

He picked one up – a short wooden affair – and blew it, producing a sort of hollow raspberry.

'Duck,' he said. Then, picking up a slightly larger metal tube, he blew again. A bass burp sounded through the store.

'Moose,' he announced brightly. Then indicating each of these strange instruments in turn, he reeled off: 'Goose – Bear – Quail – Wild Turkey. Every one a perfect imitation.'

The list sounded endless. I still looked blankly at him.

'Don't you follow me? Look, Sir, when the hunting season opens, New York empties like a broken thermometer and thousands of excited and heavily armed hunters enter our great forests upstate. They are all carrying these animal calls. The underbush is thick and the hunters are inexperienced. As soon as they hear this,' he blew a duck call, 'or this,' he sounded a goose honk, 'they blast.'

'Blast?' I echoed.

'Blast!!' he repeated. 'Hence the bright costumes! Like camouflage in reverse!'

The next day his extraordinary demonstration was proved right in every respect.

'7 DEAD SO FAR AS HUNTING SEASON OPENS' blared the *Herald Tribune* headlines.

New York is so different from any other city I know. For one thing it is laid out like a huge rectangular graph and the streets are numbered rather than named. For another thing, which tends to confuse me, almost any part of it could be almost any other part of it. I can only orient myself by reading the street numbers east and west on the corner lamp-posts.

The whole city feels vertical rather than horizontal and the realisation that all those people are piled on top of each other disturbs me greatly.

I always get the impression in New York that I am taking part in a gigantic three-dimensional movie. Frankly, it scares the hell out of me.

Just how different it all is, Clementina found out one day when she went to get her hair done. She walked into a very smart shop which she took to be a beauty parlour, with its marble front and elegant front window displaying a wig and make-up.

A frock-coated man approached, rubbing his hands.

'And what can we do to help madam?' he asked in a vibrant voice.

'I'd like a shampoo and set,' answered Clementina, taking off her headscarf.

The man drew himself up icily.

'This is a funeral parlour, madam!' he intoned, showing her the door.

Apparently the wig and make-up in the window was to show how well the undertakers could 'do-up' the departed.

One strange news story I read in New York told of the plight of the upstate New York mink farmers. They had a contract with the chicken farms to supply them with chicken offal for their minks.

The chicken farmers had started to caponise their fowls by giving them large doses of Oestrodiol – the female sex hormone. This had produced a breed of chickens with very large breasts, cocks as well as hens.

The hormone had settled in the chicken guts which were sold to the mink farmers and this had affected the minks as well. The male minks had turned 'queer' and refused to mate with the female minks – preferring their own sex.

This had resulted in a nil breeding return and a New York court was at that moment solemnly listening to this dramatic case.

The headline was: 'Upstate Mink Farmers Sue Chicken Moguls for Sex Failure.'

I thought then how different our two countries were.

*　　*　　*

The dollars melted away, mainly because of our phone calls to Britain, where Nursie, bless her, was an ever-reassuring bulwark of the family. We were both desperately homesick for Fus and Gus and every detail Nursie gave us brought us all that much closer.

The babes had been out in the double pram that Nursie manoeuvred so adroitly. While she was getting some fruit, an elderly woman had clucked over the children, who really looked like heavenly twins.

'Dadda,' said Fusty, clutching a photograph of me.

'Oh, let me see,' said the enchanted matron.

Fusty forthwith handed her one of my publicity handouts which showed the mad Professor character horribly plainly – mop hair, frizzy beard, grinning teeth and eyes wildly crossed.

The poor woman nervously dropped it back on the pram cover.

'Dadda,' repeated Fusty proudly.

Surviving financially in New York was a whole time business and funds had to be set aside for home as well, so when Lou Walters offered me a cabaret date, I seized on the opportunity hungrily.

The Latin Quarter was the forerunner of the big night club cabaret restaurants and Walters had, like Jenny Grossinger, seen me work the Palladium.

He invited us to a cabaret floor-side seat to see the show which headlined the one and only Sophie Tucker, the large and expansive singer of schmaltzy songs, who was then in her seventies.

She had a magic which was unique as she belted out *Yiddisher Mama* and other saccharine filled ballads, and which carried total conviction. Her enormous personality was as imposing as her large emotion-laden chest.

To my dismay, Lou Walters had arranged for her to introduce me. She proceeded to do it with just as much sentimentality and quivering huskiness as she had just put into her songs.

Grasping me warmly round the shoulders she looked into my eyes with a loving motherly gaze, as she near-tearfully quavered: 'This young man will soon be entertaining you in the wonderful way that only he knows how.

'This great artist is a stranger to our shores and I know you will welcome him with all your wonderful hearts.

'I shall be there when he opens next Monday. Cheering him on with all the love in my own heart.

'Wonderful, wonderful – Michael Bernstein!'

The fact that she had never set eyes on me before nor had the slightest idea of what I did made no difference to that wonderful, wonderful introduction.

The next week I opened and closed in two nights at the other Walters' club – a new one called the Gilded Cage, complete with a full size dummy girl on a moving swing. The packed night club audience just didn't know what the hell I was doing.

When I get nervous I work much too fast and try as I might I couldn't slow down. The audience heard me out in a puzzled silence with no interruptions, probably because through sheer speed I didn't give anybody a chance to get a word in edgeways. My act just didn't fit into any recognisably accepted category of comedy and was totally unfamiliar to them.

The Americans, being very much creatures of habit, are highly suspicious of any departure from the normal, and that must have been how the audience viewed me. I walked off the cabaret floor to the sound of my own feet.

But the other artists on the bill had watched with interest and appreciated what I was getting at.

Ben Blue, a gloriously funny dead-pan vaudevillian of the old school, who did a hilarious Swami act – that is a fake comedy mind-reading bit, with a straight man in the audience – gave me some valued advice.

'For Chrissake Mike! What do they know! You got a great idea – work at it. *Translate* it. They're foreigners.'

However, Lou Walters didn't feel quite the same about me and neither did one New York critic, whose words I still treasure: 'Michael Bentine, a recent importation from Britain, makes Terry Thomas look like a genius.'

Terry had been murderously slated by the same critic, only a couple of weeks before.

Bloody but unbowed, I listened to Lou Walters' surprisingly cheerful: 'It's horses for courses here, Mike – another club might love you.'

This advice came along with a much needed cheque, so we continued to eat until the next Sullivan show.

Meanwhile, the brawling, clattering clamour of New York, now mantled under a heavy fall of snow, seemed to be less of a nightmare. As we met more and more New Yorkers, mainly through Hans, we got to realise just how friendly and generous the people were.

In those days, mugging hadn't reached the heights or depths of today and, apart from Central Park and dark side streets, you could walk abroad in the City most of the day.

Jere, who had been with us in *Starlight Roof*, now reappeared in our lives. His wit is caustic and funny, drawled languidly from a mouth always ready to break up.

Describing a famous radio and TV star who emoted easily, Jere once remarked: 'His trouble is that his kidneys are too close to his eyes.'

But it was Hans who helped us the most. Always interested in the occult, Hans's real experience then lay in two areas – numismatics, in which he was an authority, and journalism, in which he made a very good living, running a news service.

His numerous long conversations with me and his fascination with the supernormal lead me to suggest he should write books on the subject. He certainly did and became famous as the 'Ghost Hunter' and, now is Professor of Parapsychology, at the University of New York.

In those days, however, his first love was show business and he urged me to write a show with him. Armed with do-it-yourself records of his music and folders full of lyrics, we started on a rough draft.

Hans will perhaps never write a great musical, but I must give him an 'A' for effort.

Once he had been pounding on Tin Pan Alley's doors with a tune which had a perennial lyric – that is to say Hans changed the words to suit the mood of the moment.

'*When it's Apple Blossom Time in Old Kentucky* became, in turn, *When it's Cherry Blossom Time in Old Tsintao* and *When it's Chestnut Blossom Time in Gay Paree*', depending on whether *The King and I* or *An American in Paris* was favourite.

We did have a lot of fun writing, though, and Hans even brought Mike Todd along, to get the full descriptive treatment of a revue from me.

Todd liked the idea but must have had other things on his

199

mind, or maybe he had seen me at the Gilded Cage, because I never saw him again.

Visual humour is more or less universal, but, for a foreigner to capture the mood of a New York audience, in those days, was almost impossible.

Only artists of the stature of Noel Coward and Maurice Chevalier, Edith Piaf and the immortal Marlene Dietrich achieved that sort of success.

The current hits on Broadway were *Guys and Dolls* and *The King and I* and *Top Banana* with the great Phil Silvers. Television's top show, for me, was Sid Caesar's and Imogene Coca's blissful *Show of Shows*. Superbly funny, it still remains unbeaten for originality and professionalism. Carl Reiner, later to become a close friend and the creator of the Dick van Dyke show, at this time played Caesar's straight man. That really was a show of shows.

Ida Patlanski, a visiting British friend of ours, summed up New York's humour for me. Arriving for tea, still chuckling, she told us that she'd just bought a new hat at Sak's Fifth Avenue and swept out of those imposing doors, feeling like a dog's dinner.

With a squeal of brakes, a yellow taxi cab pulled up opposite her and the grinning driver leaned out.

'New hat?' he asked brightly.

'Why yes,' replied Ida, blushing with pleasure.

'Don't do nuttin' for you,' he said and drove off.

The City itself slowly exerted its strange fascination. By the second Sullivan show I felt quite at home with the polyglot crowds and their seething tempo. I also realised that their dialogue was largely repetitive and the same slick phrases would be used again and again.

Johnny Puleo, the small and intensely alive comedian, who was the hub of Borrah Minevitch's Harmonica Rascals, and an old friend from my Palladium days, took us to the Italian quarter in New York.

Johnny, whose personality was in the inverse proportion to his small stature had a sense of fun all his own. At our first meeting as I came off the Palladium stage he said confidentially: 'My name's Johnny Puleo – I'd like a word in your knee.'

He always pulled the tallest and prettiest birds and I never saw him without one of these long willowy beauties beside him.

As he once described this phenomenon to me: 'Mike! I guess I'm a natural born mountaineer!'

The Italian restaurant he invited us to was exactly like the ones you see in gangster films – all chequered table cloths, voluble Sicilian waiters and temperamental chefs.

At any moment I expected the Italian character actor Henry Armetta who always played 'Mama mia' type head waiters, to appear.

The food was sensational – better even than Italy – and obviously everyone loved Johnny.

One dear old white haired man was especially interesting and told us all about his early immigrant days and how he longed for the sunny vineyards of his native Sicily.

Clementina and I were magnetised by his poetic description of that lovely island and the fascinating stories about the Italian construction workers who had built the great skyscrapers. Only later did Johnny gleefully tell us that our charming elderly friend was the local Capo di Mafia.

The intense cold and lack of funds kept us indoors a lot and we became television addicts, following the programmes through to the early hours of the morning, while we munched giant apples in bed.

The second show I did with Sullivan went much better, because I had slowed down a lot and now spoke with a slightly flatter accent, and Ed was duly pleased. His stocky build and seemingly immobile neck gave him an unbending image, but we found him helpful and friendly. He knew about first night nerves and told me he suffered the pangs of torture every time he went in front of the cameras. Anyway I was asked back for the third and final shot, in two weeks time.

In the meantime, Norman Wisdom had arrived in town and was due on the Sullivan show the following Sunday. He was a friend of mine, from the Nuffield Centre era, and was being groomed for stardom back home.

His appearance on the Sullivan show made my two night 'shtick' at the Gilded Cage look like a triumph. It was so embarrassing, we hurriedly switched channels. The next morning, at the office, we tried to cheer him up, but he was inconsolable and flew back the following day.

To our amazement, the British papers hailed his appearance on American television as a masterpiece and Norman made an immediate smash-hit opening in London, becoming one of Britain's biggest stars.

Many years later he went back to New York and opened on Broadway, in a musical and this time he deservedly wowed them and one critic even suggested that America should adopt him. That's show business!

Peter and Spike rang me, from London, urging me to come home as another Goon show series would be starting in the New Year. As we only had one more firm booking with Sullivan and were desperately homesick for the family, we decided to go, but the breaks were just coming and, through the contacts I had made in the profession, many people were now interested, especially in my creative writing.

Max Liebeman, the producer of the *Show of Shows* liked my material and felt it would suit Caesar. Liebeman especially approved of my short blackout sketches which are really stage versions of a captioned cartoon.

Being a cartoonist, I have always enjoyed devising these and one that Liebemann liked was a cave scene with two hairy Stone Age men in skins huddled together in a howling wind.

Their Stone Age axes clash together as they shiver uncontrollably and the resultant sparks start a fire in a pile of twigs.

They draw back in terror but, as they feel the warmth they excitely mutter 'Ugh' at each other and then try to find a name for this welcome miracle.

'Glug', 'Wug', and 'Mug' don't seem descriptive enough. When one of them tries the sound 'Gire' the other encourages him, as in charades, as he tries 'Wire' and 'Bire' and then, triumphantly hits on 'Fire'!

'Fire! Fire!' they excitely yell – and a helmeted Stone Age fireman comes on and puts it out with a bucket of water.

I don't claim it's a great blackout, I just state for the record that Liebeman liked it. He encouraged me to continue on these lines and wanted to see a lot more material but I was hot for home.

The last appearance with Sullivan worked even better and he also urged me to stay and find my niche in American show business.

Hans, too, was very reluctant to see us go and, quite rightly advised us against it, but the pull of home was too strong. Anyway, our transatlantic phone bill was getting ridiculous.

Shortly before we flew back, I was driving down Broadway with Chaz Chase, the diminutive Puck-like character who I had worked with in *Folies Bergères*, and I got the same brotherly advice.

'Stay, Mike,' he growled. 'You're breaking through – stick with it.'

Chaz was another of the hospitable and friendly Jewish community who really went out of their way to help me, an unknown, foreign comedian to get started. Chaz had been with us for eighteen months at the London Hippodrome and I had watched him nearly every night.

His act, which was as closely international as you can get, consisted of standing silently while his music was played, dressed in a sort of Ascot outfit of top hat and frock coat while he ate everything from his botton-hole carnation to a lighted cigarette and a burning book of matches, finishing by consuming his dicky shirt front.

Then he rounded off his 'shtick' by giving a very funny impression of an American striptease dancer while the band played *Take 'em Off*. I never once saw it fail.

He himself was a small, gruff-voiced, Brooklyn Jewish gnome of a man with a wonderful fund of funny stories punctuated with the word sonofabitch, and we all loved him dearly.

It was with Chaz that I got pulled in for speeding driving down Broadway though I couldn't have been doing much over the limit.

Two giant New York Irish cops, armed to the teeth, surrounded us.

'O.K. Leadfoot, where's the fire?' bellowed one, while the other's hand hovered near his gun. A dramatic moment at which I felt very vulnerable. Chaz laid a restraining hand on my arm.

'Take it easy Mike,' he said, and I must say I felt that any sudden move on my part would have had the .38 police special drawn and blazing.

I explained I was a stranger to the City and, reluctantly, the two massive fuzz let me go, but only after checking every document we had and even having us both out of the car and frisking us. An unnecessarily unpleasant experience.

A few weeks later I was driving my battered old Wolseley in London, slowly progressing down the Mall, when the whole exhaust assembly fell off, directly opposite a detachment of the Life Guards.

The red-hot rusty pipe rolled under the leading horseman and, as the horse reared up, the sergeant was thrown off, landing with a clang, as his breastplate hit the asphalt.

A motorcyclist swerved to avoid the prostrate soldier, and skidded into a tree, while a following motorist mounted the pavement and an old lady fainted.

As I jerked to a halt, to try to help sort out the carnage, a very large and solid London Bobby proceeded majestically towards me.

I had just got out of the car as he reached me.

His helmeted head inclined gravely towards me and his words were delivered in a deep sonorous voice:

'Well now,' he said, 'We're not being very clever this morning – are we?'

I knew I was back home.

21. Bumbling along

Our return from the States reunited us as a happy family. That nearly made up for the relatively long parting, and made me realise what family men must have gone through in the war.

It also marked the end of my professional association with the Goons, though not my personal relationship with them.

Another comedian, Graham Stark, had joined the show and did a number of programmes with us. Although he was a good performer, I couldn't quite understand how this fitted in with the original idea, and felt that the series must be well established, indeed, to make such a radical departure from our original conception of just the four of us.

I also felt that four could well be one over the magic number, because the Ritz Brothers, the Three Stooges, and the Marx Brothers, ex-Zeppo, who provided the romantic interest anyway, were made up of three people – so, who needed either the other comedian or, for that matter, one of us? After all, the Musketeers are based on a threesome – D'Artagnan merely joins them – the title is 'The Three Musketeers'.

In life I can only go by my instincts, and any time I ignore them, I go completely wrong. I knew, intuitively, that the Goons would really get off the ground in a big way, if there were only three of them, and, as I, at that time, with the exception of Spike, was the only self-contained writer-performer unit, I felt the choice of the one to leave must be me.

The conviction grew on me, until I told Harry what I felt, to get his reaction. He was very upset, but he did see my point. As he was having a phenomenal success with another radio programme, and his growing popularity would bring more listeners to the Goon Show, it would have been ridiculous for Harry to leave. Anyway, he was the key man, around whom it all revolved.

Peter and Spike were very sad about the break-up, but I

pointed out that no one had seemed put out about a fifth Goon suddenly joining us.

Then a P.R.O. at the B.B.C. must have talked to the Press, because they smelled a story and proceeded to blow the whole simple business up into some personal feud between the four of us.

This, understandably, upset Spike even more and the situation became very unhappy – after all, I was the one who, in my innocence, was doing the 'Captain Oates' bit.

Thank heavens, we can all laugh about it it now, but in those days, we were more impressionable.

So, I left the Goon Show. A few months later I reappeared on it, so that we could prove that the quarrel bit was a load of bunk, but at the time it was a sad business. I've never regretted that decision, and I did have the great pleasure of hearing their next series without knowing what was going to happen, though obviously I could often guess the pattern through that strong association we enjoyed when we created the show in the first place.

The contribution I made to the Goons was in real terms: firstly the publicity I had received with my second Hippodrome season was national and helped a lot to get us on the air. Secondly, creatively, I supplied a lot of ideas and lastly I offered a broad range of characters.

At that time Harry hadn't yet broken through into Educating Archie and Peter was only accepted as an impressionist, while Spike was then the virtually unknown. Of all the Goons, the only national publicity and top West End exposure as an original comedian had gone to me.

From the Goon Show, Harry would emerge as a top flight entertainer, Peter as an international film star and Spike as an original TV personality, script writer and author. I followed along well behind, till I won my way back.

* * *

Contrary to the B.B.C.'s dismal prophecies, at the time, I was busier than ever and a new idea was forming in my mind. For no accountable reason, except that I wanted to do it, I decided to make a children's series for television.

Before having children of my own, I don't really remember being overly fond of them, but by now I was intensely interested. I had also become alarmed, in America, by the growing number of films and television programmes that seemed to say: 'If it's alien, kill it!' I felt strongly that this was a bad influence on growing minds.

This expressed itself in science fiction epics to a marked degree, and I felt impelled to make a series of short pictures for television about friendly and cheerful visitors from outer space. These I drew as a simple egg shape, and gave them big boozy noses and a perpetual grin.

I showed them to Fus and Gus and tried various names on them, to get their reactions. They both loved the drawings and chuckled at them; their best reactions being to the words *Dumblies*, *Grumblies* or *Bumblies*.

Dumblies didn't sound quite right, somehow, and the figures were anything but Grumbly looking – so we all settled for Bumblies. No doubt about it, the whole family decided that these were definitely Bumblies.

When it came to naming the three small characters, there was a sharp division of opinion and, to keep the peace, I numbered them One, Two and Three. Number One was the professorial one, Number Two the plump and jolly one, and Number Three the right twit who got everything wrong. The family was adamant about their method of transport – they had to fly.

Not knowing very much about either children's programmes, or the techniques of film making, I went along to see the head of children's television at the B.B.C., Frieda Lingstrom.

Her name conjured up a vision of a sort of latter day Brünnhilde and, in a way, I wasn't disappointed. That formidable lady, who ran the excellent Children's Department, could well have broken into a rendition of the Valkyries. If she believed in something, she would battle for it. After taking one look at the Brumblie drawings and hearing why I wanted to make them, she then and there said yes.

To pay for them, I worked as much variety and night club cabaret, as possible. Finally I got together enough money to have the Bumblies made and the production started.

In my usual arse-about-face method of working, I decided I would pre-record the Bumblie voices and my own lines as well – then mime to my own playback, while Clementina worked the puppets to their sound track. Their mouths would have to be in synchronisation with the tape, as well as my own. It all seemed so simple at the time.

I went along to a special effects expert, Richard Dendy, and showed him the drawings. Had he not been an extremely nice person, and honest as well, he could have bankrupted me. But I had been guided to the right man and he not only agreed to make the Bumblies, but he also undertook my instruction in filming them as well.

The Bumblie drawings were now changed into three dimensional characters by the skill of Angelo de Calferta, an expatriate Spaniard, whose hands had been crippled by a sabre cut right across them during the Spanish Civil War. While recuperating in France, he had started sculpting, on medical advice, to regain the use of his terribly wounded hands.

Those hands are still the most beautiful ones I have ever seen, long and sensitive, but with tremendous strength, a superb example of human creation. They moulded the Bumblies into three lovable small people, who eventually captured the hearts and minds of millions of children.

When I finally went to see Miss Lingstrom again, and put the first three painted moulds of the Bumblies on her desk, she spontaneously clapped her hands and called in everyone in the Children's Department to come and see them.

It was all so exciting that it never occurred to me how much it was all costing. All I knew, or cared about, was that a small team of people totally believed in them and, somehow, we were going to make them into a television series.

We hired and used a clockwork camera, called a Newman Sinclair, whose lethally powerful springs had to be wound by hand. The technical problem of synchronising this camera to an electric tape recorder was a minor miracle in itself but, so long as the speeches were short, they didn't lose their synchronisation too apparently.

We made the actual films in an attic attached to Richard Dendy's workshop. The weather was so cold that, on one occasion, the camera actually froze up. Production was brought to a chilly halt while we thawed out.

Jo Jago, our cameraman, a Cornishman who had been on such films as *Sound Barrier*, entered into the spirit of the thing completely. During one tricky shot, where we were all fully occupied with making the effects work, he got so excited that he joined in and helped one of the Bumblies to fly across the screen. The little scene worked out marvellously – except that, in the general confusion, Jo had completely forgotten he was the cameraman and hadn't filmed it.

It was that sort of a happening. Right in the middle of it all there was a lightning strike at the laboratories. It looked like curtains for the Bumblies but, luckily, George Elvin, who was then the reigning head of the Union, had seen the Bumblies and was an enthusiastic fan. Apparently he put the whole thing to a vote and got a unanimous 'Yes'. I do believe we were about the only little film that got processed during that complete stoppage.

When I thanked him for this consideration he winked and said he'd only managed to swing it because the Bumblies were extraterrestial – and therefore outside the Union's jurisdiction.

As mad as a hatter and lovely with it, Angelo had done a wonderful job. From the moment we saw the 'rushes of the first day's filming, everyone fell in love with the Bumblies. I knew that all that terrific effort would be worth while.

Angelo fascinated me with his stories of his life as a sculptor, and took me back to his studio to see his work, which was quite breathtaking. A definite one-off, as they say in engineering, Angelo was the incarnation of the true artist in his total dedication to whatever he was doing. I am certain that the immortal character of Gully Jimpson was partly based on Angelo.

He inscribed tombstones for his bread and butter, when his other work packed up. Obviously, if you mis-spell a carved word on stone, it is wellnigh impossible to eradicate or correct it. And occasionally, Angelo would make a mistake. One lovely example, which stood in a corner of his littered studio read: 'In loving memory of Miss Mary Anne Walters, who pissed away' – and there, obviously, the inscription ended.

It was, I think, the association of ideas that caused that mistake to happen: Angelo, probably, was happily smashed when he did it.

Another story he told me, which I'm sure is true, was about his first big commission, to sculpt a life-sized Birmingham city councillor, on a horse – why on a horse is anybody's guess!

Angelo was, as usual, nearly starving at the time but, on the strength of the contract, he borrowed enough money for the assured rent of his fourth floor studio and the down payment on the clay for the matrix. This material he had to hump upstairs, on his back, a third of a hundredweight at a time.

Slowly, the great sculptor progressed, until a recognisable figure of a man, astride a great charger, took shape in the studio. Angelo worked on it, night and day, until the noble and impressive statue was complete and ready for the plaster casting. At this stage, it was viewed by one of the city fathers, who had commissioned it, and who was so ignorant of the methods of the artist that he asked how they would get it out of the door.

Armed with a further stage payment, Angelo went out for a much needed feast, having lived on bread and tea during this whole period.

He met a few friends, of the sort who always seem to gravitate towards people who had received interim payments, and the pub meal turned into a celebration. So it was past closing time, in the afternoon, when Angelo returned to his studio.

Outside the house was a fire-engine, and an interested crowd. In the basement was a very misshapen councillor on a very flat horse. The combined weight of all that matrix, with its heavy wet clay covering, had been too much for the floor.

Angelo promptly persuaded the landlord, who was insured anyway, to rent him the basement to finish the job. His argument was unanswerable – he couldn't pay for anything, till he had.

As it was lunchtime when Angelo went to the pub, everyone who lived in the intervening three floors had, mercifully, been out at work.

* * *

Slowly the Bumblies progressed as we filmed in the bitter cold of that attic, with Clementina huddled, swathed in layers of sweaters, underneath the table on which the Bumblies moved. We kept going on hot tea and coffee, which Angelo laced with rum.

Finally I delivered the finished film prints to Miss Lingstrom and they were an instant success.

I nearly gave up when the B.B.C. accounts department paid me about £40 a programme, as this didn't even cover the cost of the film stock. I had in my naïvete, thought that the B.B.C. would pay for the bare costs.

It was my own fault, however, for not getting the situation properly clear, with the accounts and the copyright people, but I was so excited about making the Bumblie series that I just hadn't approached the business properly. So I had to pay every penny by my own efforts and the Corporation had their cheapest children's programme ever.

Mind you, it was no fault of Miss Lingstrom's – she was very upset about it.

I was already committed to make up the series to thirteen, and so had to shift the whole operation to my own garage, where we completed the series, under even greater difficulties.

It puzzles me to see the B.B.C. pleading poverty and asking for ever higher licence fees and, then, announcing that most of the artists working for the Corporation earn less than £2,000 a year. I can well believe it!

The most important thing, however, was that we had kept faith with the young. Practically every week nowadays, someone grown up and with a family of his own, comes up to me to tell me what pleasure the Bumblies gave them, and that makes everything well worth while.

All this had bankrupted me, as near as dammit. My next contract was in Australia and I had, somehow, to borrow the fare. After the misery of being apart from the children while we were in America, I intended to take the whole family this time. Although my fare was paid, I had to find the money for the rest of us.

My mother-in-law turned up trumps by lending us the fare — which is why I never do gags about mothers-in-law.

Before we left for Australia we all went through a dismal time, because Nursie, who was now very much a part of the family, wasn't coming with us, as her elderly father was taken ill.

This put a complete dampener on the preparations, for what should have been an exciting new adventure, and we all felt terribly depressed, except Fus and Gus, to whom we hadn't yet broken the news.

Then, miraculously it seemed, her father took a turn for the better and absolutely insisted that Nursie should accompany us. This was good news, but other difficulties reared their heads — for one thing, the booking of the cabins had been done and there was no more room on the crowded ship.

I went to Pop and told him my troubles. He thought quietly for a moment before saying: 'I pick up that Nursie will go with you and that you are not to worry — you will be away for quite a long time, and both Nursie's father and I will be perfectly all right till you get back!'

When I got back home, a phone call from the shipping line had told Clementina that the ship's bullion room was being converted into a cabin for this one trip, and that we could have it at no extra cost — incidentally, outside the first class suites, it was the biggest cabin on the *Oronsay*.

So Nursie was to come with us, after all, and Pop's prophecy was spot on.

Before we left, among all the bustle and panic of packing, there was a knock at the door. When I opened it, a middle-aged man, in the generally accepted version of a civil servant's rig out, handed me a card and introduced himself.

'Ministry of Defence. I'd like to have a word with you about your Bumblies.'

Thinking that here was a family man, whose children wanted an autographed picture of the Bumblies, I asked him to come in. He thanked me, but after I had produced the photograph, he didn't show any sign of leaving.

'That's not exactly what I've come about,' he said, cautiously.

'Well, how can I help you?' I replied, wondering what dinner dance or other function I was to be required for.

'Let us be frank, Mr Bentine. We at the Ministry, are deeply interested in the Bumblies.'

I expressed my delighted surprise.

'We are very intrigued as to how you do it,' he went on.

'Well, that's a trade secret, really, but I use a sort of remote control.'

'Exactly what I told my chief,' he exclaimed, triumphantly. 'You see, Mr Bentine, he would have it that your puppets were filmed, with single frame action, and I said they were under some sort of control.'

'Well, now that we've settled that, perhaps you'll excuse me – we've got a lot of packing to do.' I made for the door.

For a moment, almost a look of panic crossed his face.

'You're leaving the country?' he asked in alarm.

'Yes. We're off to Australia.'

'I see,' he looked relieved. 'Then may I ask you, point blank, if you are using some sort of shielding to cut out studio interference, with your radio control?'

I gazed at him blankly, and then the penny dropped. This misguided civil servant imagined that I had hit on some kind of remote control, which he could adapt for some other use.

'May I ask which department of the Ministry you work for?'

'Well, let us just say that we are interested in remote control systems,' he countered.

The light dawned brighter.

'You're in guided missiles!' I said, almost accusingly.

'You might call it that,' he wavered, uncomfortably.

So I explained to him, roughly, how the Bumblies worked and he got quite embarrassed, thanked me hurriedly, and left.

A glorious thought crossed my mind, as I closed the door and leaned, helpless with laughter, against it.

It was a picture of Bumblie Three, jammed into the nose cone of an intercontinental ballistic missile, with that idiot grin on his amiable rubber features, as he says: 'O.K. fellows – here we gooooooo!!'

I still remember that momentary look of panic crossing my visitor's face, when, for an instant, he thought I was defecting behind the Iron Curtain.

22. Waltzing Mashuga

The voyage out to Australia on the S.S. *Oronsay* was not without incident.

From the moment at Tilbury, when the giant ship's siren scared the living daylights out of Gus, who screamed in unison with it, to the almost tearful farewell from our homosexual steward at Fremantle, we found ourselves up against problems.

Fus, however, took it all in her stride and didn't seem too put out by this upheaval in her life. Nursie, too, sailed over it all with a calm detached interest while Clementina, being ballet-trained, had soon become a firm favourite with the stewards.

Gus stoutly refused to eat with the other children and Fusty, as always, stood by her brother. As I looked at their defiant four and three years of bewildered childhood, I wondered if it all hadn't been a terrible mistake and that we should never have set out on this long journey.

Beset by these doubts, though by now I really should have had more faith in my father's gift of prophecy, I changed into a bathing costume and dived into the small ship's pool to cool my fevered brow.

Beside the pool were two Australian women who were bedecked in long dresses with pearls and accessories of a frilly and delicate nature.

My diving leaves much to be desired and my all too solid body met the water, almost horizontally, with a painful smack. As I rose from the water, I realised that my entry into it had emptied a fair portion of it over the two daintily overdressed spectators seated close beside it.

In fact I had drenched them from their elaborate hair dos down to their ankle strapped shoes.

'Stupid clumsy Pommie bastard,' one yelled shrilly.

'Peruvian Pommie bastard madam, if you please,' I corrected

instinctively before apologising profusely for my whale-like plunge.

Going ashore at Port Said and Aden made the trip for Nursie who loves shopping anyway, but I was easy meat for the wily Egyptian and Arab merchants, who clustered round us in their bum boats and tried to sell us everything in sight with such blandishments as: 'A real bargain Mrs Windsor!' 'To you four pounds!'

To me: 'Hey Solomon! Don't miss this opportunity of a lifetime, guaranteed satisfaction camel saddle! To you, Abraham Lincoln, special price – five pound ten!'

We did, however, buy a camel skin suitcase, which weighed about half a ton, and carried the Bentine family possessions round the rest of the world before its cardboard frame eventually came apart.

We slowly boiled our way through the Red Sea. On a brief stop at Aden, we all piled into an antique taxi driven by a Somali of great persuasive charm, who took us out to see the oasis of Suliman. After a long and dusty drive, this turned out to be a strip of grass about the size of a cricket pitch.

However the journey was made worth while by one magnificent moment. Some Empire-building character, complete with a topee, who was playing golf on a course that looked like one gigantic sandtrap, raised his eyes off the ball long enough to gaze out into the empty infinity of desert and shout – 'Fore!'

Colombo, in Ceylon, also provided us with some joyous moments when a passing local gent, wearing only his dhoti and an expansive smile, remarked to me apropos of the steaming heat: 'Varm for de time of year!'

While Nursie took the babes back to the ship after a quick visit to the Colombo Zoo, Clementina and I went shopping. Here a wonderful game developed, sparked off by a friendly reporter from the *Ceylon Times*, who had asked me if I knew anyone in his country.

The only person who came from Ceylon, that I'd ever met, was an extraordinary man called Victor Danapala, who I had been introduced to some years before. Victor was something of an enigma and a man of mystery who, I remember, lived in a large ground floor flat in Balham furnished with all the riches of the East. As they say.

He was a forceful and very amusing companion and was determined, without knowing a thing about me, that I was to go and make films for him in India, but he never pursued the matter further.

I hadn't seen him for a couple of years and mentioned him casually to the young Ceylonese reporter. The effect was electric, as the photographer with him nearly dropped his camera and the journalist actually did drop his notebook.

We never found out why Victor's name had this puzzling effect on the people we met on that one day in Colombo, but we spent the rest of our few hours there trying out what I called the 'Danapala effect'.

This consisted of going into any shop, ranging from ones that sold saris to elegant jewellery stores, and casually mentioning Victor's full name as a friend. Immediately, either the price dropped fifty per cent or you were asked to leave.

We just caught the last boat back to the ship and shared it with some of the crew who were as drunk as lords. We never found out why Victor's name had that extraordinary effect.

One last long leg of the sea voyage brought us to Fremantle, the port that serves Perth and Western Australia. With our now 'ship-hardened' family, we stepped ashore to the start of our two years Down Under.

Fremantle was as nondescript, corrugated iron roofed and ugly as Perth was attractive, in its uniquely beautiful setting of the winding Swan River.

I was contracted to work for David N. Martin, who was a well-known if not exactly well-loved Australian accountant turned entrepreneur – or as the word came out when he said it 'Onturprinure' – suggesting some form of artificial fertilizer.

He had, in turn, subcontracted me for the Perth season, to two elderly expatriate British comedians, called Edgeley and Dawe, who were then knocking seventy and had become the lessee management of the theatre in Perth.

Meanwhile we settled into a four-bedroomed bungalow on the outskirts of the town and opened a show, topped by that fine entertainer Donald Peers, who had just flown out from Britain. Donald, as usual, did very well with his polished professionalism but I was a bit too revolutionary for Perth audiences.

My first gag, based on my wild hair and beard, was: 'Good evening – you probably think that I am wearing a false wig and a false beard – well! you're quite right. (Then taking them both off). This is what I really look like!' (Showing the audience that I looked exactly the same underneath.)

Normally this gag was a stonecold certainty to get a laugh, but

I knew I was in for trouble in Perth, when I did it on the opening night to nothing – not a titter! Only a clear nasal voice saying: 'Why does he wear a wig Ethel? He's got enough hair of his own!'

However, by dint of rejigging the material and slowing down a lot, I got the act over to the local public who, when you met them individually, turned out to be some of the most hospitable and good natured people in Australia.

I also met my mother's two brothers, Uncles Frank and Arthur, who had emigrated to Australia before the First World War.

Uncle Arthur was in hospital and Uncle Frank did the honours by taking me to see his brother and smuggling him a bottle of muscatel which Uncle Arthur, with a wink, slipped under the bedclothes.

Uncle Frank had been captured in Gallipoli and spent most of the 1914–18 war as a prisoner in Germany, nearly dying of starvation in the process.

Uncle Arthur, on the other hand, although he'd joined up at the same time, never left Australia and for some reason enjoyed about three times his brother's pension. To me they seemed to be older, smaller and Australian versions of Uncle Jim.

Our next date was Melbourne, right across the awe-inspiring Nullarbor plain of the great Australian desert. We went by train, or rather by four trains, because for some reason best known to the political geniuses responsible, the railway lines in individual parts of Australia were each of a different gauge. When you came to the end of the State line you had to get off and change on to another train.

On that incredible journey from Perth to Melbourne we had to do this three times. The first change was at Kalgoorlie, a ghost-like Western style shack town on the borders of the Nullarbor plain. The second was after crossing that unbelievably large and arid area of the earth, where the relief train had actually fallen off the lines and was sitting there ploughed into the sands with not one window broken. The third was at Port Pirie where we changed, yet again, into an elderly train equipped with bum-numbing wooden seats. This one took us on the short run into Adelaide where, utterly exhausted, we boarded the luxurious Pullman train to Melbourne.

This beautifully laid out city seemed to me to be much more British in climate than the rest of Australia, complete with cold winter winds and lashing rain, but in summer the surrounding

Dandenong Hills and the nearby beaches made it a very pleasant place to live.

We moved into what was described in the advertisement as: 'A genuine Tudor residence in Toorak.'

Here once again I met David N. Martin, whom I had first encountered at the Palladium, a year before. This bald-headed, steel-rimmed bespectacled accountant showman was already something of a legend among the artists whom he brought out from England, and the myths were hardly flattering – but, he treated me completely honestly and in no way made life unpleasant. In fact he was a fan of my humour, which I still believe he didn't really quite understand.

He didn't even have a go at me for my lack of success in Perth, but told me that he believed the act would go well in Melbourne. Which, thank heaven, it did – resoundingly so to excellent notices from the critics, who really did affect the business in Australia, especially if they gave you bad write-ups.

I had written some sketches into the show – principally my light-house keeper one, where the two aged keepers have been marooned for weeks and wait stoically for the relief to come.

The sketch starts off with them carrying a mermaid down from their bedroom and chucking her back into the sea. Then the head keeper says in a puzzled voice: 'There must be a way!'

This gives some idea of the high tone of intellectual humour set by the sketch, which is filled with sight gags, like the one where the barometer drops off the wall to the accompanying line: 'The glass has fallen.'

Every time the assistant keeper goes to look out of the port hole, he gets a bathload of water in the face, complete with fish. As these were cheaper to buy fresh rather than have made up as expensive props, I never knew what fruits of the sea I was going to get in the kisser – and one night a new prop man actually used frozen ones that nearly fractured my skull.

I played this sketch and another one, set in an airliner, where an elaborate meal is served during a bumpy flight. This was the sort of pure slapstick that tickled the Aussie funny bone of the day with lines like: 'Federal Airlines is proud of our motto – Wing your way with sweet F.A.!'

My partner, in these pieces of deathless music hall prose, was John Bluthal, a young Australian Jewish character actor of multi-accented talent. We both had a ball doing them.

Every night we would change the characters for the sketches and become Scottish, Irish, Welsh, Indian, American, Chinese and Jewish lighthouse keepers. In the aircraft cabin shambles, we played any other nationalities we might have missed out earlier. One night John played the whole sketch in Yiddish, but David N. Martin sent us round a note about that. It said simply: 'I'm not paying you to speak French.'

John told me some of the the stories about David N. and swore blind they were true.

Once, while auditioning an excellent American ventriloquist, David N. who, never booked an act without personally seeing it, said: 'Mr Canfield Smith – would you mind holding the dummy closer to the microphone, I can't hear what he's saying.'

On another occasion, one of the Tivoli theatres he owned in Brisbane was invaded by flying ants and he received a telegram stating: 'Show stopped by flying ants.'

He is supposed to have replied by cable: 'Book them for a further week.'

Whether or not these stories are apocryphal or not they do help to illustrate the man himself.

He had quite a flair for feeling what would go over with his audience, but didn't know very much about show business itself because he had come into it later in life than was usual.

He once asked my opinion on what he called a native Australian act, who turned out to be the fastest apple-wrapper in Tasmania.

David N. auditioned him, with the idea of including the lightning apple manipulator in a finale of 'Australiana'. This huge Tasmanian solemnly stood there, with a large box of apples on one side and a heaped pile of tissue paper on the other. The rehearsal pianist struck up *William Tell* and the Tasmanian disappeared in a frenzied whirl of activity and paper, during which David N. proudly announced to me: 'He wraps a gross of apples in under three minutes.'

I diplomatically suggested that the cost of the apples would become prohibitive, and this talented craftsman was reluctantly dropped from the finale.

John also told me of David N.'s publicity stunt with a British strong man act called, I believe, Wilfred Briton. I had seen this immensely broad and chunky little man at a music hall in Kingston, and had been amazed by his feats of strength. The final one consisted of his lying on the stage, with a huge wooden beam across his chest, on which about ten members of the audience stood nervously, while two girls on fixed bicycles at either end of the beam, pedalled furiously away and waved Union Jacks.

In Melbourne, when this stocky mini-Hercules arrived, David N. as a publicity stunt suggested that he should pull a double decker bus up Elizabeth Street, with his teeth. The strong man agreed to do it and set about making a special jaw harness.

He actually pulled a double decker bus up this incline, straining every muscle in his powerful frame and, incidentally, loosening most of his teeth in the process.

When he had finished he was utterly exhausted and couldn't understand why, until the driver said: 'I didn't trust yer, mate, on the hill – so I had me brakes on!'

The mind boggles.

In Melbourne we were joined by Andrew Briger – who had known Clementina since they were children and who had been one of the very few people who approved of our marriage. He had been a good friend when we needed him and, as he recently lost his mother, I had invited him out to Australia.

One of my favourite people, Andrew is of Russian descent and the son of a pioneer of Russian aviation who had, after the revolution, brought his family out of the country and eventually settled in England.

Andy was also Madame Legat's nephew and had known Clementina since she started learning to dance at his aunt's Ballet School.

To show what a land of opportunity Australia was in those days, Andrew landed in Melbourne with just the clothes he stood up in and a few pounds in his pocket. He became one of Australia's leading architects, a happily married and proud father of a fine family. Recently he was given the full red-carpet treatment on an invited tour of his native Russia, as a visiting alderman of Sydney. Not bad for nineteen years of hard work! In Britain, before he came out to us, he had just about made ends meet as a junior architect.

In Melbourne the show was headed by David Hughes, the young Welsh pop singer, who had far more than just good looks and a fine presence going for him. His voice was a really first class tenor. David, of course, I knew from Britain. When his fiancée, Anne, came out for a cathedral wedding in Melbourne, David asked me to give the bride away.

Anne, a truly beautiful girl, had brought some tranquillisers to help her through the ceremony, but I got a bad attack of wedding nerves and so she gave them to me. Together with a fortifying glass of pre-nuptial champagne this really tranquillised me – and the proxy-father-of-the-bride kept nodding off in the limousine on the way to the cathedral and twice fell asleep, standing up, during the service.

The best man, Gordon Humphries, an ex-Spitfire pilot and our chief dancer in the show, had to hold me up. Gordon, being one of those quiet, good humoured types who can cope with anything, carried it all off and me out, beautifully. Anne, who is a jolly lass, got the giggles.

Our next stop was Adelaide, that lovely city of broad streets and many churches in Southern Australia. On arrival, we were joined by a troupe of American dancers from Harlem, billed as the 'Ten Norma Miller Dancers'. They were led by Norma Miller, an arresting pencil-slim dusky torch-battery of nervous energy. To say that this animated group of groovy hoofers surprised sleepy Adelaide is putting it mildly.

The girls had contrasting dyed hair, which they spent hours straightening. The lads ranged from the king-sized 'Stoney' to the small dapper drummer, Michael Silva, who used to spend many patient mornings teaching me the finer points of his musical craft and who later became Sammy Davis Junior's anchor rhythm man.

Clementina and I were enchanted with them all and Norma, who was a real character delighted me with such spontaneous remarks as: 'Mike. It's so quiet out front you could hear a rat piss on cotton!'

And on another occasion when she was asked to do a free concert for charity: 'Shit man! I wouldn't even give a crippled crab a crutch!'

In her defence, I must explain that in the U.S., under the Equity rules, you get paid for charity shows.

The show went marvellously well in Adelaide and one critic, having heard I was half Peruvian, described me as: 'One of Britain's best loved coloured comedians.'

The Norma Miller Dancers were highly accident prone. Stoney was badly injured when he came into collision with the accidentally released Iron Curtain, which nearly severed his ankle. Then two of the other boys dropped out, with sprains and illness, reducing the act from ten-to-nine-to-eight and, finally, with yet more casualties, to six Norma Miller dancers out of the original ten.

In Norma's own words: 'Shit, man! We're a dancing act, not that goddam Nursery Rhyme!'

When we finished our season in Adelaide, the company went right across to Western Australia, where I had already played, leaving me to take my contracted thirteen-weeks-out in Adelaide, which we all loved. We rented a flat in a house on the sea shore at Glen Elg, and had a marvellous time exploring the beautiful coast of Southern Australia, with its great rolling downs and wattle covered hills.

Then off we all set for our final season in Sydney, where we settled in a house at Pymble, on the north shore of that breathtakingly beautiful harbour, in a suburb served by an electric railway which ran red trains, all of them the twins of the London Metropolitan Line.

Melbourne had been a stately and rather reserved city, but I found Sydney or, as the Aussies called it, 'The Big Smoke', a brawling, sprawling, growing-in-front-of-your-eyes complex of complete contrasts, from the new skyscrapers just starting to rear up on the skyline, to the antique open trams which the Sydney folk called 'toast racks'.

Melbourne also had trams, but they were modern and more-or-less silent ones, whereas the Sydney ones were smaller clanking old heaps. We all loved them, especially Fus and Gus, and even Nursie, who swung athletically on and off them like a dignified Olympic horizontal bar champion.

David N. Martin had now headlined the show with Mell Tormé, the velvet voiced American singer, who also played great drums and had one of the richest funds of Jewish show business stories I have ever enjoyed.

One lovely one he told me was about Clark Gable, who was looking for a new agent, but who was apparently highly suspicious of Jewish people. He finally picked an agent but, before signing with him, asked him directly: 'You're not Jewish are you?'

The agent replied quickly: 'Not necessarily!'

Also with us on the bill was Irene Ryan, the American comedy character comedienne who much later made such a smash hit as Grannie Clampett in the *Beverly Hillbillies* series.

She also was a friendly person and told me stories of her Hollywood film career, during which she had been cast repeatedly as a wisecracking maid, opposite the imperturbable English actor Arthur Treacher, who always played British butlers.

They acted these parts so often and so recognisably together that, while they were resting between pictures, they often got firm offers to enter domestic service.

Apart from show business parties, there was now a general acceptance for us on the Australian social scene, which had its own society columnists who wrote up the barbecues and beach parties, dances and formal 'deb' balls.

These ultra snobby articles referred to them as functions, and there were lists of guests with synthetically double-barrelled names, like the Fred-Smiths and the Bert-Joneses.

I must say I like the 'dinkum' side of Australia, rather than the so-called social scene, but then everywhere in the world, this bores me to tears. I dearly love a get-together and a good giggle with a few friends, but the other nonsense I never could cotton on to – maybe its the Inca in me!

At one party we went to, the hostess, along with a number of the distinguished guests, was smashed out of her head. As we left rather early in the proceedings, the swaying party-giver said to Clementina: 'Do come again dear, you've been no bloody trouble at all.'

Don't get the impression that this was typical. Sydney, like Melbourne, had a very real and lively interest in the arts and boasted a fine symphony orchestra. Ballet companies and operas, plays and playwrights were also emerging strongly from their much neglected background, as Australia began to realise, probably under the influence of the new Australians immigrating from Europe, that you didn't have to be raving queer to be a lover of the Arts. As an artist, however, you were still looked on with some suspicion by the average Sydneysider:

Here I met Leon Thau, my present television producer and a close friend, under slightly unusual circumstances. He was appearing in *The Duenna*, which Lionel Harris had come out from Britain to produce, at the Philip Street theatre. He was playing the part of an elderly drunken monk, in which he was totally believable and very funny.

I went round after the show, especially to congratulate this obviously old 'pro' on his performance. When I asked to see Mr Thau, a young, curly haired, Aussie appeared and said: 'Hi. My name's Thau. What can I do for you mate?'

I asked him to pass on my congratulations to his father, and to tell him how much I had enjoyed his performance.

'Jesus,' said Leon, 'My old man's not on the boards – you stupid bastard, that was me!'

Along with a lot of other excellent Australian actors, like Ray

Barrett, Leon made a good living out of radio, mainly from playing in the endless soap operas, that ranged from Fu-Manchu type thrillers to *The Blue Hills*, which was a sort of Australian version of *The Archers*.

I once went round with him to the studios where, in small soundproof cells, these radio dramas were churned out. In two hours Leon had nipped in to about four of these battery coops and played two 'heavies', both very sinister figures, one honest son of the soil, and an elderly Chinese herbalist. All without a single trace of the broad Aussie that he normally spoke with, off microphone.

Leon told me that the writers would often forget the continuity of their stories in the rush to turn them out, and that you could find yourself out of a job in the middle of a serial.

He cited one case where a diminutive Sydney actor, who was adult in age but specialised in playing children's roles, had indignantly protested to the producer because, in one radio session, he had left the microphone with the words: 'Right! Well I'll just have a look-see up in the attic,' – never to return to the story again.

As the small actor downed a large schooner of Sydney's best beer he said plaintively: 'That was years ago – I'm still bloody up there!'

I spent as much time as possible with my family, and we went on visits to that excellent Zoo, with its enchanting Koala bears, and played all over the beaches, from Sydney's main City one, at Bondi, which was disappointingly urbanised, to the smaller north shore ones like Woy-Woy and Curl-Curl. We even went right up the Hawkesbury River, where we had a marvellous few days on a cruiser hired from Bobbin Head.

That river is really beautiful, with its winding progress between high wooded hills and the sudden surprisingly English names of the little towns along its banks, like Datchet and Windsor, Maidenhead and Marlow.

We had now been almost thirteen months in Australia and my contract was coming to an end. David N. Martin wanted me to stay on and play New Zealand for a tour, but I wanted to get back home. It had all been marvellous experience and I had emerged much more as a writer and sketch performer, rather than just a music-hall act.

So Clementina and Nursie started to pack up the house and I went down to see David N., to arrange about shipping us back to Britain. Then, out of the blue, an Englishman called Eric

Pierce rang and offered me a year's work, writing and recording my own radio programme. Out of courtesy I went to see him and found a pleasant customer eager for my wares. But I was feeling the pull of home very strongly and didn't really want to do the show.

The more reluctant I was, the more keen this enthusiastic man was to have me do a series for him so, to make certain I would get out of it gracefully, I asked for what was then a helluva lot of money. That certainly shook him and I went back to help with the packing up.

To my astonishment he then rang up and said he had accepted the offer.

Any married man with a growing family, especially in show business, will understand why I could now hardly refuse and, after talking it over with Clementina and Nursie, I agreed to do it.

This virutally meant staying on in Australia for at least a full six months more. This we did, teaming up with John Bluthal and another young writer/actor of sound experience, called David Nettheim.

David was a sensitive actor, with a splendid narrative voice. He hadn't had much experience of comedy although he had a lot of credits for adapting books and plays into radio scripts and, therefore, was ideal to work with me in getting my ideas down into radio terms.

I called the show *Three's A Crowd*. Between us and a very skilled recording engineer called Stefan, we multi-recorded it, playing an enormous range of parts between us and pioneering a lot of new effects.

The series did very well and played round Australia long after I had left but, at that precise moment, the Goon Show started in Sydney and Melbourne and instantly became a cult show.

Naturally, we had to take second place to that one. But I was the first of the Goons to play Australia and make a break through with way-out humour, just as I had been the first one of us to play the U.S. and for that matter, the Palladium and the West End of London.

Pioneers, however, seldom get much material reward, in comparison with the ones that come after, and that has been my experience right throughout the many facets of show business.

The Sydney New-Australians fascinated me, with their extraordinary mixture of mittel-European and the odd Aussie slang. Their conversations in the Kings Cross area of the city sounding something like: 'Czin dobre bluey! How you goin'? Kak pashi vaya mate! Pani maya my bloody Holden car! Proschum panouf! My bloddy sheila, etc.'

With them they brought their culture and their food, and Sydney burst forth into a colourful bloom of foreign restaurants.

The Australian wines, in both their economic quantity and quality, appealed to the Europeans as different from their own vintages. They had a slightly eucalyptus flavour, due to the ubiquity of that tree and the subsequent fall of its aromatic leaves which, in turn, find their way into the rivers and finally, through rainfall, into the grapes.

The Australian wines are really very good – I just wish they would stop calling them claret or burgundy, which they are definitely not, and have the pride in naming them by their Australian origins – such as the fine Cawarra and Coonawarra red wines or the excellent South Australian whites.

Their flavour is very reminiscent of the South African wines, which also seem to carry the slight but distinctive tang of pine or eucalyptus.

Wine authorities will probably say I don't know what I am talking about, but I have been enjoying wines in many countries for many years and can probably tell a good wine from a fine wine as well as most people in the trade. As for bad wines, any fool can tell those by the terrible effect they have on the unsuspecting drinker.

Australia also had its own food specialties, starting obviously with kangaroo tail soup, through the magnificent oysters and lobsters to the delights of tea brewed in a billy. All delicious in their separate ways.

I found the real beauty of Australia in the sweeping magnificence of its great canvas of a landscape and the long swathes of sandy beaches of its enormous coast line. I am, unashamedly, an unreserved Australophile. It's a wonderful continent, with room for twenty times its population – at present huddled together in the peripheral coastal cities and in one tiny centre at Alice Springs.

At the end of our long stay on this hospitable continent we packed up our traps and, as they used to say in those pre-war travelogues: 'Said farewell to Sunny Australia, land of the sheep and kangaroo – and lean bronzed men and women!' Then we boarded the good ship *Tahitien*, a Messageries Maritimes vessel of the French Merchant Navy.

We were waved off from Sydney Quay by a large crowd and a near weeping Andrew Briger. The propellers frothed our ship out into that beautiful harbour till the long strings of balloons which stretched to the Quay broke – and with them our ties to the land which had generously supported us for two years.

23. It's free – and they give you fruit

The long voyage home, via Noumea, Espiritu Santo, Tahiti, the Panama Canal, Curacoa and Marseilles, took us over two weeks longer than the scheduled time. This was not exactly a hardship, though Clementina and I nearly missed the ship in Noumea, after a camera-film shopping expedition, and we had to, literally, jump from the quayside to the gangway, as the *Tahitien* pulled away. We just made it, over a gap of ten feet of rapidly widening water, while Nursie and the babes watched horror-struck on the deck above.

In Espiritu Santo, an island in the New Hebrides, we were berthed, for ten days, in the enormous natural harbour of the Segund channel, while our cargo/passenger ship took on copra.

Thanks to the kindness of a local planter, a Frenchman called Jo Burgess, who was straight out of James Michener's *Tales of the South Pacific*, we were able to explore the island. It was a paradise of jungle green, speckled with exotic flowers and plants, hiding the completely engulfed remains of a large American wartime bomber base.

Jo himself, a powerfully built, tough Marseillais, had, in fact, worked for G-2 Intelligence during the war, operating a hidden radio set, reporting back on the movements of Japanese ships.

Cutting my way through the dense undergrowth, my machete rebounded off metal. On clearing away the tangled vines, I was amazed to find I had uncovered a complete B-29 bomber. This huge four-engined monoplane, still loaded with all its machine guns and ammunition, was sagging down on a collapsed under carriage, as though it had crash landed and just been left there, in that last mad island-hopping scramble for Tokyo.

The Americans had also abandoned hundreds of jeeps and trucks by driving them off a cliff into the sea beneath. This part of the island was known as 'Million Dollar Point' and Jo, who

228

was also an experienced diver, used to go down to the piled up mass of automobiles and machinery to bring up gearboxes and other items that he needed.

He showed me a generator which he had salvaged, in perfect condition and still in its original grease-packing after over ten years on the bottom of the sea.

One wonderful day we picnicked with Jo and his beautiful wife Toinette, on one of the small islands in the lagoon. Together with Nursie, Clementina, Fus and Gus, in a piroque outrigger canoe, Toinette paddled while Jo and I swam alongside, looking down into the crystal clear warm water.

Seeing some large fish below us, I asked Jo what they were.

'Requins,' he replied with a slow smile. 'Sharks, Michael! But don't worry, there are too many fish for them to eat anyway, so they're not hungry for us!'

Having had four cases of shark deaths, in Sydney and Melbourne, while we were in Australia, I was not too happy, but Jo obviously knew what he was doing.

While the babes rushed about on Jo's little desert island, Clementina, Nursie and Toinette helped us collect oysters from the mangrove roots, which were sticking out of the water. Jo kept chickens on that island, so Fus and Gus had boiled eggs for their tea, and we sat entranced while he told us stories about Father André and his Mission.

Earlier I had met this small grizzle-haired elderly French priest and instantly felt a great affection for such a remarkable but simple man who, arriving on the island, as an 18-year-old ship's carpenter, had received the 'call' and returned to France to become a priest.

When he came back, he brought a ship's lifeboat load of coconuts with him, and planted the island's palms, which had developed over the years into the thriving copra trade.

Nuns and a Mother Superior had joined him and Father André had built them a small convent, a church and a Mission Hall, all with his own skilled carpenter's hands.

By the outbreak of the war, Espiritu Santo had a lively and happy Mission operating on the island, providing for the French and British planters and their families, as well as for the local Melanesian people.

Suddenly, one morning, their peaceful idyllic life was shatteringly changed and Father André woke to find five hundred ships dropping their anchors into that huge natural harbour.

Jo's stories of the small alert French priest's efforts to keep his very lovely nuns and the eager beaver Americans apart, had us fascinated. With the help of God, and a permanent armed guard of U.S. Marines, who also watched each other like hawks, Father André managed to preserve the status quo.

When I met him he was a sprightly 80 years old and had just wrecked the tenth jeep of the dozen the Americans had left him as a parting gift. Battered but unbowed, he was explaining to me the advantage of driving fast over the coral roads, once wide but now narrowed by the all-devouring jungle. His theory was that the faster you went over the potholes, the less you felt them, and he waved a heavily bandaged arm about to illustrate his point.

The Mother Superior, who was a gentle sweet-faced woman, with a steel core, had confiscated the two remaining jeeps and locked them up until Father André's wounds were fully healed, and she muttered to me: 'Father richly deserves Paradise – but not yet!'

A copra barge, unloading alongside the *Tahitien* caught fire and had to be cut adrift – finally drifting on to the shore and burning out in a red shimmer of heat.

We all loved that island and left it full of regret and a shipload of copra beetles. These little brutes got in everywhere, from your morning coffee to your goodnight kiss.

Life aboard the *Tahitien* continued its frenzied round, as we lazily dipped across the Pacific to Tahiti. A French family called Miot, with two sons and a daughter, were returning to France from consular duty in Australia, and we got along fine with them. Pierre, the youngest, was Fusty's age and he was as near to a changeling child, as I have ever seen, with a wickedly merry face and pointed ears. I think a pointed tail should have gone with the outfit of this junior French Monsieur Spock, but he was enchanting.

I'm sure our two families were about the only ones on the ship who kept to our own cabins, in the French nightly game of musical bunks.

At Tahiti the crew left the ship, like rats from the *Titanic*, and we had to make our own way ashore. The First Mate explained that many of the French crew members aboard had girl friends in Papeete, and that it was a case of first served first come.

A French film crew was at work on the island and it was the time of the great dance competition, between all the islands in the group – Morea, Bora-Bora and Tahiti.

Those dancers made a gorgeous picture, in their grass skirts and shell headdresses, with that lovely long black hair of the Polynesians. They wriggled their hips and rolled their slim brown bodies in a marvellously rhythmical way, which was utterly natural and, oddly enough, almost sexless.

My own idea of what constituted a pretty Polynesian girl was not shared by the average Tahitian, who only gets turned on when the ladies tip the scales at around sixteen stone. I will never forget my first look at a 'real' Tahitian beauty against the sunset, or rather as much of the sunset as showed behind that ample wobbling shape.

One day we found some giant tortoises, of the 200-year-plus age group, underneath the old tumbled-down Parliament buildings, and they graciously allowed Fus and Gus to ride on their huge shells. Throughout our time in Papeete, we explored the island by day and slept in our all-but-empty ship at night.

At the same time the Marquesas island racers – tall beautiful sailing ships from San Francisco, were berthed alongside the quay and their crews of blue water yachtsmen wandered about the town, with a girl on either arm.

We met an eight-year-old princess, of startling beauty, and her grandmother, the last of the old family line from King Pommeri. This lovely elderly lady had waist length hair, that she could sit on, and her adorable little grand-daughter lovingly combed and brushed it.

They were on a French-Government-sponsored trip back to France, where the princess was to go to school. Her grandmother told me about the old king and how he had died from drinking Benedictine in huge quantities – in fact, I had seen and wondered at the stone Benedictine bottle which tops his tomb outside Papeete.

Even as we glided out of the lagoon entrance and looked back at Tahiti, the island left a lasting impression of light, which must have been the inspiration of Gauguin and I felt that here was the last remnant of a dream.

That dream turned rapidly into a near nightmare, when both Fus and Gus, along with nearly the whole ship, went down with a vicious bug called 'La Grippe Tahitienne'. We had no official ship's doctor and the worst of the epidemic didn't hit us until after we had cleared the Panama Canal.

That long, steamy, fever-loaded cutting through the isthmus must have brewed it up to vicious proportions. After we were through the Panama Canal, I managed to get sufficient penicillin at Guadaloupe – ransacking the few pharmacies in the unbelievably filthy town of Point-le-Pitre, and persuading a young doctor, who was travelling with us, to give the babes the injections. Frankly, I could have done it rather better myself, but memories of my Folkestone A.R.P. exercises had long since quenched my thirst for medical practice.

A fortnight or so behind schedule, we finally crossed the grey Atlantic. Passing by the Rock of Gibraltar, that we had last seen over two years before, we slid up the coast of Spain and through the heaving Gulf of Lyons, to drop anchor at long last in Marseilles, where we arrived broke to the wide.

For three days we wandered around the port, while I waited for a money draft to arrive at a Marseilles bank. Although we ate at the small family hotel where we stayed, we hadn't a centime to spend outside.

Gus saw a French couple about to enjoy a large plate of snails and his expression of amazement and disgust quite put them off their lunch. Just as though, for the first time in their lives, they actually realised what they were going to eat!

At last the money arrived – I paid our bills and we boarded the overnight train to Paris, where, in our sleeper berths, we had the most enormous and delicious midnight feast of long French loaves, cheese, fruit and wine.

As we slowly rolled out of the Marseilles Terminal, wordlessly munching great mouthfuls of our impromptu picnic, Clementina sighed happily.

'What an experience,' she said. 'I only hope Fus and Gus remember it.'

'Still,' added Nursie, 'it will be nice to be home.'

And it was.

24. The House of Commons and other junk

When we arrived back in Richmond we found the house in one hell of a mess. I suppose the agency which had let it for us, during our two year period away, had checked up on it, throughout this time but we literally had to scrub the walls down to get off the grease and muck.

Meanwhile I set about getting some work with the new television companies that had sprung into being as part of the commercial setup.

I had been away for over two years at the other end of the world and the theatrical agents' reactions were enlightening. They ranged from:

'I remember the face but the name eludes me,' through:

'There's two other blokes already doing your act,' to:

'I thought you were dead.'

But the coming of commercial television had put paid to the old B.B.C. monopoly of the air waves, and there was plenty of work going if you wanted to risk your reputation in front of the television cameras.

Lew Grade saw me do a couple of successful T.V. appearances and invited me along to discuss some writing for A.T.V. but these only lasted for a couple of shows. Still, they were a temporary help in keeping the ever-present wolf from the door. That creature is so familiar to me I often wonder if it doesn't wear a collar round its neck with my name and address on it.

The Goons, meanwhile, had taken off on their separate ways while collectively holding their well-deserved number one place as the top radio show.

Goon humour is extremely difficult to transfer to the television and film screens because it relies heavily on the imagination of the listeners and was really designed for radio, where it very successfully evokes wonderfully ridiculous images in the imaginative mind.

Everyone had a different idea of what each Goon character looked like and to each listener they were different.

Their television equivalents in the *Telegoon* programme, of necessity had to pin these images down to a distinct puppet and these couldn't possibly match the individual images already created in the Goon fans' minds.

So Peter and Spike had teamed up and made some very funny shows using a parallel sort of anarchic approach. These series of shows were called *Fred* and *Son of Fred* and were produced and directed by a young American unknown called Dick Lester. The Press loved them.

Peter had another six shows to do from his original contract and as Dick had left Rediffusion, the producing company, and Spike was busy on a film, Peter asked me to write and appear in them.

As David Nettheim had just arrived in England I roped him in and set about getting the short series down on paper. I called it *Yes, Its the Cathode Ray Tube Show*. Each show dropped one word of the title so that the last one was called *Yes*.

The opinion of the critics was definitely 'No' on the first one but as we progressed the write-ups got more approving and although we weren't a substitute for the 'Fred' shows the Press decided that we had merit.

Peter was, by now, developing into an international comedy star and his performances were splendid. I wrote him two pieces which he particularly enjoyed.

The first was a prop sketch with Peter as an old gardener with an original way of getting rid of snails, by destroying their confidence in their virility. This he accomplished by using a dummy sexy female snail which spurned their ardent advances.

The dummy female consisted of a snail shell on Peter's finger with a sexy pair of tiny lips and false eyelashes painted on his finger tip.

As the male snail, sobbing its heart out at its failure to win over the aloof dummy female hurled itself in despair over the edge of the table, Peter sadly remarked: 'He's committed insecticide!'

Another sketch had Peter as the oldest film extra in the world. He was magnificent in this one as the sad-eyed old performer with his long film career as a crowd artist behind him – with lines like: 'Then I struck a bad patch – I was out of work for twelve years.'

Later on he says: 'I made a number of films with Mister de Mille. I was in the motion picture where, in a battle scene I was struck over the head with a battle axe. Then in another of Mister de Mille's pictures I was struck behind the knee with a broadsword – and I remember yet another one of Mister de Mille's pictures, a biblical one, where I was picked up and thrown into a sacrificial fire. Yes, indeed Mister de Mille often had me in his motion pictures. I can't think why – I never did him any harm.'

Slowly I was developing a comedy style of writing which was born of observation and a sort of strange logic.

Through this series with Peter I met Dick Lester and we found a mutual enthusiasm in comedy, so much so that Dick came in with me on a radio series I had been writing and recording called *Round the Bend*.

This show was produced by my old and valued friend Pat Dixon, that tall academic of immense integrity and lively humour who had been responsible, originally, for the Goon Show and had battled relentlessly for it through its rather rocky stages at the start.

My respect for Pat was total and he helped me in my writing enormously. Together we tried out all sorts of radio gimmicks, like multi-recording and varying tape speeds to achieve character voice effects and the show really took off into the realms of comedy fantasy yet somehow retained a documentary style.

One sketch I remember was set at the Farnborough Air Show and featured the voice of the flight commander of the R.A.F. aerobatic team which was relayed over the public address system, in the style of air displays, so that the enthralled crowd could hear his instructions to his aerobatic formation.

Through a fault in the landline he gets connected to a public call box where a young man is trying to phone up his girl friend.

At his orders: 'Close up there – you're lagging behind', the phone box takes off and joints the jet fighters in loops and rolls in the circling formation above.

This is a pure radio picture sequence that you would never get away with on a screen in the visual media but it does work marvellously in pure sound.

We had a ball making that strange effective series – but in the middle of it all Pat was tragically stricken with cancer. We heard about Pat's condition from Pat Hillyard, the head of

B.B.C. light entertainment, who was as upset as we were.

Pat Dixon insisted we continued the series with a different producer, Charles Chilton, another old friend of mine, who had the same genuine relationship with Pat that we all enjoyed.

I will never forget going to see Pat at St George's Hospital for the last time. He summoned up sufficient strength to keep the whole tone of the visit as cheerful as possible – his entire concern being to tell me how much he had enjoyed working with me over the years and how I must keep on with the original line of comedy that I was developing.

He emphasised how important he felt genuine laughter to be, especially the kind that rose from the imagination which had been stimulated by original comedy thoughts, and he really was very concerned that I should finish the series for him. A comedy series seems such a small and insignificant thing against the life of a man, but he looked at it, in terms of the enjoyment it could bring to others.

I was deeply moved, that, in his tragic terminal condition, he should be so selfless. But this was typical of Pat.

Mercifully Pat's passing was as quick and painless as possible and, at his funeral, his coffin was draped with the Confederate flag and Kenny Baker played the *Last Post* as a blues.

That may sound ridiculously trite, but it combined Pat's two great enjoyments in life – his amazing knowledge of the American Civil War and his love of New Orleans Jazz.

Pat's death left a gap in our lives and we all felt the best way not to break faith with him was to write and perform a good series.

From experimental radio, Dick and I decided to try another television series. While we were getting it off the ground, Clementina produced our second son, Richard, or, as he for some inexplicable reason became known – Peski.

Unlike Fus and Gus, whose arrivals had been at panic stations, Peski sailed into the world serenely and without fuss or bother.

I was present at his birth and helped Clementina through an easy delivery. I can only recommend the experience of seeing your own children born as something every couple should try. The miracle of birth is still the greatest antidote for people who are ever more constantly being subjected to the fear of death.

Peski's arrival seemed to spark off enormous energy in me and I carried Dick along with it into the new television series.

We called it *After Hours* and made it live from Birmingham.

The studio was minute and Dick had to crowd his cameras back to back while we worked round them.

We minimally rehearsed at Chelsea Town Hall and the cast included such old friends and stalwarts as Clive Dunn, David Lodge and Benny Lee plus the then much neglected Dick Emery, a fine performer in his own right, but almost unrecognised except as a comedy support.

Right from the off, it felt right and we enjoyed that marvellous feeling of comradeship that you only get when you know you are part of something worth while.

Bruce Lacey, the genuinely eccentric artist who really does ride a penny farthing bicycle for enjoyment, made my props for me and helped me build my first invisible flea circus.

At Bruce's semi-detached house up by Alexandra Palace, you knew you were in for a slightly different experience when you pressed the door bell and six knife handles sprang out of the front door, surrounding you in outline like a knife thrower's partner.

Inside the house, which was loaded with props and junk, the hall was dominated by a full sized stuffed camel which you had to crawl under to get in.

The first little flea circus that he built consisted of my original version just as I had seen it in my mind – a few jumping effects that shot the sand into the air as though the flea was indeed jumping, then the little ladder whose rungs bent as the invisible flea climbed up to the springboard, which bent under its apparent weight, followed by a springy release and a spout of water from a tea cup underneath, giving an amazingly real effect that the intrepid flea had dived into the cup.

Bruce must have had nearly every type of gadget and prop jammed into his overflowing semi. I remember once ringing him up to ask if he had such a thing as a 16-foot crocodile.

'Not a 16-foot one,' he replied, thoughtfully. 'Will an 18-foot one do?'

Our final rehearsals for the show we held over Sunday lunch in the dining car of the train up to Birmingham, to the delight of the stewards and the occasional spilling of the soup.

These rehearsals weren't exhibitionism, but were dictated by necessity. When, one Sunday, the train was stopped because of track works on a steep bend for twenty minutes, we continued going over the sketches at an angle of about twenty degrees, which we compensated for by leaning the other way.

We would arrive at the studio at around three o'clock. Three run-throughs later we were on the air with most of the props still being painted, and pieces of scenery still being brought into position. But it worked and, through some magic bred of the sheer excitement and keenness, the shows were a great success with the small late night audience that watched them.

I dreamed up all sorts of ideas, from interviewing the top half of a head-to-head balancing act, who was suspended upside down in mid-air because his partner had quit show business, to a luncheon party given by the mayor of a flooded town, with the entire dinner table under water, but the formal lunch still continuing without interruption, while live ducks snapped up the floating bread.

We had guests as well, including one famous cricketer and an American character actor, both of whom went out after their run-throughs and got fairly well oiled, so that most of the questions and answers had to come from me, virtually shouting my elated guests down when their language went over the top.

This was pure basic television at its strange impossible best, where the sense of immediacy comes straight through the screen.

Some critics, who saw a relay to London, demanded that the series should be shown down south, but internal politics between the contracting companies put the block on this and brought me into violent opposition to Val Parnell.

He had always treated me with great fairness, and I was taken completely by surprise at his adamant refusal to bring the show down South and his open criticism of it as: 'Rubbish!'

Lew was upset by the publicity this incident received and called me in to see him.

'Why have you no respect for Val?' he asked me directly.

'But I have. He's a great showman and understands theatre and music hall backwards – but he is wrong this time! Anyway, when you say respect – I have respect for many people, not necessarily in show business.'

'Like who?' asked Lew defiantly.

'Well, for example, Albert Einstein! I've got unlimited respect for Einstein!'

Grudgingly Lew admitted I had a point there, but came back with: 'Who else? – go on Mike! Who else do you respect?'

'Schweitzer,' I answered immediately. 'I have enormous respect for Schweitzer!'

Lew looked puzzled. Then he said slowly: 'I don't understand you at all Mike – Albert Einstein, yes! – but why Freddie Schweitzer?!'

The only Schweitzer that Lew knew personally was Jack Hylton's brilliantly funny comedy trombonist.

I didn't say so then, but I have great respect for Lew as well, for rather different reasons.

After Hours, never did get to London, apart from one late night showing, but happily continued to gain momentum and a devoted viewing public up north.

It also gave Dick and me a great deal more experience in visual comedy on the small screen. Dick, after one disastrous attempt to translate the show on to stage, left us to become a highly successful and now internationally known film director – but I think he learned a lot of his comedy from us.

The stage show was called *Don't Shoot We're English*, and it was a disaster. Dick hadn't had sufficient stage experience at that time to put the show on in a fail-safe way and we had troubles right from the start.

The cast couldn't be faulted, with Dick Emery, Clive Dunn and Ray Barrett knocking their brains out to make it work. But it was a complicated show to stage with a lot of props and it needed a hard-headed and very stage-wise director to get it set right for the theatre.

On the opening night in Newcastle, of its twenty scenes, nineteen went wrong and one was cut for time. One of the spotlight operators didn't show up and Dick had to go up into the lime box and operate that as well.

Incredibly the audience in Newcastle adored it and we finished the show to cheers.

As compère I had spent the evening ad-libbing my way out of the various disasters and this had somehow given an odd impromptu quality to the show which the audience thought was part of it.

Among other things, the designer had lumbered us with a strange structural background that looked like, in Dick Emery's words: 'A Zeppelin in a steep dive.'

The whole show was a shambles, yet somehow it still worked – but Dick Lester left, after a row with the backers, and we still hadn't got it right by the time we opened, at the Cambridge Theatre in London.

The critics, who only wanted the current fashionable satire, tore it to shreds – not that I blame them – but Sir Bernard Miles defended it in print saying it was pure comedy, in the real sense, and very funny. We couldn't survive those damning notices however and, as there was no more money in the kitty, we folded in two weeks.

The critics seemed vindicated, but over the next five years I performed every one of those sketches on television to rousing critical acclaim. It really is a strange business!

The strain of this sad affair had been a bit much, because I had to carry the whole responsibility and keep cheerful on stage as well, and, right in the middle of filming a small part with Ernie Kovacs, a couple of weeks after we closed, I went down with pneumonia.

Kovacs, in whom I found a really genuinely kindred spirit, spotted I was in for trouble.

'Mike,' he said, 'I don't want to seem an alarmist but you are steaming in the arc lights.'

So I was, and that night I developed a dangerously high fever and was well into the throes of pleurisy.

My doctor, Ralph, rushed me off to hospital and pumped antibiotics into me, but the virus wouldn't respond. Finally they gave me a new antibiotic, that was reputed to be a wonder drug. It nearly killed me, as massive clots formed in both legs and I developed a pulmonary embolism.

Within hours the pain was nearly insupportable and the specialist shot me full of pethedine. That eased the situation and I drifted off into a rosy, euphoric dream world. By the end of a fortnight my right leg was developing gangrene and I was receiving five needles of pethedine a day.

It says a lot for having a violent rejection mechanism, which my battered body was equipped with, that I wasn't by then well on the way to becoming an addict.

Pop was confined to bed with acute bronchitis but Florrie, his housekeeper, who, like Pop, was an able healer, came to see me. Florrie had come to look after Pop when he returned from Peru. This she had done magnificently while her gift of healing, which she had discovered in her childhood, had helped my father through the latter stages of his life.

This large, jolly, Northumbrian lady had the ability to charge you up like a battery with positive energy. Many times I have benefited from her remarkable gifts – arriving to see Florrie in a depleted state, only to leave within a few hours thoroughly replenished with her abundant healing powers that she dispenses so cheerfully.

It is an extraordinary gift and one which Pop also had in abundance, but in his later years his health had inhibited him from using it as freely as he would have wished. Whether you call it spirit healing, magnetic healing or faith healing, I have no doubt myself that Florrie can transfer her own vital energy into a person desperately in need of it.

'We're not going to lose wor leg,' she said, in broad Northumberland, as she placed her hands on my left thigh. I felt a wave of warmth pulse through the whole leg, just as though I had been placed under a strong infra red lamp.

After she left I fell into a deep sleep and, when I woke, that awful black colour had been replaced by a red and blue bruising, and I knew I'd still be a whole man.

The specialist, a wise elderly man of great skill and experience, examined the leg and clucked solemnly: 'I was going to amputate that but – well! God works in mysterious ways.'

I told him about Florrie and he didn't seem in the least bit surprised.

'Wouldn't be the first time I've seen something similar,' he grinned over his half-moon glasses. 'Incidentally, you're coming off the drugs as from now.' He went on, 'By the way, it won't be pleasant, but you'll find it an interesting experience, no doubt!'

You could call it that. I don't think I would want to live through the following 48 hours again for anything. But I can say, with honesty, I now know what some withdrawal symptoms are like.

By the end of the first day the pain, which was still acute, drove me to begging for the pain-killing drugs and by the second night I was screaming for them.

Then Sister came in and told me that Clementina had given birth to a daughter.

That did it – the pain seemed to recede into the distance and once again I fell into that amazing deep sleep that totally heals.

All through the whole rotten business, Clementina, who was again heavily pregnant, had never missed coming to see me twice a day and Sam and Marty had come whenever they were allowed to. Bennie Lee never missed a chance either and many show business friends turned up or were turned away. One or two people I thought I knew well didn't even phone and that surprised me a bit, but then people can be very sensitive about serious illness and so choose to ignore it.

My longing to see the new baby and be home again did more for me than any wonder drugs. And Marty's chicken soup, which she brought every visit, worked wonders – as she described that delicious beverage: 'Jewish penicillin.'

16   241

Suki, our new daughter, who in the general panic of her birth had nearly been born on the loo, was a great joy, as she still is, and once home I made rapid progress. With the help of our old friend Peter Goodall, who showed endless patience, I got back to walking again.

My experience at this time was that the most unlikely people took the greatest trouble to help. Pete, who was a childhood friend of Clementina's and had become a good friend of mine, had always struck me as a very unsentimental and down to earth person, always ready to give a hand at fixing things around the house.

The effort he put into helping me to walk again was touching and surprising as together we staggered around, with me shuffling behind a kitchen chair which I pushed in front of me while Peter alternatively encouraged, kidded and bullied me into walking, until I could, at last, stumble about unaided on that rocky left limb.

That took three months but my leg stood up to it and still supports me today, though it does protest from time to time.

It has always been my experience that a long down-period invariably is followed by a rapid upswing and as soon as I could move about without falling over I was straight into a new B.B.C. television series.

It was once again 'live' and we called it *It's a Square World*. Johnnie Law joined me in writing it and from the off it felt right. I used much the same cast, but this time, Joe Gibbons, Frank Thornton and Leon Thau swelled the ranks of our team.

Barry Lupino produced and directed it and its fast-paced demands on my writing and performing were the best therapy I could have. *It's a Square World* was a kill or cure panacea and I loved every minute of it.

It rapidly caught on, in much the same way as the Goon Show had, all those years before, attracting a small but dedicated audience and slowly building up into a big figure show.

The special effects department of the B.B.C. now turned up in my life, led by an effervescent streak of a man, called Jack Kine.

This wild enthusiast helped me to develop my invisible flea idea into a wonderful series of animated models, translating my concepts and quick sketches into a detailed miniature world of jumping sand and tiny explosions, that captured young and old alike.

The first model he made me was a wonderful imaginary new

242

town on the Irish border, next to an old world village, from which invisible leprechauns made an I.R.A. style raid across the border, and robbed the new bank, finishing up with a tiny miniature shoot out with the invisible police – fire engines and a complete mini-battle. We thought the whole effect was marvellously funny then, but, God! how terrifyingly prophetic it was.

Jack and his gloriously extrovert team of pyrotechnicians and model makers would often work far into the night, in cramped conditions and with budgets that they had to bend, to fit in with the demands I made on them.

I devised, worked out and designed the animated models while the effects team actually built the 'Flea Olympic Games', where invisible fleas jumped hurdles and pole vaulted, a Norman castle which was attacked by unseen peasants with miniature battering rams and model cannons till it sank into its own moat and a masterly reconstruction of the Invasion of Ancient Britain by Julius Caesar, complete with little Roman galleys that rowed themselves through the water and an opposing invisible army with catapults, chariots and flights of tiny arrows. Truly they were all masterpieces of the model maker's art.

I worked along with them, when I could, and spent many happy and constructive hours on those delightful models.

Bob Godfrey and Keith Larner of Biographic Films made us special cartoons from my ideas, literally at cost, and these we combined with live action – breaking through all kinds of conventional television barriers to gain our effects,

One especially successful item was a 'steel lecture', where I delivered a straight talk on steel production, against a background of a graph of figures and machinery, that eventually became bored with my lecture and started to have a party, which degenerated into a fight and a locomotive and car chase.

The fact that the shows were still live, at this time, made the challenge all the greater and I only took the minimum time off to sleep, while the rest of my life seemed to be filled with the thousand and one problems that this pioneering type of comedy demanded.

The team of comedians who worked with me caught the spirit of it all and knocked themselves out, sometimes literally, to get the effects I wanted. Somehow the effect of all this hard work and enthusiasm sprang out from the small screen and we were immediately rebooked for another series.

This time we started recording shows, on the comparatively

new videotape machines, which for some reason were hired from and located at the commercial studios in Birmingham. This entailed feeding the show, by landline, to the Midlands and being in constant telephone communication with the recording end.

In the middle of one show, a gang of G.P.O. engineers dug up the landline and cut off the recording in mid tape.

Dick Emery, quite rightly, emerged from the series as a star – this splendid character comedian at last got his break.

Dick had been born in the traditional prop basket and had spent all his life in the business but somehow, despite his fine talents as a character actor he had been overlooked as a major star.

I had always considered him to be a splendid performer and in *Square World* I created a varied assortment of character situations which fitted him like a glove.

He was very funny indeed and took full advantage of the opportunities I gave him and, in return, brought to the show a wonderful collection of vague elderly colonels, bloody minded old Cockneys and unctuous parsons all of whom helped Dick to eventually blossom out into his own highly successful series.

John Law, who now worked full time with me, pointed out that I was concentrating more on the other comedians than in building up my own comedy image, but, strangely enough, it is so much easier to see another comedian's performance than to stand objectively back and write for yourself. Anyway there wasn't time for thoughts like that and the show had to come first.

In the writing I essentially came up with the concepts and the visual ideas and Johnnie and I worked them up together – for John was above all an adroit and skilled wordsmith. It worked splendidly and an enormous flow of material passed into the show's format.

Whereas, in music hall and cabaret, years of repetition put a final professional polish on every word, move and gesture in an act – television series demand just as high a standard of performance and a constant change of concept, while allowing practically no time at all for these necessities.

It's think or sink as far as the writer goes and for the writer-performer there is no second chance – if it goes wrong he has only himself to blame.

On top of this you must add the many other things that can screw you up in the studio – props that don't work, under-rehearsed cameramen or, sometimes even, inept direction. It really is a wonder that television comedy works at all.

Often, the fascinating little models went wrong, or rather didn't quite pan out as we intended, but I could always turn this to advantage by shouting at the invisible performers until the effect happened.

Sometimes we would have to go back and repeat a sketch, which I always thought would have killed it stone dead with the studio audience. But I found that, by being completely honest with them, and telling them what had gone wrong, they stayed with us and even seemed to enjoy it more the second time round. Perhaps some of them hadn't quite got the point the first time.

I'm sure one reason this odd pattern emerged was that all the sketches were largely visual in concept and, therefore, no matter how many times you played them, they always came out slightly different.

We became more adventurous and, at the end of the series, with the small amount of pre-filming facilities I had been allotted, I decided to sink the television centre with all hands.

That great man, Jack Hawkins, consented to be the fall guy. As he had just finished the highly successful *The Cruel Sea*, and was well known for playing rugged sea captain roles, I interviewed him on a rocking set – that is to say a rostrum which is mounted on a rocking device.

As the straight interview progressed, Jack – who played it all marvellously poker-faced – slowly slid from end to end of the set, while behind us a back projection screen showed scenes from *The Cruel Sea* and finally settled into one long shot of the great heaving waves of the Atlantic.

We then cut to a submarine interior and a U-boat commander looking through his periscope. In the centre of his torpedo sight lines, he sees the B.B.C. Television Centre.

'Ach, so,' he chortles, 'Fire vun!'

A torpedo streaks out and, immediately, its track appears on the projection screen behind us, coming straight at our rocking interview set.

Two large explosions occur behind our chairs and, immediately panic breaks out in the studio, with various make-up girls and technicians hurriedly putting on lifebelts, etc.

Jack immediately takes command of the situation.

'Don't worry Mike,' he says. 'I'm very experienced at this sort of thing. This is your captain speaking! Now hear this – Abandon Television Centre! Woman's Hour and Children's Hour first!'

From then on, we cut in and out of various parts of the building, with well-known artists sliding down life lines, jumping out of windows and every other gimmick I could persuade my long suffering friends to undertake.

It was a good idea, but Jack made it magnificent and that is how I always like to remember him.

The newspapers began to acknowledge our existence as a show, with something different about it, and we slowly took off on the four-year journey that lay before us.

I say us and we, because *Square World* was truly a team show. Everyone in it, or associated with it, really became a part of its whole structure, because one weak link would have destroyed it.

By now, John Street was producing and directing it and, having been basically a film man, he got us more camera time for pre-filming.

John was a bland reassuring person whose height and distinguished features combined with his white hair to give him an impressive presence. I called him 'The Bishop' and he certainly helped us to get facilities that up to then I had only hoped for. The main bulk of these facilities were those connected with filming and these helped enormously to change the character of the show.

John Street was also a great model train enthusiast and so when I suggested using the lovely scale model Romney, Hythe and Dymchurch railway to reconstruct the Great Train Robbery, he set about arranging it with a will.

The idea was that an idiot gang led by the superlatively good character actor Derek Guyler, who had taken Dick Emery's place when he left, had planned to rob the seaside mail train, not realising it was in fact a miniature railway.

Duly they set about the actual robbery, racing alongside the track in an old Austin Seven saloon – leaping aboard and fighting over the carriage tops. Why we weren't killed I shall never know, because even using the speed-up techniques of the under-cranked camera we still had to belt along at thirty miles an hour.

John's secretary, Hetty, an enthusiastic and super-efficient Jewish lady, who clucked over us all for some three years like a mother hen, stood by with sticking plaster and iodine and Clive Dunn actually played throughout the whole train sequence with a broken arm.

Hetty's long and anxious tending of our various minor wounds and many soakings, which she countered with large bath towels and hot tea laced with brandy, earned her the title of 'Golda Nightingale'.

We had opened up quite another dimension and I was allowed to pioneer some of the techniques that are now part of every show of this kind.

Each final episode in the current series, I devoted to an attack of some sort on the Television Centre itself. We surrounded it with cowboys and Indians, like a beleaguered wagon train; escaped from it, by tunnelling beneath it and passing the displaced earth up through various well-known programmes; destroyed it with a giant man-eating orchid, that had escaped from a *Gardening Club* programme and, finally, sent it into orbit with a huge rocket, set off inadvertently, by Doctor Who, with a *Sky At Night* commentary by my good friend Patrick Moore.

In fact we laid the foundations for some of the flattering copies that exist today and do sometimes bear a startling resemblance to quite a few of my shows, especially in the end spots.

All the mayhem delighted the viewers, but the B.B.C. itself didn't quite appreciate the service we were rendering it.

After one weekend filming the attack of the cowboys and Indians, I came in early on the Monday morning, to find a small group of the administrative staff huddled round the entrance.

'He burnt it!' one said angrily. 'That damned Bentine has burnt it.'

He pointed to a brick, which had undeniably been scorched by one of the smoke-pots that figured prominently in the Indian massacre.

The next day, John and I got a memo which I still treasure. After the normal preamble of restricted distribution etc. its message read: 'Under no circumstances will you allow the Television Centre to be used for purposes of entertainment.'

Other repercussions followed. Tom Sloan, with whom I had a constant running battle – which, I'm glad to say, terminated amicably before his tragically early death – called me in after our tunnelling-out episode. Johnnie Law, who by now was the Editor of the comedy script department, had the unenviable job of being in the middle.

'Michael,' said Tom, fuming. 'That break-out from the Centre – you had the B.B.C. looking like the Gestapo!'

'Oh, I don't know,' I replied. 'The armbands distinctly said B.B.C.'

I knew what Tom meant though – it was during the escape sequence from the Television Centre where Dick Emery, as the

B.B.C. security chief in a German style S.S. uniform, straps himself into a tiny Messerschmitt car which, with its perspex bubble top looked rather like an M.E. 109, then chased me in my long combs. round the V.I.P. car park firing machine-guns like a fighter plane till I shot him down with a machine-gun mounted on a typical German prison camp guard tower.

The Messerschmitt burst into flames and Dick baled out with his backside on fire. As you can imagine it was a highly intellectual piece of comedy.

Despite our differences, Tom backed the show to the hilt, and it was through him that we were entered for the International Television Show at Montreux.

This Montreux International Television Festival was a sort of combination of 'Who's Best' and a global mini-golf match.

When the contestants weren't becoming square-eyed from watching their various rival entrants' efforts, everyone played a quick round of mini-golf on the small course which adjoined the Baroque-style hotel where the Festival was held, on the shores of Lake Geneva.

I remember partnering Johnnie Law on behalf of Scotland, Britain and Peru against the formidable opposition of Germany and Japan, and actually beating the ex-Axis partnership by two holes.

The *Square World* which was shown to an almost empty viewing room at the start was soon being enthusiastically watched by contestants who came hurrying in from the bars, attracted by the delighted yells of laughter which greeted the show.

It finished to an incredible climax of thunderous applause and Tom Sloan, his face radiant, actually hugged me and shouted 'We've won! We've won!'

I couldn't believe it but it certainly looked that way and I suppose we might well have won the Golden Rose itself, but for an odd coincidence which perfectly illustrates my banana skin thesis.

To our amazement we won the Grand Prix de la Presse and, I believe, had I not had a cut-in of Kruschev, singing *Black Eyes,* thumping the desk with his shoe, we would have won the Golden Rose as well, but fate and the banana skin decreed that we would have a Russian judge on the Montreux jury.

I don't blame him, because, after all, he could hardly pass that fateful 'edit', but echoing the words of the splendid Sammy Davis Jnr, when he saw the show and heard the story: 'Mike, you was robbed!'

Sammy, who was over in Britain for a Palladium stint, had seen my Montreux effort on its British transmission and loved every minute of it. He had then rung me up to congratulate me. As I only knew him through mutual friends I was very touched by this spontaneous gesture. He had then consented to come on one of my shows, which he did as part of a Northern club audition scene I had specially written.

Sammy came on after a dog act which had gone wrong beautifully and intentionally and started singing *What Kind of Fool Am I?* The delighted and surprised studio audience gave him a terrific ovation as the club manager stopped him and said: 'Thank you, we'll let you know!' Then, turning to me, the manager continued 'Another bloody Sammy Davis impression!'

That prize and exposure at Montreux really caused a revolution in international television comedy, and many subsequent entries, even from us, bore the unmistakable stamp of the *Square World*.

Anyway, it all added to the fun and quite a lot of that stemmed from the extraordinary things that happened while we were filming the end-spots of the shows.

For one of these I conceived the idea of Chinese junk sinking the Houses of Parliament with cannon fire. The idea came to me when I saw a Chinese junk, moored up river, above Molesey lock, on the Thames. Previously, during another episode we had been filming near Limehouse, I had been talking to a delightful Chinese doctor, who was bewailing the disappearance of London's China Town.

'Great shame!' he protested. 'The London County Council just pulled it all down without really consulting the local Chinese people.'

The two incidents fermented in my brain and I came up with the suggestion at my next writing session with Johnnie.

He loved it and, in his dry Scots way, commented: 'That'll show the bloody Sassenachs that we Scots mean business.'

John delighted in projecting a bloodthirsty stage-Scots anti-Establishment attitude, though he was the mildest and most international of men.

My invaluable aide-de-camp, our studio floor manager, who had been a yeoman in the Navy and thrice torpedoed, gleefully set about procuring the junk for us and getting permission, from the Port of London Authority, to film in Westminster Reach.

I left these matters to him after I failed to get the necessary clearance for a Moby Dick episode I wanted to film up the Thames, using a huge rubber whale.

When the Thames Conservancy asked me how long the vessel was, that I wished to navigate in their reaches, I replied truthfully: 'Twenty-eight foot, overall.'

'Beam?' asked the official, noting down these particulars.

'Seven feet.'

'Draught?' he went on.

'Two foot six inches.'

'Method of propulsion?'

'Outboard motor.'

'Any sanitary appliances?'

'Not necessary, as we will only be aboard a couple of hours,' I explained, cautiously.

'How would you describe the vessel – a motor cruiser?' he inquired.

'Not really!'

'A motor yacht?' he pressed on.

'Definitely not!'

'I see. A launch then?'

'I'm afraid not,' I said slowly.

'How would you describe it then?' he said finally.

I took a deep breath.

'It's Moby Dick – the great white whale.'

'Good morning, Mr Bentine,' he said pointedly.

So now, my splendid ex-yeoman friend did all the negotiating.

A few weeks later, we found ourselves aboard the Chinese junk, with Clive dressed as Doctor Fu Manchu, and the rest of the team done up as Chinese warriors. It was a mild Spring morning and, as yet, there were few people about.

The cannons, marvellously made by the resourceful Jack, were loaded with pyrotechnics and plastic cannon balls. The war junk made a brave sight as it slowly drew alongside the Mother of Parliaments.

The bombardment commenced and, soon, polystyrene cannon balls were bouncing off that famous building.

For two hours, without disturbance of any kind, we filmed and fired away, while the business of London and Parliament continued unabated.

I suppose if you were a Londoner, crossing Westminster Bridge, and you saw a Chinese junk, bombarding the Houses of Parliament with cannon balls, you wouldn't turn to some passing stranger and say: 'Look! There's a Chinese junk, bombarding the Houses of Parliament with cannon balls.'

Just in case, after all, there wasn't a Chinese junk, bombarding the Houses of Parliament with cannon balls.

Nevertheless, it was a full two hours before a police launch slowly appeared, from underneath the arches of Westminster Bridge, and a quiet voice addressed us, through a loud hailer: 'Ahoy there!' it said. 'Do any of you gentlemen speak English?'

I don't know any other country in the world where that could happen.

25. A flea in my circus

In the middle of this exciting year, when things seemed to be going really well at last, Pop died.

Florrie rang me to tell me the news.

'He just went out like switching off a light,' she said gently. I went off by myself and sat down to try and adjust to the ending of my father's earth life and found myself surrounded by a wonderfully secure feeling.

I had no doubt Pop was with me at that moment, and I decided to go ahead and record the next show as scheduled.

The last week of Pop's life had been filled with incident. He was always rather upset that I had gone on the boards, even though he himself had been a keen and accomplished amateur actor. And, in some ways, he regretted my not continuing on the scientific course that he had set me.

But in this last week he had seen an edition of *This is Your Life*, and thoroughly enjoyed it – because even though I had always sworn I'd never get caught on that show, Eamonn and Clementina had so planned it.

The excuse given to allay my suspicions was so logical that I didn't question it.

John Street had told me that he wanted to make a trailer, that is to say a preview, of our next show, at the B.B.C. Television Theatre at Shepherd's Bush.

This, of course, was standard operating procedure and I had suggested interviewing typical members of the British public, who lived in the Shepherd's Bush area, about their reactions to *Square World*.

The gag was to be that all of them were either Indian, Chinese, Japanese, or Arabs – in fact anything but typical Britons.

John and I had been filming all day down at the seaside and I was bone-tired when we arrived outside the television theatre,

252

which had lights and cameras already set up, as well as my team done up as Arabs, etc.

As this seemed to be what we intended to do I didn't think it out of the ordinary when, led by Frank Thornton, they rushed forward and picked me up. I just thought it was all part of the gag, which in the case of trailers we often ad-libbed.

Even in the presence of an audience inside the theatre didn't wise me up to what was really happening, because we often used other shows' studio audiences, to get a reaction for a trailer.

Only when I came face to face with a grinning Eamonn Andrews, whom I had known for years, did the penny finally drop.

All I could say was: 'You rotten bog-Irish bastard!'

To which the dacent boy replied: 'You bloody mad Peruvian!'

Neither of these immortal quotations appeared on the programme, I'm sorry to say.

Eamonn quickly added: 'We've brought your friends from all over the world for this one Mike!'

So what the hell can you do?

The B.B.C. had treated me royally over this programme, bringing Andrew Briger from Australia, as well as many friends, including my beloved tutor, Bill Hope Jones, and many others.

It was really a very wonderful experience though I told Clementina I never fully trusted her afterwards – as she'd been far too successful in hiding it all from me for about six weeks beforehand.

M'Tutor summed it up for me when he said: 'I haven't had so much fun since the headmaster's braces burst!'

Pop, however was too ill to take part in it and watched it, delightedly, from his bed at home.

When I went to see him, for the last time, he told me that in the past week he had realised clearly and happily that my real work lay in his old business which would give me the contacts to carry out my other work.

Florrie told me that, during the past few days, Pop had been in light trances for hours on end, awakening from them to tell her in minute detail the places he'd been and the people he'd seen and talked to.

While we were talking he did precisely the same thing, and I sat beside him holding his hand until he came out of it, some considerable time later.

Sure enough he happily chatted about Ma and Uncle Jim and his brother, my Uncle Ricardo – describing them clearly and recalling exactly the conversations he had just had with them.

These were mainly predictive and, incidentally, in my case they all came exactly true.

At no time did my father give the impression of waffling or rambling in his mind. Up to his passing that razor sharp brain of his remained as clear as ever.

One story in the 'Life' programme which had amused him a lot is worth telling.

Kelly, my West Indian pilot friend of our swanning trips round Germany, had long returned to his island home.

We had corresponded over the years, for we had been full of plans for charter cruises and shark fishing parties. In the course of time, however, our relationship had become one of Christmas cards and then finally silence. We were both so busy with our individual lives that the experiences we had shared were just a happy memory.

When we were moving house, Clementina decided she couldn't have me under her feet at that time. So I went off on a short trip by banana boat to the West Indies, writing a new series on the way.

This ship was one of a fleet owned by Fyffes, the banana importers, and called at each of the West Indian islands in turn.

On arrival at Barbados, memories of Kelly Kelsick came flooding back. Going ashore, I went along to the offices of the local newspaper and asked them if they could give me Kelly's address, or if they had any word of him.

'Very sad,' said the editor, in that lovely, soft, singsong accent of the island. 'He shot himself you know.'

I was staggered. It was about the last thing on earth I would have expected Kelly to do.

'Why?' I gasped in horror.

'Incurable disease,' the editor shook his head sadly. 'Yes, your friend was Chief of Police hereabouts, and when the disease came he shot himself. 'He's buried out at the military cemetery. Perhaps you'd like to see the grave?'

Naturally I wanted to pay my last respects to my good friend's remains, but somehow I just couldn't believe it all. The whole thing was so utterly unlike Kelly.

The editor got a taxi for me and with an elderly driver we belted out to the cemetery. On the way I explained my sad mission.

'A good man,' murmured the driver. 'Many people loved that man.'

When we arrived at the overgrown walls of the grey and depressing military cemetery, we found it to be a mass of trees and bushes, and here we met the gardener and asked to be shown the grave.

'Outside!' he said. 'Man, they don't bury suicides inside the cemetery. Only outside, man, for the poor bastards who kill themselves.'

I was furious! Here was my friend, who had left his beautiful islands to fight for freedom in the cold grey European skies, dumped outside this military resting place like some pariah dog.

Perhaps it was the heat of the sun and a couple of consoling rum punches the driver and I had consumed on the way that caused my next decision.

'Show me,' I grated out. 'And if they haven't marked his grave – I will.'

The gardener walked over to a plain stone without even a head marker.

'That's it man,' he muttered. 'Unconsecrated ground too.'

'Right!' I cried. 'Back to town and we'll get a stone right away.'

Several angry rums later we had found a stonemason who was willing to cut the lettering then and there. By this time I had been joined by several sympathetic people, who had heard the story from the driver. The driver, by now, was embroidering my sentimental gesture into a saga of brotherly love. The sympathisers had brought more rum.

I hadn't realised the power of that delicious rum punch and stood there weeping at my own saintly behaviour in honouring my dead friend's remains.

The stonemason, who, by now, had also joined us in a few drinks had just about got to the 'In Lovi – ' part of the rather flowery inscription I had dreamed up, when the editor arrived with a photograph.

He foresaw a fine story for his paper in this spontaneous sentimental gesture and as he handed me the picture he said: 'I thought you'd like to have this last photograph taken of your dear friend.'

I looked at it through a rummy haze and then it dawned on me.

I'd never laid eyes on the man in the picture before.

I gulped and then asked the editor in a strangled voice: 'How many people are there with my friend's surname?'

'Hundreds,' he replied. 'Why?'

I had to explain. The West Indians, with their great sense of humour, got the message. I staggered all the way back to the ship followed by a triumphal procession of hysterical people, gleefully passing the story on from person to person.

Dear old Kelly himself was there on the programme to confirm the story, as an extra bonus.

Pop loved it all and chuckled over it when I visited him.

His passing was peaceful and I knew the best way I could show him that I had profited by his teaching and affection and that I really believed in survival, was to carry on doing the shows. Much later I did the same thing for my eldest son Gus – but in neither case had it anything to do with that phoney show biz saying: 'The show must go on.'

The Montreux Show, which I had virtually made up of sketches that I had written before I worked with Johnnie Law, had brought us the Press prize, which consisted of a handsome silver pot, instead of the more usual silver rose.

This the B.B.C. put away somewhere inconspicuous, as it didn't, in someone's opinion, match up to the neat array of gold and silver roses that they so proudly displayed.

I showed the videoscope of this prize winning edition to Jack Parr, the American comedian, who was over in England doing a show with my old mate Jonathan Winters.

He insisted that I allow him to show a piece of it in the States and chose several extracts from it, including the one of the bowler-hatted and umbrella-carrying guard of honour, marching over Westminster Bridge to raise the Union Jack in front of the House of Commons, saluting it by firing their umbrellas.

Jack Parr's whole team loved it, and he promptly invited me to do a special shot with him back in the States, as soon as I was free to do so.

Tom had been telling me that the B.B.C. couldn't continue to fulfil its contract with me on the same terms. John Law and I were definitely under the impression that the series was finished, unless we could cut down the facilities and the number of shows contracted for.

This, virtually, meant the end of the *Square World* so, when I went over to the States to do the Jack Parr Show, I felt free to discuss further work in America, should it be offered.

As I explained earlier we were greeted by the same immigration officer and passed into the States without further formalities. That is to say, until I went to collect my flea Olympic Games from the Customs Hall.

Jack Kine, whom I brought over for the show, with the B.B.C.'s blessing and the use of his leave, was guarding the packing case that contained it.

'They won't let it in Mike,' he said, looking worried.

'What's in the box?' demanded the Custom's official tersely.

'Theatrical props for the Jack Parr Show.'

'Specifically! What is in the box?' went on the Customs man.

'The Olympic Games!' I said shortly.

'The Olympic Games!' he repeated slowly, then turned to his friend.

'George,' he said, 'we've got some kind of a nut here.'

'No, honestly,' I explained. 'It's a sort of trick effect – the Olympic Games – with fleas.'

'With fleas,' he echoed. 'The Health Department ain't gonna like that!'

'No! Not real fleas – invisible ones,' I continued desperately.

'Judas Priest,' he looked goggle-eyed at me. 'Now the man says dere invisible.'

'Why don't we open the box and show him?' interjected Jack with quiet reason, and so we did.

By this time quite a gathering was crowded round the mysterious box and, when I went into the routine and Jack made the sand jump and the effects work, we got cries of wonder and a round of applause, the Customs department's being the loudest of all.

Everything on that trip seemed to work wonderfully well.

On the way in from Kennedy Airport we had the first awkward taxi cab driver I had ever met in New York. This one was determined to be offensively rude.

'By your accent you're British,' he started aggressively.

I agreed.

'From Great Britain, huh! Tell me – what's so great about it?' he went on in a sneering tone.

'What language are you speaking?' I asked gently.

'English,' he replied.

'That's what's great about it!' I said and we finished the journey in silence.

I normally never use my professional techniques with anyone outside the business, because the tongue is a sharp weapon and the trained tongue can cut deeply, but in this case I think he deserved a put-down.

On the Parr Show I had another trick effect that caused a mild sensation. I gave a short talk on how to put ships in bottles, finishing up, with one bottle empty, and one filled with a little model oil tanker. I explained that this model had been made by a retired British Admiral and the empty bottle had been sent to me by a German sailor.

As soon as I put the empty one down on the table, opposite the other one, a tiny submarine rose inside it and torpedoed the oil tanker, which sank out of sight through the bottom of its bottle.

The results from the show were extraordinary, and I immediately flew out to do another successful one in Hollywood.

When we landed at Los Angeles Airport I was as excited as a schoolboy to see, at last, the movie capital of the film world of my childhood. Like all things you ardently look forward to, the reality never quite comes up to the anticipated image.

In Hollywood's case I had the feeling that the buildings that lined the great boulevards would, like film sets, have no backs to them.

Hollywood seemed all front. Some bright city father of this enormously strung out suburb of Los Angeles had thought up the idea of putting the names of screen stars on the paving blocks along Hollywood Boulevard.

The named paving stones started, recognisably enough, with Gary Cooper and Gloria Swanson. But this street is so long that the names tailed off into the not so famous ones like Rod La Rocque and Lupe Velez, to struggle on till they offered you Milton Sills and Baby LeRoy.

It became quite a guessing game and I was fascinated by it all, noting, *en passant*, that some dog had expressed itself on Ronald Reagan and someone had thrown up over George Murphy.

*　　*　　*

I had an introduction to Carl Reiner, who was then producer and head writer of the Dick Van Dyke Show, which, for sheer polish, and timing, I have yet to see bettered.

Carl had run my Montreux film for that talented and friendly cast and, when I sat in at their read through, they readily accepted me as one of them.

Carl, who proved to be a marvellously outgoing and generous person, took us to the Bistro restaurant which had originally been Mike Romanoff's famous meeting place for the Hollywood mighty.

Clementina was all agog to see the stars in their natural setting. While Carl went off to get us a table she asked a small, slim, elderly, bald-headed man sitting at the bar if he knew any of her screen idols.

'Well,' he replied slowly, 'a few of the faces do come in here from time to time. Stick around!'

Clementina then asked him why he was wearing an empty lipstick refill box on one of his fingers. He told her he had hurt his finger in a car door and that the little box protected it perfectly. By this time Carl had come back and as he ushered us to our table my beloved wife said: 'Well! I don't see any stars yet, but that nice little man said that they come in later.'

'For your information, honey,' drawled Carl, enjoying every word, 'that nice little man is Frank Sinatra.'

The show I did for Television was at the El Capitan Theatre, just off Hollywood Boulevard and, thank heavens, went very well.

Compèred by the slightly vague but charming Gig Young, the show was called *The Hollywood Palace Show*, and the old El Capitan Theatre had been redecorated and renamed to house it.

Gig Young seemed to be at a slight loss in memorising words, probably because he was in the middle of becoming a father, and had cue boards with his words on them, dotted around the place.

The first one, believe it or not, read: 'Good evening – my name is Gig Young.'

For my bit, I had got the studio prop department to make me some bits and pieces, among which I put an instant masterpiece gag.

A wall flat was brought on with three elaborate, empty, picture frames on it. The spaces inside the frames were, apparently, unpainted canvases and I explained that I was going to demonstrate a new British invention, 'Instant Spray on Masterpieces.'

I then produced two aerosols, one marked *The Laughing Cavalier* and the other, *Mona Lisa.*

The effect worked beautifully. As I sprayed the mist from the aerosols, the Laughing Cavalier appeared in full colour in the frame, and I followed this by producing the Mona Lisa in the second frame, by spraying it with the other can.

Then I sprayed the third empty frame with both cans at the same time – producing the Mona Lisa with the moustache and beard of the Laughing Cavalier.

Garry Moore, a talented veteran comedian with his own TV show in New York, had seen my performance in *The Hollywood*

Palace Show and promptly booked me to fly straight back East and do one with him.

We packed up and left the next night, seen off by our new found Hollywood friends, and were met at Kennedy Airport by Hans Holzer, my old friend, who by now was well established as the number one parapsychologist in New York.

This constant flying between the two coasts gave me the odd feeling that America only consisted of New York in the East and Los Angeles in the West, with three thousand miles of cloud in between.

While I rehearsed a sketch for the *Garry Moore Show*, I took time off to visit with Jonathan Winters, one of my all time favourite people who, some years before, I had literally bumped into outside Green Park Underground station in London.

He had been doing a British television show and, for years, mutual friends had tried to get us together. We finally met entirely by chance and immediately set out, then and there, on an instant ad lib routine, in front of the entrances to the Underground. We were completely unaware of the hurrying crowds, as we switched accents and non-existent languages in a glorious release of pent up comedy energies.

Johnny is an ex-Marine who has a natural born talent for creating voices and sound effects, and his routines are great – one typical one being a reconstruction, with wonderfully acute comedy observation, of a Marine attack on a beachhead. How such an unpromising subject becomes so funny is the secret of Johnny's immense gift for comedy characterisation.

The sketches I had chosen for the Garry Moore Show were a short one – based on how to get rid of worms in your window box by using a specially trained hunting tortoise – and a NATO sketch, where an international team of military experts get loused up by their interpreter, played by me, as they try to plan a battle with model tanks on a large sand tray.

The interpreter fouls things up when, accidentally, the German General's tank gets smashed by the British General's swagger cane.

The situation gets out of hand when he translates the German General's swear words, and develops into a free-for-all, when he tries to convey, in Turkish, the literal meaning of the American General's Texan drawl: 'Tell that no good son of Bedouin to take his cotton pickin', chicken pluckin' hands off my tank!'

The end of the sketch finds them degenerating into a mini-scale shoot-out with the tiny guns which, obviously, is going to escalate into the Third World War.

The sketch was a total success, brilliantly directed by a thoughtful and painstaking ex-B.24 bomber pilot, called Mickey Ross who got more laughs out of that one sketch than I had believed possible in a whole show. We became then, and have remained ever since, good friends.

The upshot of it was that the producers of the show, then and there, offered me a twenty-six part series – at, to me, an enormous fee. To say that I was taken aback by this fabulous offer is to put it mildly, but the 'banana skin' decreed otherwise.

Unfortunately for this deal, Tom Sloan had just arrived from England and heard about it. Surprisingly, in view of our previous conversations, he demanded that I come back to complete my B.B.C. contracts.

I was absolutely nonplussed, because I had agreed to do the American shows, and I felt such an idiot when they were told by the B.B.C. representative that I was already under option.

I could hardly drop John Law into the inevitable squabble that would arise if I invoked him as a witness to Tom's earlier attitude, which we had both understood to mean that the B.B.C. would not take up the option.

Tom was adamant about using the option and so I returned, with a great show business opportunity missed completely.

However, I am a great believer in Fate and, who knows whether I was really ready to handle such a demanding series, anyway. That may sound like sour grapes, but it is a genuine belief that things happen for the best.

Back home we did one more series for the B.B.C. and then I packed it in, but even the last series I made for them was worth doing. This was the one where I sent the Television Centre into orbit. Somehow it seemed an appropriate way to finish.

There was one hangover from the *Square World*, which Johnnie Law told me about.

Some weeks after I left, a Jaguar car pulled into the driveway which runs up to the Television Centre at Wood Lane, and some men, wearing stocking masks and carrying pick-axe handles, leaped out.

The security men, on duty, smiled tolerantly.

'Hello Mr Bentine. Back again?' he remarked, tipping his cap nonchalantly.

The men ignored him and dashed into the cashier's office, laying about them with the axe handles, and rushing out with several thousands of pounds, in cash, in a bag.

As they jumped into the car and drove off, Johnnie swore blind, that the security man called after them: 'When is it on?'

If the story is true, and no one has ever denied it, the poor security man can be excused, when one considers the number of times he had seen me and my team do similar sorts of stunts, involving the Television Centre. Anyway, he probably saved himself a nasty crack on the head.

26. The Woolwich Alps

When I finally left the B.B.C., to go back to commercial television I took most of my performing team with me, but naturally, I couldn't include Jack Kine and that unique group of special effects wizards.

A.T.V. hadn't got anything like the enormous resources of the B.B.C., but, with the keenness of the talented people they had got, we managed to do another series of 13 shows.

One of these featured a 'pirate' bus company's double-decker being engaged in fiery broadsides, from cannon mounted on its open upper deck, with a town Corporation bus done up as a Nelsonian ship of the line.

The buses were crewed by my faithful and smoke-blackened gang of comedians, dressed appropriately as salty pirates or smart matelots. They were driven by members of the companies that had been persuaded to let us use their transport. If anything, they entered even more into the spirit of this nonsense than did the slightly apprehensive professionals.

Leon conducted the pirate bus, dressed as Long John Silver, complete with a wooden leg and a parrot on his shoulder.

We had immense fun filming this battle down at Southsea, which is known for its quiet retiring respectability. During a lull in the noisy festivities, the pirate bus, complete with figurehead and false poop deck, pulled into a 'Request' stop for the crew to have a quick smoke.

Immediately, an old lady, who had been waiting at the stop, attempted to board the bus.

Leon gently explained to her that we were filming for television and that this was supposed to be a 'pirate' bus.

'Oh,' said the lovely little lady, 'when is the next one due?'

Another time, we were doing a gag with a Victorian post box,

263

made by our long-suffering props department. We unloaded the post box for a moment, to get at some other things we needed, and put it down on the pavement.

At once, an elderly man came up and posted two letters into it.

It is, I am sure, the natural reticence and native politeness of the British, that leads them to this detached attitude to the unusual. The finest example of British sang-froid, discounting the Chinese junk episode, was when we were filming a sequence about a Russian expedition which had come to Britain to climb the highest point in Woolwich, which happened to be the Corporation rubbish dump.

The idea for this had come to me when I passed a building, near Twickenham, that had a sign on it – *Isleworth Explorers' Club*. It set my mind thinking about what these intrepid explorers would, normally, explore. Surely not *Isleworth*!

I shifted my imagination to Woolwich, which has always exercised a fascination for me, and where I had already filmed the 'Sinking of the Woolwich Ferry', giving it a dramatic treatment worthy of the *Titanic*.

In this case I visualised a Woolwich Explorers' Club, setting out to climb some remote mountain in Siberia. In return, a Russian team of climbers would be invited back, to climb the highest peak in Woolwich.

Before we spent an uncomfortable and odoriferous day climbing the actual dump, during the course of which we were supposed to be nearly wiped out by a sudden rubbish slide, we had some opening sequence shots to take of the Russian climbers arriving in London. They were to disembark from the old *Discovery* which is moored alongside the Embankment.

No one showed the slightest curiosity or interest as the four of us, heavily equipped with oxygen masks, full climbing gear and skis, roped ourselves together and proceeded from the ship's gangplank, along the Embankment pavement, to the zebra crossing.

At this moment, a policeman, without any hesitation, held up the traffic so that we could ski across in safety. We disappeared down the nearest Underground station, totally unremarked by the busy London passers-by.

Although a lot of good material went into *All Square*, as we called the programme, and it did get high figures from the viewers, we just couldn't compete with the standards of production that we had set ourselves with those four years at the B.B.C.

I had written the series with another old friend – John Ennis. Johnnie Law, as a B.B.C. contract writer, couldn't switch channels, and it certainly wasn't the material's fault, nor the performances, from such stalwarts as Derek Guyler and the regular team.

Looking back at my many misakes I see that I left the B.B.C. at a critical time in what is laughingly referred to as my career. I hadn't calculated on the difference made by splitting the programme in half with a commercial break and didn't then realise how you have to woo your viewers back to the programme after the advertisements.

John Ennis and I met when he came to write a short article about me and stayed to collaborate on a mad series of features for his Sunday paper. These were based on the sort of thing John had written seriously about for years – like the great Bombay explosion or the night the Tay Bridge collapsed. I just set up a parallel series of ideas of the same sort such as *The Day the Food Dump Blew Up*, or *Flying Saucers! Are They Powered by Cold Tea?*

I only hope the readers had as much fun as we did writing them. Clementina fed us regularly, between snorts of joy, as one or the other of us would think up some idiotic gem of schoolboy wit.

But then, writing comedy should be like that. I quote from notable comedy experts like Hal Roach, who later told me of the long gag-fests of Keaton and his team, and the glorious days of Laurel and Hardy, and, when I met another great maker of funny films, Harold Lloyd, he also confirmed this for me.

Like Harry Secombe, I've always felt a bit guilty that my living should give me such pleasure. We seem to live in an age where the self-appointed voices of our conscience constantly hammer our guilt home to us, in all the media. If you don't believe that, read any of today's newspapers, or switch on practically any edition of television or radio news, all of which seem to spread doom and gloom around the room.

Thank God for the funny men like my old friends Morecambe and Wise, Tommy Cooper and the Goons, Jonathan Winters and Carl Reiner, etc., etc., etc. – and especially for that timeless phenomenon, the great silent era of movie comedy, that still can rock each new generation in turn.

John Ennis and I eventually wrote three books together, with varying degrees of success, starting with *Fifty Years on the Streets.* This was a saga of Fleet Street, in which the first printer's error is in the title, which is supposed to read *Fifty Years in the Street.*

This book turns up on the shelves of many comedians and comedy writers. It featured the intricate and exciting story of a great Fleet Street reporter, Herbert Beck-Jones, who had never quite made the big time till he joined the staff of the mighty *Sunday Morning Treat,* which every true blue Britisher had after Sunday morning breakfast.

Herbert's various jobs ranged from Foreign Correspondent with *Exchange and Mart,* to the Crime Reporter of *Our Feathered Friends,* while some of his crusading journalism was contributed to the pages of *Farmers Weekly* and the *Matrimonial Gazette.*

Herbert never quite got things in perspective, but continued throughout his life to write articles like *Our Friend the Kaiser* and his 1929 Editorial, *You Can Count on Wall Street.*

The other books were *The Book of Square Games* and one on *Square Holidays.* To our surprise, these three excursions into a written version of my square world of comedy, did well.

A rather weird occurrence, or coincidence, happened when we were making *All Square.* The end-spot that I had chosen to do was a Go-West-Young-Man idea, based on a newspaper article, which was about there being too many people living in South-Eastern England. To get the Go-West idea over on the screen, we packed our team into mini-mokes, a sort of tiny jeep, and put covered wagon-type tops over them. Led by an A.A. Scout, with a feather in his crash helmet and a ten-gallon hat brim round it, this mini waggon train set off for Wales and the West, where they were attacked by the wild Welsh miners, who lived in tepees with coal-pit winding gear on top. They were led by their redoubtable chief, played by Harry Secombe, wearing a huge Indian style headdress, with leeks in it instead of feathers.

It had all worked out very well indeed, and I was editing the programme with the producer, when someone came in and mentioned that there had been a disaster, in Wales.

I went cold, and asked him what had happened.

'A slurry tip has collapsed on to a school and killed a lot of children,' was the grim reply.

Then I realised that, in the commentary I had made a couple of weeks before, I'd talked about the 'great black hills of Aberfan' as our cameras panned over a huge slurry tip.

I rang Lew and we changed the programmes round immediately. I then remembered another odd thing; that we had nearly failed to do that particular end spot on the show when, for the first time in my experience, the film laboratories mislaid the film print and I had to keep the studio audience amused for a whole hour before it turned up.

I don't say that there was anything necessarily paranormal in this experience, because it had been of no use in warning anybody of the coming disaster. I merely state the circumstances, as an example of the odd things that occur in my life.

I was very upset when somebody leaked the story of our film to the *Psychic News* which, without consulting me, made a great play of the whole thing, as though I had had a premonition of this terrible tragedy.

In spite of all the difficulties in making the series we got good figures on the ratings and, after we had finished making *All Square* a B.B.C. spokesman came out with an interesting statement to the papers. As I read it in the *Daily Telegraph*, it said that the B.B.C. had claimed the two top comedy programmes of the year, according to their ratings. One was *Till Death Us Do Part*, which was Number One, and the other was *All Square*.

They didn't even know I'd left.

27. Me and Atahualpa

Quite suddenly one day I felt the strongest urge to go to Peru. Clementina knows the signs when I am certain of something, and immediately started packing.

I sent a cable and it crossed a letter which was on the way to us. Cousin Peter, always a great favourite with me, had died from a heart attack. The family was plunged into deep mourning but, the following day, a cable returned from them saying they would love to see us. This, I felt, must be the reason behind the impulse that made me decide to go in the first place.

Our journey there was typical of the sort of thing Clementina has come to expect in our life together.

The P.R.O. of B.O.A.C. insisted that we receive first-class treatment, but that I must only pay tourist rates. I said that it was very kind of them, but I was quite willing to either pay first-class fares and go that way or pay tourist fares and go economy.

No! insisted B.O.A.C. First class for economy fares – which was apparently, something that they didn't normally do.

When we turned up at London Airport and boarded the plane we were seated in the tourist section.

I explained the situation to the steward, who told the pilot, who radioed the tower, who asked the P.R.O., who confirmed the arrangement, rather like the sequence of the House-that-Jack-Built.

Duly we were seated in the first-class section – that is until we reached New York. Here a relief crew took over and the new steward promptly and rather disdainfully showed us back to the tourist section.

When he was rude to Clementina that lit my fuse and I let him have it.

Once again the insane House-that-Jack-Built routine started but luckily, on board, was a charming man who ran the South

American end of B.O.A.C. and he fixed things for me.

Once again we were ushered back into first-class seats and apologies were followed by some rather sickeningly solicitous service. I would have been much happier back in the economy section but Clementina's Scots blood was roused and she wanted the 'works or nothing'.

We arrived in Lima, at Jorge Charez Airport, at 0240. For some extraordinary reason the magnificent revolutionary quadruple jet VC 10s flew in at this ungodly hour and left at dawn, as though they were ashamed of being seen.

Fourteen members of my family had nobly turned up to meet us and surged forward, forming up in a line, like a Peruvian football team, so that I could pass along them, giving them all our, *Abrazo Criollo*, a sort of hug, kiss and pat on the back, all in one.

This we solemnly did. The last one on the line I hugged close to me turned out to be the Customs Officer. Being Peruvian, he returned the embrace and we all moved off in a great gaggle, with everyone talking at once.

Antonio was waiting for us at the Country Club, where he had booked us a suite and filled it with a riot of flowers. Normally a very formal man, he gave me a bear hug, for we had known each other from the time I was a baby.

Clementina couldn't believe it all, being used to the more restrained atmosphere of British families – though her own is a very affectionate one – but here she was instantly accepted as a Bentin. The few of us that didn't speak English all chattered away to her in Spanish, German or French depending upon which country we had been educated in.

The next morning even more flowers arrived, this time from B.O.A.C. Rosita, my niece, thoroughly approved of our choice not to wear mourning.

'Look at us,' she said, 'we all look like crows and you brighten us up.' And she rushed us all over Lima, where we met every Bentin there was, from the oldest and most venerable to the newest and wettest arrival.

At one family reunion there were 58 Bentins; the sum total, bar one or two, who were overseas, of the entire family. Most of them I knew by name and had met before, but the latest thirteen children, all belonging to one of my nieces, were just labelled: one to thirteen.

I should explain here that the son or daughter of your *primo hermano*, or cousin, is your nephew or niece. I was *Tio Miguel* – Uncle Michael – to them all.

I also met the remarkable Angelina, who was well into her nineties and had been Pop's nurse when he was a little boy. Angelina came from the mountains, where Uncle Ricardo had adopted her and brought her down with him to the coast.

I was very moved to see, at one giant family reunion, that, as Angelina was the most senior member of the household, everyone – from my white-haired eldest cousin to the very youngest Bentin – kissed her first.

The family Bentin fortunes had really been founded by grandfather, Don Antonio, who was a silver miner up in the mountains. We are all proud of the fact that he was the first mining engineer really to look after the needs of his miners by building them proper houses and schools and a hospital as well – mining for silver being a dangerous business.

He, and his son Ricardo after him, lived for years in the Sierra, at Cerro de Pasco and even higher – well up into the rarefied air of the Great Cordillera.

Grandfather was a tough hombre, but Uncle Ricardo was even tougher. Pop told me that this eldest brother of his, whom he adored, could actually lift a mule on his massive shoulders. Knowing Pop's hatred of lying, I am sure the story is true – what puzzles me is why Uncle Ricardo should want to do it at all.

Both of them were subsequently elected vice-President, and both died President-elect, after serving their people for eight and twelve years respectively.

They were intensely humane men who believed passionately in their people and fully realised that our mixture of bloods gave us double responsibility where the Indians were concerned, without being paternalistic.

From time to time, for political reasons, one or other of my family found themselves in jail, which is probably why Pop brought Tony and me up to be non-political animals.

Pop had been sent to England, at the age of thirteen, at a time of great political strife in Peru. To the day of his passing, he had no interest whatsoever in politics or politicians. My brother and I take after him, and it has often struck me as odd that, in the many strange situations in which I have found myself, when I desperately needed help of some kind – be it from a pilot, a navigator, a doctor, a dentist, a good shot, or for that matter a lovely woman I never remember needing the services of a politician. I'm sure that must mean something.

270

My family has always kept closely together and been far more interested in business. and its social responsiblity, than in political power.

When Uncle Ricardo was mayor of Lima, the representative of a large British biscuit manufacturing company came to see him with an introduction.

'Could Don Ricardo help me establish my line of biscuits?' he asked.

'Of course, but naturally we will have to have samples,' suggested my uncle.

'Oh, I have those – a one-ton wooden case of them,' he replied brightly.

'May I ask where?'

'Certainly. They're down on the docks.'

My uncle rose from behind his desk. 'Come with me, young man,' he said, 'for here beginneth the first lesson in South American salesmanship. Never leave the samples alone on the docks.'

When they got there, not only had the Indians eaten every last crumb, but a large family was already living in the packing case.

*   *   *

Lima was exactly as Pop had so often described it – the scars of many earthquakes showing on the lovely old Spanish colonial buildings.

The great squares, like the Plaza de Armas and St Martin, are still gems of that period of Peru's chequered history, while great tree-lined avenidas sweep across the city to the garden suburbs of San Isidro and Mira Flores.

Those greedy Spanish ancestors of mine, with their gold-hunger, only matched by today's race for gilded possessions, founded this city just inland from the port of Callao.

Presumably, they came from a misty region of Spain, because the Neblina – a sort of damp sticky cloud – can still make Lima unpleasant in certain winter months. But in summer it really gets hot and the Limeñas flock out of the city to the endless beaches that stretched in great sweeps from the north of Peru right down to the Chilean border.

I have never enjoyed anything more than going with a party of my family to one of these Pacific coast beaches. It reminded me so much of my early life with the British side of the family, chasing each other in those vintage cars round Shoeburyness.

But one thing shocked me deeply.

Around the city itself, the Indians, who came down from the mountains, where work is so scarce and the living so hard, huddle together in *barriadas* which would have disgraced my grandfather had he ever allowed them to be built in his mines.

A tap for running water is a luxury in these miserable shanty towns.

Yet, everywhere, among the straw matting and flattened tin walls of the *barriadas*, I found television aerials. When I was invited inside a hut, in its dimly lit and earth-floored interior was a television set, round which, for the consideration of a couple of *Sols*, the people sit inscrutably, watching every flicker of the screen. I realised how much it had become the new opiate of the people.

The Peruvian Government, which is always short of money because of its necessarily heavy dependence on outside investment to develop the enormous potential mineral wealth of the country, does its level best to get rid of the *barriadas* and to properly house the Indians. But as fast as they clear up one shanty town another springs up in its place.

I can see that Peru is slowly emerging from the long and savage division of the very rich and the very poor. Unfortunately, its fantastic potential wealth, especially in oil, makes it the target of many unscrupulous would-be exploiters, both private and national, from all over the world.

Juanito, one of my nephews, and my cousin Rosa's boy, was a keen shot and had arranged for me to meet the head of the P.I.P., the *Policia Inspecion Publico* – our equivalent in Peru to the Special Branch in Britain.

The commander asked me to demonstrate the hand gun to his officers, the following day. Juanito duly called for me at the Country Club.

He had brought an assortment of weapons but seemed a bit worried. On the way in to the range he said: 'By the way, Uncle, you can shoot? I hope!'

I told him it was a bit late to start having doubts and I started my usual demonstration to a handful of not particularly interested young detectives. They were armed with the hopelessly inadequate .32 police revolver and I had Juanito's .357 magnum and a .38 police special.

When I finished my short talk about safety and the theory of hand-gun shooting, I jumped round, without warning them, and pumped two shots into the centre of each of the three single man targets, standing 20 feet behind me.

This I can still do in about three seconds and, when I am in practice, in two seconds.

The greatest expert of all, a strange tubby little Montanan called Ed McGivern, could get the whole of five shots off in under 3/5ths of a second – something many hand-gunners, including me, have tried and failed to do.

This demonstration on the police range was impressive enough, however. Within the next hour, such is the power of the word of mouth, plus the swift rattle of gunfire, that the range was filled with P.I.P., eager to try their hand.

The whole demonstration could rapidly have become lethal, as their idea of gun safety was minimal, but I bullied them into taking care and they listened. Funny how people always listen to a man they know can shoot straight.

Finally, a young Air Force sergeant turned up, with a Madsen 9-mm. sub-machine-gun, and an Uzi, which is an excellent Israeli make of the same type of gun. I chopped the man targets in half with short effective bursts.

Shooting is an odd human accomplishment. Like its ancestor, the bow and arrow, it seems to be a part of man's atavistic background. Once learned, you never forget it.

I think Juanito was far more relieved that he hadn't lost face because of a duff uncle, than he was interested in the demonstration of new techniques in self defence. I was glad to see, however, that by my next visit to Peru the methods I had demonstrated – and their attendant safety measures – were in full use among the Peruvian Police.

The best thing about the whole unfortunate business of policemen using guns, is that, if the policemen are properly trained, at least the innocent public are less liable to be hit accidentally in a shoot-out in the streets.

However, to return to more peaceful pursuits:

For those people, like me, who are interested in Peru's fascinating history, the *Museo de Archaeologica* has a magnetic attraction.

Clementina and I were quite fascinated as we took in the beautiful ceramics and textiles of this small but superb museum.

Even though I had read a lot about Peruvian pre-Columbian civilisations, it was only when I was confronted with the marvellous intricacies of art forms that I realised what a fabulous heritage was mine.

I really felt intimately connected with the beautiful *wacos* (drinking jugs) and the stunning feathered cloaks, while the sculpture and murals completely captured my imagination. With all due respect to Doctor Pavlov, blood is thicker than water and race memory does play, in my experience at least, an enormous part in genetics.

Erich Von Daniken's researches have awakened a lot of interest and speculation as to the origins of Tiahuanaco, on the Bolivian side of the border and the strange markings on the plain of Nazea.

Antonio flew us over and orbited these markings. I must agree with Von Daniken that they certainly do look like a well-laid-out airfield with long, wide runways and hard standings for huge aircraft. The extraordinary truncated top of a nearby mountain does seem to have been cut off and levelled, for some kind of long take-off ramp.

We next flew up to Cuzco. Among the many extraordinary sights and wonders there is the inexplicable, dominating statue of Montezuma of Mexico in the main square. It is only matched, I understand, by the statue of Atalhualpa in Mexico City. I can only suspect a slight administrative hitch, somewhere.

Cuzco itself is a mixture of Spanish colonial, Inca and pre-Inca buildings, which in the latter case consist mainly of walls, and heavily restored at that. Not so in the case of Saxahuaman. This we found to be very different and quite breathtaking, for the colossal stones of Saxahuaman are part of a gigantic fortress complex, that was the last stronghold of my Inca ancestors.

I've tried, but I can't get a narrow knife blade between the mortices of these blocks, some of which weigh an estimated 150 tons, and come from a considerable distance away.

The rock is hard and enduring and modern chrome steel alloys soon blunt. When I tried to work the stone, I could hardly scratch its surface. So how the Incas, or their predecessors, who built most of these monolithic structures, worked to such fine limits with bronze implements, is again far beyond my comprehension – unless, as Von Daniken and others now suggest, lasers were employed, or, perhaps, some even more sophisticated ultrasonic device.

It's all a fascinating mass of conjecture, and the latest discovery of the extensive square-cut subterranean tunnels, in the north of Peru on the Ecuadorian border, long rumoured but only recently located, once again confounds modern scientific explanation.

274

Nature can't cut square tunnels out of the living rock – subterranean water courses or rock faults are invariably rounded by the action of water. But square-cut tunnels . . . surely these must be the work of man – and what men at that!

Pedro, whose passing had coincided with my decision to make the trip, had spent years of his life among the mountain Indians of the Cordillera and Alti-plano – the great high plains of the interior. When he came to see us in Britain, he had told me that he was convinced that they had once been a very advanced civilisation, until my gold-hungry ancestors had destroyed them and turned them into slaves.

As a child, I had listened enthralled as he explained that the Incas were comparatively recent and had invaded Peru from the north, building great roads to consolidate their conquests.

I remembered him telling me that, along these roads, were posthouses which housed the Chasquis, the long-distance runners who bore the knotted message cords, or *quipus*, as they were called.

These bunches of knotted woollen strands apparently contained an encoded message relating to many things, from the number of llama flocks to the amount of crops which had been grown in some specific area.

The Incas, amazingly enough, had no written language – a fact that made the Conquistadores despise them until they saw the incredible works of their hands and minds.

Now, at last Pedro's fascinating stories were realities before my eyes. I could touch the actual stones that my ancestors had so mysteriously worked. To Clementina it was astounding and impressive, while to me it was nearly mind bending.

Long before the Incas, there had been many civilisations in Peru, Ecuador and Bolivia – such as Tiahuanaco, with its massive Portals of the Sun and that inexplicable harbour, 12,000 feet in the air, and the Mochica, Chimu and Chavin civilisations of the high plains.

Among the Chavin ruins, I have seen sculpted heads that are so alive they seem to speak across the great bridge of time.

Miguel Mujica, another cousin of mine, who was educated in England, spent his life – and his fortune – gathering together the gold of the Incas to save it from leaving the country and finding its way to foreign museums and private collections, or even being melted down into bullion.

This incredible collection of gold artifacts has been presented to the Peruvian people, and, with it, his fascinating collection of beautiful feathered cloaks, which once adorned the Incas and their priests.

Together with Linda Johnson, the tall, slim daughter of the then President of the United States, Miguel had taken us around his unique collection, which was housed in a sort of semi-underground fortress. This instantly gave me the idea of calling him 'Goldfinger', a nickname which has since stuck, and his Japanese valet we christened 'Oddjob'.

His collection is quite remarkable. But the gold, beautiful though it is, pales into insignificance beside the feathered cloaks. They really are the most beautiful example of the use of natural materials I have ever seen.

One delightful incident occurred during our visit to the museum, when Miguel kept trying to keep between Linda Johnson and some exhibit in a glass case behind him. She was equally determined to see what my cousin was concealing.

Eventually she said, 'Do you mind, Señor?' and managed to insinuate herself past him to gaze with astonishment at a superb example of early Inca erotic art – a small, squat, golden Indian of the Cordillera, gazing proudly at his enormous sexual organ, in full erection.

I well remember her hushed: 'How about that?'

I couldn't resist it. 'Either early Inca or late Texan,' I declared, knowledgeably.

Nowhere would those incredible feathered cloaks have been seen to more effect, than at the great Inca festivals. People from all over the world come to see the Inti Rymi, the old Inca festival of the Sun, which takes place, at the change of the year from winter to spring, in front of the gigantic fortress of Saxahuaman. The great stone walls are crowded with thousands of enthralled spectators for this brilliantly colourful spectacle.

Commercialised though it now is, it still commands a stirring in your blood, whether you are Peruvian or not. I have some film of it and still watch it with a catch in my breath, even after many viewings.

At this time my cousin Antonio was the *Gerente* of the Peruvian Internal Airline. He had started the airline, after training as a pilot in England, with a Texan partner, named Slim Faucett. The airline bears that tall lean American's name.

I long treasured a photograph of Slim and Antonio walking side by side: the Texan, with his six foot four inches height, deep in conversation with Antonio's compact five foot four – both with their hands, characteristically, crossed behind their backs.

As my cousin, who had survived his business partner by some ten years, was already thinking of switching to jet aircraft, I extolled the virtues of the Trident Tri-jet. But my cousin sadly explained that, despite many requests from him, Hawker Siddeley had still not flown a Trident out to Peru. He eventually went to Braniff and ordered one of their splendid Boeing 727s. It arrived, on proving trials, painted in the Faucett livery. Even the American hostesses were dressed in the same smart Faucett uniforms.

It seemed to me that we really had an awful lot to learn from the Americans, when it came to sales know-how.

* * *

Next off we dashed to Macchu Piechu — that fantastic hidden city of the Incas which the American Hiram Bingham had discovered, in the early part of the century.

This beautiful mountain fortress-city bestrides a great saddle of rock, high above the Urubamba river, whose seething white waters rush past a thousand feet below.

As I wandered about among its lovingly reconstructed terraces and wonderfully laid-out water courses, amid the typically Inca buildings, I felt that here there existed a peace, which I had found very seldom anywhere else on earth.

The condors, which circled above the ruins, seemed symbolic of the long-past power of the builders who conceived this extraordinary city, so cunningly concealed from the steep narrow valley below as to be totally invisible — which is, of course, why the Conquistadores took so long to find it.

As I stumbled about the ruins, communing with my long-dead ancestors, Clementina found and ate some delicious wild strawberries. 'Pity I finished them,' she grinned, 'but you seemed a bit lost in thought — and I didn't want to disturb you!'

Almost as soon as we touched down again back in Lima — and my cousin Rosa, Antonio's sister, had finished scolding him for risking a heart attack in the high altitudes of the Cordillera — Antonio had, characteristically decided to rush us both off into the jungle.

Rosa's daughter, Rosita, who is one of my favourite nieces and enormous fun to be with, accompanied us on this trip. Within a few hours, we had risen from the coastal plain of Lima and flown high over the Gran Cordillera, till I could see the bare snowy collossi of the Andes fall away into the jungle-covered ridges of the great razor-backed foothills that point the way to the Selva itself.

On our flight I could see just how hairy it must have been for 'Slim' Faucett and Antonio to pioneer these flying routes. Their aircraft, carrying nitro-glycerine to the mines had literally to circle like condors to get into the updraughts that would help carry them over the mountains.

Below us I knew there were whole mountains of copper and rare earths. God alone knows what immense resources lie in the transitional hills between the mountains and the jungle proper.

At last the plane touched down on the runway at Iquitos, the last port before the Amazon breaks into its three mighty tributaries: the Napo, the Ucuayali and – the actual source river itself with its old Aymara name – the *Marañon*.

During the flight the pilot, Captain Sanvitti, a first-generation Peruvian of Italian descent and an immensely experience pilot of 10,000 hours flying time, told us of his undoubted encounter with a flying saucer, near Nasca.

This was later confirmed by another first-generation Peruvian pilot called Captain Kling, whose experience in the air matched Sanvitti's.

Both of these airwise pilots had been flying on the Lima to Arequipa route, which passes near to the plain of Nasca, their flights being within a few days of each other.

Part of the routine safety measures for flying, in such a mountainous area as Peru, are to make regular radio position checks, with the airports you have left, and then change over to the airport radio frequency of your destination, as you reach half way.

In both their experiences of a U.F.O., the object had appeared quite suddenly in the vicinity of the Nasca area, and immediate radio silence had followed.

The U.F.O. had circled and kept pace with them in the clear night air that is such a feature of this region. It was visible, not only to the flight deck crew, but also to the passengers in the cabin as well.

The sighting continued for about 15 minutes, and Sanvitti and Kling described the strange pulsating light in identical terms.

When you consider that both these pilots had just about seen every natural aerial phenomenon in the course of their long flying experience, they both make impeccable witnesses.

Meanwhile, both Lima and Arequipa had become concerned at the sudden radio silence and the subsequent departure from normal safety regulations and started to fear the worst.

In both cases the U.F.O. performed a series of passes ahead and alongside them, but made no obviously hostile move. Both pilots are quite clear in their conviction that the source of the light was not a conventional high-speed aircraft.

As soon as the U.F.O. finally accelerated away at a breath-taking speed, their radio returned to normal, indicating that the interruption in their signals had been caused by the presence of a very high intensity magnetic field.

I put forward all the usual arguments, like lenticular clouds and reflected images, but these were invalidated by the total absence of cloud at those times.

My other suggestion – that they might have mistaken the planet Venus for a U.F.O. – they greeted with polite silence.

Antonio told me he would go bail for both of these airmen. He knew them well and trusted them implicitly. I could see that neither of them were the type who practise practical jokes. Anyway they would have had to let their cabin crew and all the passengers in on the joke, as well.

Naturally, they both reported their separate experiences to the Peruvian Air Force, who were intensely interested, when they checked up and found that none of their French Mystère or British Hunter jets had been anywhere near that area.

'Besides,' said Sanvitti, 'if we ever find a jet fighter that can do those sort of manoeuvres without coming apart, we would be well advised to buy it.'

I was still pondering over this strange business, when we landed at Iquitos, but the wonder and beauty of the Amazon soon entranced me and my thoughts turned to its delighted appreciation.

Iquitos itself is a crumbling port of many styles of buildings, ranging from a marvellous house completely covered with brightly coloured tiles, to concrete and stucco villas and a peripheral floating shanty town of leaky houseboats and straw huts on stilts. It has a shopping centre which sells just about everything and boasts an ornate, Victorian-style, ironwork bandstand – the exact twin of the ones on the Folkstone Leas.

It is also headquarters of the efficient *Ejercito de la Selva* – the Peruvian jungle army, and provides the harbour for the *Flotta de la Fluvia* – the small but well-run river fleet of gunboats that serves as a vital link to all the settlements. It's British-built, flat-bottomed ships look as though they had floated straight out of *Sanders of the River*.

I was amazed at the variety of British goods that find their way to Iquotos, mainly by way of the efficient Booth shipping line, who sail 6,000-ton shallow draft ships over 2,200 miles up the Amazon to this last port, before the river breaks into three.

Pat Nichols, a cheery, Billy Bunterish character, who was the Booth Line representative at Iquitos is a marvellous extrovert. In his house, outside the town, he keeps a large anaconda happily living underneath the raised floors.

'Keeps the rats down,' says Pat, as though he's got a cat there.

He also has the only haunted billiard room I have ever seen. On specific nights, a number of people who have stayed with him, as well as Pat himself, have heard the billiard balls rattling and rolling in a ghostly game.

Discounting the snake using itself as a cue, it is difficult to explain, except for the obvious reason that it is a game of billiards played by some discarnate entity, reputedly the shade of the previous manager, who shot himself after brooding on accidentally shooting a young boy.

Haunted billiard table, snake and all, Pat is a marvellously cheerful and effective person. It was largely through his efforts that so many British products found their market in Iquitos.

Clementina and I even ate a Lyon's Maid ice cream on a stick, in the upper reaches of the Amazon.

One day Antonio took us, in two fast motor boats, to visit the Jaguas, a once proudly fierce people who hunted the great jungle cats, that gave them their name, but who are now pathetically dependent on tourists and intermittent work on the Iquitos docks.

They listlessly posed for photographs, in their long raffia skirts and head-dresses, which they had probably just changed into from their ragged shirts and jeans. Disinterestedly, they demonstrated their prowess with the cerbatana, the long, bark-covered blow pipe, with which they shoot their deadly curare-tipped bamboo darts with great accuracy.

As a boy, I had been given a blow pipe, by my cousins, and I was able to make a fair showing with it. This started to rouse their interest and, suddenly, from a remote, almost detached attitude, the Jaguas became a cheerful competitive tribal family group, vying with each other to show their tremendous skill and laughing and jostling round my small tape recorder, on which they heard their own voices for the first time.

They knew I appreciated them as people and not as some interesting curiosity, to be photographed and tipped. As one of my luckier shots ripped into the cigarette packet target, they banged me on the back with an enthusiastic *abrazo criollo*.

We left them in a rather different atmosphere from our arrival. As they waved and shouted to our fast disappearing boats, I felt they looked on us as something rather more than just inquisitive passing *gringos*.

That meeting stirred something inside me, and I realised how much work there was to be done in the rain forest. While Antonio and I were freeing the propellers for the umpteenth time, from the thick clinging water weeds, I quite clearly saw a hovercraft cross the horizon where two tributaries met.

It was only a subliminal flash of vision, but I knew then that I would come back with that machine, to try to open up this gigantic and undeveloped land.

When I told Antonio what I had seen and knew about the capabilities of the hovercraft he listened intently and agreed that the machine had great possibilities.

On our return to Lima he, very correctly, approached the President, who was then Señor Beleaunde Terry. He, in turn, consented to see me and hear about the hovercraft.

It all seemed slightly unreal that I, the *cordero negro de la familia*, the black sheep of the family, should be going to tell the President of my other country about a machine that I had visualised on the Upper Amazon.

Clementina and I were received by President Beleaunde, in the suite he would normally use for important State conferences, and he soon put us at our ease. This is quite normal for Clementina, who seems at ease anywhere, but difficult for me, because I am ridiculously shy – that is, until I get myself going on the pet subject of the moment, when I will enthusiastically discuss it with the Pope himself.

On this occasion I had a pre-sold audience in the matter of the hovercraft, because this stocky and contained middle-aged man, who spoke such shame-makingly good English, was as interested in the possibilities of the machine as I was.

The fact that a few years later he was removed from the presidency, by an Army coup led by the present President, General Velasco, is neither here nor there, because I have no understanding whatsoever of politics – only of facts. I state as a fact that when I talked to President Beleaunde, in that ornate presidential salon, where my grandfather and uncle had often sat with their presidents, I spoke to a man who was intensely concerned with the development of the rain forest and the future of the Indian peoples who lived there.

He told me that, if I could persuade the hovercraft manufacturers to bring their machine into the jungle, he would take a personal interest in seeing the trials. I explained that I was a comedian and not a magician but, feeling that I was now committed, I promised to try my damnedest to get the machine out to Peru.

Clementina had the last word, as we left the Presidental palace.

'You do get yourself involved,' she said simply.

How prophetic her words were.

The whole family held a farewell party for us at which most of us were in tears, mainly of laughter, and, as we took off from Lima Airport, Clementina said: 'That was the most wonderful time of my life.'

As she echoed my own thoughts I chanced to look in my pocket diary. The entry there read: 'Leave Peru Thursday – open Sunday, El Latino Club, South Shields.'

Talk about from the sublime to the ridiculous.

28. Right up my Amazon

Almost the first thing I did when we arrived back in London, was to contact Eamonn Andrews, to show a piece of film that Father Pelosi, a friend of mine who is a Franciscan brother, had made of the Campo Indians shooting arrows at each other, in a test of manhood.

Small and totally alive, Father Pelosi has two weaknesses – as he thinks of them. He loves cameras and believes Scotch whisky is purely medicinal. If those were my only two sins I might just be as fine a person as the good Father.

As well as showing the film of the Indians, I wanted to make a protest about the apparent lack of interest in Peru, where selling the Trident aircraft was concerned.

Eamonn agreed, enthusiastically, to show the Pelosi film, but, just before we went on the air he reluctantly had to ask me to drop the whole Trident business.

I didn't want to get him in any trouble, so I agreed to let the matter go, but I wanted to know why. Eamonn told me that Hawker Siddeley had asked me to come along and see them before letting such a story loose on the air.

That seemed fair enough and we went ahead with showing the dramatic film extract of the Indians duelling with those lethal arrows.

To my astonishment the studio audience shrieked with laughter. Afterwards, one man came up to me and said: 'That was one of your best yet. Funny idea that, but you can't fool me – I recognize Wimbledon Common when I see it.'

He genuinely thought it was one of my filmed end-spots for the *Square World* – like my expedition by canoe to discover the source of the Thames, only to find that it was a dripping tap.

The next day an apologetic P.R.O., from Hawker Siddeley, phoned up and asked me to lunch with them. I was curious as to why the Trident had failed to show up in Peru, and I knew that, wherever John Cunningham was, I would get a truthful answer.

The lunch was instructive and friendly and, afterwards – as a sort of consolation prize, I suppose – they let me fly in the lovely little H.S. 125 executive jet, which was a joy to handle.

I explained that I wasn't trying to mix any puddings, but was genuinely shocked by their failure to demonstrate the Trident in Peru. They told me, quite bluntly, that the plane, in that early configuration, would not have shown up well in performance at high altitude air fields, with high temperatures, such as Cuzco.

The later Trident models had, apparently, vastly superior take-off weights and the power was to be increased greatly.

They had answered the question that had been nagging at me and, in return for not pursuing what obviously was a delicate situation in the British aircraft industry, I asked if they could help me with an introduction to Hovercraft.

That the P.R.O. was only too happy to arrange. I said I would come down to Yeovil to see the Westland people as soon as I started my summer season which, by an odd chance, was at Weymouth, only a few miles away from the Westland factory.

I also asked for a further introduction to a top sales representative at the British Aircraft Corporation, because I had some rather important news for him. This, also, was arranged and I duly phoned the particular person, whose name was well known in aviation circles.

When I got through, I explained that I would like to meet him, but he was apparently extremely busy. So was I, but that didn't seem to matter very much.

Couldn't I tell him over the phone? he then queried.

'If that's what you want,' I replied. 'I have reason to believe that the sales agreement to sell Lightning fighters to the Peruvian Air Force is going to be blocked. I know the Peruvians would like to have these fine machines and naturally, being Anglo-Peruvian, I have a simple patriotic interest in warning you of the snags that may prevent this.'

I got a very chilly reception at the other end, while the well-known airman told me that the whole deal had been clinched and assured me that there was absolutely no question of there being any difficulties whatsoever, implying, probably quite naturally, that it wasn't any of my business anyway.

My information had come from neither Peruvian nor British sources, but via an old chum of mine from the war. Being aware of his Intelligence background, I felt convinced that it was correct.

I apologised for taking up the expert's valuable time and rang off, feeling frustrated and angry, that I should bother to stick my neck out.

About a fortnight later, the papers announced that the deal was off, as the Americans had objected to the whole concept of Peru having such an efficient machine.

I often wonder how the well-known expert reacted, but I was sad that the Peruvian Air Force had lost such an opportunity to gain experience with these great British planes.

I felt even more determined that, at least, a British hovercraft would be the first one of its kind up the Amazon. I arrived at Yeovil full of enthusiasm, ready to make my points of argument.

These were simple enough. The rain forest of South America is extremely difficult to traverse because roads are almost impractical over much of its area; and, anyway, the cost of building them is prohibitive.

There are thousands of roads there already, but they happen to be rivers. These flood or dry out, at different seasons, and are often clogged with weeds and fallen trees.

The one machine capable of navigating these rivers, in any conditions – even during the tropical rain storms, which immediately ground all aircraft, including helicopters – is the hovercraft. The machine I knew to be ideal for the job was the S.R.N. 6.

By the weirdest coincidence, I had written a technical script on British industry, for a projected film by Jack le Vien, and the hovercraft was one of the revolutionary machines I had to learn about. In actual fact I had never been on one but, because of the research I had done, for the film script, I had a very good working knowledge of its capabilities.

Luckily, at the meeting, there was a splendid man, called Tony Gawade, who totally supported my every argument. He had been trying to break into the South American market for some time, and asked me, point blank, if I could get President Beleaunde to see his films on hovercraft.

'That's up to the President,' I pointed out. 'But I'll ask my family to approach him.'

I cabled Antonio and he agreed to try to help.

When I had been discussing the idea with Tony Gawade he asked me what I wanted in return.

'Nothing!' I replied, a little surprised.

'Well we must do something,' he pressed me.

An idea came to me as to how I might help further, in my other capacity in show business.

'I tell you what,' I said, 'give me the film rights for South America. That'll cost you nothing and it will obviously make you feel you're reciprocating. And I may well be able to persuade someone to come and film the whole trials.'

And so that fateful agreement was made. Had it not been, I don't think the hovercraft would have ever been the first British machine, of its type, to make the Amazon trip almost up to its source.

The American company would probably have tried it, and undoubtedly would have, had I offered them the same facilities.

My weeks were now busy, with the summer season, which looked like being the hottest one for about a hundred years. This didn't improve our business at Weymouth, where the weather plays a very important role, apparently. When it rained our first houses did well but, when that broiling sun shone, who would be silly enough to miss its warmth on those lovely sands!

As Alfie Ravel, who was in the show with me said: 'The weather is so hot and the beaches are so crowded the Punch and Judy man has lost his voice.'

Voice or no voice, he was playing to bigger audiences than we were. However, we broke about even and I learned a bit more about show business.

Meanwhile I had contacted a V.I.P. at the B.B.C. and told him about my projected idea of a trip right up the Amazon, which was to be a British first.

'What in?' asked the V.I.P., a man for whom I had a great admiration.

'Well I can't tell you yet, but I will let you have the first refusal,' I said cautiously.

'Fine, Michael!' he said, and said that he would look forward eagerly to hearing further from me.

I was cautious because the whole thing was so delicately balanced, at such long range, that it might easily fall through and I had no wish to embarrass the B.B.C. or my family or, for that matter, myself.

The cables went back and forth and Antonio, typically, put himself to endless trouble to help in every way, because he is both a patriotic Peruvian and a strong Anglophile, and had long since been awarded an O.B.E. for his past efforts to help relations between the two distant countries.

Eventually, Tony Gawade was able to go over and show various generals, and the President himself, the films he had brought featuring this revolutionary machine.

When he returned, he told me, happily, that he was sure the whole thing could now go ahead. I was so excited I immediately rang the B.B.C. and contacted my V.I.P.

When I got through he said, almost immediately: 'Now don't think we've pinched your idea – but we're taking the hovercraft down the Orinoco.'

'How very interesting,' I said, 'and how did you know it was my idea to use a hovercraft? We never discussed it, in the first place.'

I was furious, when I thought of all the trouble my family, and especially my cousin Antonio, who was by no means a fit man, had been put to.

I felt exactly as I had, all those years ago, in front of that Court of Enquiry. Obviously our whole project was to be given the old heave-ho.

'Right,' I said coldly. 'You can take the hovercraft anywhere you feel like – to hell if you want to – but, if it happens to be in South America, you can't film one foot of it. You see, I've been given the film rights!'

The V.I.P. gave a gasp – at least my reputation at the B.B.C. was enough to ensure that they knew I never bluffed.

'Who gave them to you?' he demanded.

'Hovercraft,' I replied and rang off.

I then got straight on to Tony Gawade and confirmed, that he would back me up. To his eternal credit, he honoured his word – I can think of a lot of people who wouldn't have.

He sent me a letter, as well, and then the pressure started.

Did I realise that the Duke of Edinburgh was backing the Orinoco Expedition?

'No,' I said. 'I didn't. Anyway what the hell had that got to do with filming the expedition?'

The film, of course, would pay for a great part of the costs, I was told; surely I appreciated that?

Now, had I been a politician or what is called 'a good business man' I would have demanded, and probably received – a large percentage of the take and full credit for my family's efforts.

Being an ordinary person, who only wanted to fulfil that fleeting vision I had been given in the Upper Amazon, I asked for none of these things in return for giving up those all-important film rights – only for the guarantee, that, before the Orinoco expedition, the hovercraft should undertake a trial run in Peru, right up the Amazon.

Hovercraft, themselves, insisted they paid my return fare and hotel expenses in Peru. They said it was the least that they could do.

Meanwhile, the second Orinoco expedition was already receiving its Press build-up, and a well-known night club and society gossip columnist was now to accompany the machine on 'the last great journey in the world', as he called it.

I, for one, would never have gone into the Amazon basin, the first time, if half those perilous adventures were quite as commonplace as this writer implied, and I certainly wouldn't have taken Clementina!

But the writer did go a bit far when, during a television interview, he implied that I was just running around Iquitos, with the hovercraft.

Quite a run around, when you consider that wonderful machine carried us, without any trouble at all, from Iquitos – which is well over two thousand miles up the Amazon, and at which port she had been put in the water – to Nazareth, another 450 miles further up the Marañon, which is the actual source river of the Amazon, the over the white waters of the wicked Pongo de Manseriche, the rapids that had claimed so many lives from conventional craft.

As soon as I could, I flew into Lima. As I passed through customs, I handed over two revolvers I had been carrying for the chief of the Policia Inspection Publico. Unfortunately the chief had been himself placed under arrest, for some reason, a couple of weeks before.

The upshot of it was that, the following morning, a detective from the P.I.P. turned up to talk to me. Fortunately, he had been at my shooting demonstration the year before.

Cousin Miguel Mujica came down to the police bureau with me and it finished with drinks all round and great interest being shown in the modified weapons I had brought – plus an unqualified apology for the formalities. Anyway I was glad to see the P.I.P. had finally disposed of the sadly inadequate arm that they had been using for some years, with the loss of good men in combat with better-armed criminals.

After a quick and happy round of the family, I went to see my friend David Muirhead, who was then the British Ambassador in Peru. This large, bluff and accomplished Scot had been in Special Operations Executive during the war and we talked over some of the odd things and weird people we had known in those years.

He was very concerned, because a Press campaign was attacking President Beleaunde, with the inference that he was in some way going to profit out of the hovercraft and that my own family was involved as well. This was a stupid misconstruction put on the only hurried statement I had made, reluctantly, to the Press, just as I was boarding the V.C. 10 for Lima.

A bloody good way to start off things in Peru, I thought, after all the pudding mixing already in England.

The Ambassador agreed that the best thing I could do was to go straight on to Iquitos and straighten the situation out with the hovercraft team, while he would join us later – for David Muirhead was as keen an enthusiast for the hovercraft as I was.

Flying over the Cordillera, I pondered on the extraordinary manoeuvring of politicians and gratefully thanked my father for having taught me to stay out of them.

When I first arrived at Iquitos the atmosphere was frigid, to say the least. Only Tony knew the real truth behind it all.

I always believe in taking the bull by the horns, so I'd brought along copies of all the letters I had received, containing the reasons for my being there and I let the crew read them. The atmosphere changed immediately, and I really enjoyed doing my best for that whole crew.

Tony Gawade was, as before, a staunch friend. For Don Ellis, that Francis Drake-like character, who was the captain, and an ex-Folkestonian as well, I have a specially warm spot. His skill and quiet cheerful ability always remain, in my memory, as the very best example of how to carry out a difficult job perfectly.

The technical crew were experts and knew their jobs backwards and all of them co-operated in every way. It was a great privilege to have known them and made such a fascinating journey together.

With us we had two other pilots, Commander Grahame Clarke and Captain Stuart Syrad. The first was a stocky ex-naval Lieutenant Commander and the other a young Marine Commando. Both were extremely anti-me at the start but, when they had read the detailed correspondence I had brought with me, their attitude completely changed, and we got on just fine.

Antonio flew in, with my cousin Miguel Mujica and his son, Miguelito, who I always think of as one of my own boys; and they entertained the whole crew to a dinner that went on till the small hours.

When I introduced Miguel formally to the Commanding General, José Benavides, who accompanied us, I asked if he knew him.

'Naturally,' Miguel replied. 'His father, Marshal Benavides, put me in prison three times.'

The General, who was a delight except when he insisted that I told jokes at every remote army jungle camp we stopped at, had supreme faith in the hovercraft and it was he who had chosen the Marañón, as the test area.

He certainly tested it thoroughly, and that wonderful machine never once failed, in Don Ellis's skilful hands.

Don became a great favourite with the General, who summed him up perfectly. 'Es un hombre!' he said.

After the tests for the Navy, in the rivers round Iquitos, we set out very early one morning for the major trip – a run of more than four hundred miles to the most remote farm in the world.

At four o'clock in the morning we thundered down the long concrete ramp of the Peruvian Air Force seaplane station, just outside Iquitos, and splashed on to the black waters of the Amazon.

Loaded to capacity with extra side tankage and a full complement of crew, plus the equipment we needed for the trip, we roared off up river in the rapidly increasing light.

We were all strangely quiet at first. With the Peruvian river pilot sitting next to him, Don was concentrating on the swerving course of the broad river, as it forks into the long main tributary, the Marañón.

As the brightness grew and we were able to shut off the interior lighting, the solid phalanxes of greenery rushed past us on our near side, and, slowly, the other bank of the wide tributary became visible in the pinkish haze of pre-dawn.

Like a huge dark grey highway between an endless avenue of trees, the Marañón stretched ahead of us – twisting and turning like one of the great anacondas that lie in its waters.

Suddenly I realised that at last it was all happening – the long effort and anxiety had finally crystallised into the simple fact, that here I was, in the hovercraft, belting along towards the remote white rapids of the Pongo de Manseriche – just as I had visualised it all a year before.

As the day grew warmer the heat inside the cabin of the machine became uncomfortable and, at the General's suggestion, we started to peel off our bush jackets. By midday the heat was breathless and we were mostly in our shorts, grateful beyond measure for the General's thoughtfully provided beer, packed in ice in a large insulated box.

Beside us flashed the thick green wall of jungle that lines the banks, broken occasionally by a small settlement of huts, where the Indians ran out to see us roar past. From time to time, Don sharply altered course to avoid a floating tree which, borne downstream by the current, stuck out like an upthrust spear.

As our fuel ran low we pulled in to the other side of the river, at a small settlement called Tres Unidas, where one of the commercial barges, towed by a tug, had left us drums of kerosene for our Hawker Siddeley Turbo-prop engine.

While the interested locals gathered round shouting 'Un Platillo Volador! – a flying saucer!' I wondered where they had picked up that idea – perhaps from seeing the genuine article? And as the drums of fuel were emptied into the oval side tanks I watched and filmed a colony of leaf cutter ants, stretched out in a long busy line.

They fascinated me, as they carried great sections of leaves to the water's edge and then, using them as rafts, swept out into the river. It all seemed so frenzied and at the same time pointless, much as hovercraft expedition probably appeared to the Indians who were refuelling us.

Off we bellowed again, sending great clouds of spray over our fins and rudders, as we rushed up the river towards our first overnight stop.

This turned out to be a small army camp at Barranca, set high above the Marañon on a plateau, reached by a steep line of rough wooden steps.

Here the small detachment of the Ejercito de La Selva provided us with huts, and a riotous night in the officer's mess.

As we arrived, a young Indian boy proudly displayed a baby anaconda he had caught – a mere fifteen feet long.

The dinner in the mess, which started formally enough, with toasts and speeches by the General and the young officer commanding the jungle outpost, slowly loosened up into a typical party, that could have taken place, all those years ago, in any R.A.F. mess.

At about three in the morning, after I had taught the Peruvian officers the famous game of Cardinal Puff, where every time you make a mistake in a fairly complex ritual you are made to drink a pint of beer, the General ordered me to tell them some jokes, or *chistés* as he called them.

Aided by Toby Garcia, who, like me, was half English and

half South American and was our official British Army interpreter, I launched forth into the old British service jokes, that have seen her through two World Wars, plus a couple of mime sequences of my own invention.

None of these pieces of schoolboy humour need further elucidation. Let's just say they went over very big. Eventually, Toby and I cried off and staggered across the jet-black parade ground towards our invisible huts, guided by Toby's luminous compass dial and alarmed by slithering sounds as some nameless creatures scurried out of our way.

The next morning, at first light, after waking to look up at the beady little eyes of the tarantulas or rats or whatever they were scrabbling about the rafters of the hut, we dressed in our still sopping wet bush jackets that we had hung up to dry the evening before, and off we went again. This time with an enthusiastic, if somewhat bleary-eyed, guard of honour to wave us cheerily on our way.

Our destination was a hundred miles further on and called Borja; a tiny port, which also acted as a helicopter base for the fleet of private choppers run by Alec Bristow's Company. They supplied fuel oil, cement and transport to the oil drillers, wildcatting on the rigs in the Rio Santiago area, above the boiling white waters of the Manseriche, which lies directly ahead of the port.

The object of the exercise was to pass through the few kilometres of canyon faced Pongo, and prove that the hovercraft could handle rapids as easily as it crossed to the Isle of Wight.

First Tony and Don, plus the spare pilots, Graham and Stuart, piled into a chopper and whirled off up the Pongo, on a recce.

A few minutes later they were back, smiling happily, and everyone except me got back on board the hovercraft for the first run through the rapids.

I was determined to get shots of this manoeuvre, purely for a visual assessment of the behaviour of the machine in the rapids, and John Waddington, a gangling double for a young Lindbergh, flew me in the helicopter.

Off we raced and were just in time to catch the hovercraft as Don bucked her into the first shelf of the tumbling waters. As we flew in chase, it dawned on me that normally the choppers flew high over the Manseriche – and now the reason why was obvious.

John grimly held the machine just behind the hovercraft, as it skidded round the sharp bends of the Pongo. Our rotor blade tips seemed to clear the canyon rocks by only a few feet.

In one of his steep turns, which were necessary to negotiate the snake-like twists of the Manseriche, the camera jammed and I lost some historic footage of the event. Still, I managed to get a high angle shot of the machine well below us, the next time I flew above the rapids.

Don brought the hovercraft, complete with the delighted General, through that maze of swirling waters as though he was driving a bus.

When I touched down just above the Pongo, at the strategically placed Army camp of the Teniente Pinglo, which is at the western end of the rapids, the hovercraft was just nosing into the landing stage.

The guard of honour couldn't believe that any machine could, so effortlessly, make that much feared passage of the turgid Manseriche.

Another party was set up, this time with the wives of a few of the officers present. These remarkably pretty girls had chosen to live with their husbands, in what must be the remotest married quarters on the earth. Mucho mujeres!

This got as riotous as the first thrash at Barranca but, of necessity, I had to tone down a lot of the 'chistés', that I performed, for the packed army mess, with all the open windows crowded with the short, stocky, laughing Peruvian soldiers. In that cut-off corner of the enormous rain forest, it was even more amazing to hear great gusts of belly laughter echoing out to wake up the lorros and papagayos of the jungle.

The following day I was dragged out early by the General, to demonstrate the revolver, automatic pistol and sub-machine-gun techniques of my past, his excuse being that I literally was the only person there who had ever seen guns fired in anger.

So I found myself teaching a Peruvian jungle regiment the techniques taught originally by Shanghai policemen and, what's more, they still worked.

Then once more the S.R.N.6 was tested to the full – this time to demonstrate its amazing abilities to oil drillers from up the Rover Santiago.

Jammed between four of the crew, who grabbed me tightly, I kept the camera as steady as possible and six times we bucked our way over the Pongo – whizzing past the great jagged rocks that form the narrowest part. This time, I got the plunging images on film.

High over our heads flew the helicopter pilots, on their way to the jungle oil rigs, with various spectacular loads slung below their machines.

These consisted of either a huge collapsible rubber bag of diesel fuel, a large crate of cement, from which dust trailed in a grey plume or even, sometimes, one of the self-contained air-conditioned aluminium jungle living-units, like a small flying caravan.

These pilots earned their high salaries the hard way. If the rotors stopped, it meant a certain fatal crash in the thick high jungle, where, as you fly over them, the tree tops look as tightly closed as a cauliflower head.

The pilots alternated their work and leave at ten-day intervals. Apparently, at a house in the suburbs of Lima, a perpetual party was always in progress, where this latter day flying Foreign Legion got rid of the tensions of such a wildly hairy job.

Our next task was the final leg of the river passage to Nazareth, the remote farm experiment of the Colonisation de La Selva.

Another early start, and we scudded off, in our perpetual spray cloud to run almost immediately into a full-scale tropical rain storm. This deluge, which is the nearest thing I know to standing under a waterfall, would have instantly forced down a seaplane, or even a helicopter – but the hovercraft swept through its thick sheets of rain without any bother at all.

On the way up this last 100-mile passage, we passed the usual motley collection of outboard-powered dugout canoes and over-loaded houseboats, providing us with a perfect contrast of the old and the new.

The hovercraft was not just some kind of gadget, such as had been demonstrated by a well-meaning American team who, the year before, had brought an immensely complicated jungle-flattening machine to Iquitos.

This extremely expensive piece of machinery, which looked like a large horizontal locomotive with flat feet had, after a short explanatory speech by its designer, stamped its way through the matted jungle floor to total disappearance, the designer being the last one to leave before it sank from sight.

We had, unkindly perhaps, pointed out that five hundred stainless steel machetes, at five dollars each, in the skilled hands of the local inhabitants would flatten more jungle rather cheaper.

The S.R.N.6 had genuine advantages over any other transport used in the rain forest at that time. It was faster on average, safer in any conditions and could operate for long periods, without too complicated a servicing schedule.

It's one disadvantage was that, not being built in quantity, it was hellishly expensive. The General who was by now totally sold on the idea, sadly pointed out the Peruvian forces could get two or three seaplanes for the same price, plus the spares.

At Nazareth, the whole reason for the expedition became apparent. Here, in a small farm area of about 500 acres, the Peruvian Government was producing two to four crops a year of practically anything from cocoa, through maize and cereals, to coffee, sugar cane and cotton. In fact, in that incredible hot-house climate, in top soil fed by the almost inexhaustible supply of trace elements from the Cordillera, with a constant temperature of about 85 degrees Fahrenheit, and super-saturated air, there was no upper limit to the yield.

Animals as well, including chickens, pigs and cattle, thrived in the unique conditions. Here was living evidence that my theories were right. The rain forest could easily feed the whole starving Earth and, obviously, here we were with a machine that could open it up.

The one drawback was equally obvious. With the development of the rain forest, on the vast scale that was inevitable, the passing of the Indian was foredoomed.

Whether by absorption into the new social structure, or by contact with the diseases of civilisation, the passing of the age-old way of life of the jungle Indian is the price of progress, or in this case, world survival.

Surely some brilliant brain, among all the doomwatchers who predict and prophesy catastrophe, but never seem to come up with a solution, can supply an answer: between the jungle reservation, which virtually means a human zoo, and the standard sort of preparation for absorption, which could mean slow extinction, there has to be an answer somewhere.

Having impressed the hovercraft crew with that amazing farm, and the farm with the amazing hovercraft, we turned round and set off back to Teniente Pinglo.

One final party later – and these parties were probably the most potentially lethal dangers we encountered on the whole trip – off we dashed through the early morning mist over the Manseriche, to break a large number of hovercraft records for the final return run to Iquitos. As we roared and thundered our way back, I really felt we had made a small step forward in the inevitable conquest of the rain forest.

Pedro Larrañaga, who accompanied us as the Peruvian agent for the hovercraft on this expedition, had become another good friend but he never could get used to my show business connections.

One morning, during a short break in the trip, we had been sitting on the banks of the Rio Santiago, 300 miles from nowhere, shooting at a floating log in the river, with Pedro's revolver, when he idly asked me:

'Miguel. What are you going to do after this?'

I looked in my diary and told him I was due back at the 'El Latino', South Shields.

To this day he doesn't believe me!

I won't go into a long and lyrical description of the rain forest, because either you are fascinated by it, or you leave on the next plane.

When I asked an American, who was working, reluctantly, in the area, what he thought of the Selva, he replied: 'Man, when you've seen one tree – you've seen them all!'

I still find it absolutely awe inspiring, and I'm glad we did our thing and tested that incredible machine to the very limit of its capacity.

We had, naturally, had a few tense moments, but, usually they were nothing to do with the hovercraft itself. Once I just stopped Don from going for a paddle off a sandbank into what looked like bubbling white water. It was actually a shoal of piranhas.

The hairiest moment for me was the helicopter trip with John Waddington, when, at that narrowest point, we only had about twenty feet clearance on either side of the rotor blades.

Because of political pressures, the President didn't come to see the machine, but General Benavides thanked everyone for their efforts, and we all had one hell of a farewell party about which I remember nothing.

I don't regret a thing about the expedition, but I was sad to see that when all the honours were, quite rightly, handed out after the very successful Orinoco trip, Don Ellis, who wasn't on that one, got no recognition whatsoever.

One thing both trips proved to the hilt. These hovercraft are the machines that can open up the vast areas and bring mankind the sorely needed resources of the gigantic rain forest. They can act as transport, fast-moving hospitals, supply carriers and social contacts between the isolated settlements that are scattered all over the Selva.

I find that there is nothing graceful or lovely about a hovercraft, such as there can be about a boat or a plane. It is designed and built to do a job of work and it does it better than anything else I know.

I grew fond of that ungainly squarish metal box, balanced on its great fat ballooning skirt with its inside temperature soaring above 110 degrees, while we streamed with sweat, even when we were stripped down to the briefest of briefs.

I've photographed the General for posterity, as he peed off the stern of the S.R.N.6 into that mighty river.

I've stood at the mouth of the Manseriche as the funnel of waters hurtled into the winding canyons below, leaving a white mist to hang over the flanking trees. And I've wondered at how the whole expedition started, from that one quick flash of insight, seen by an Anglo-Peruvian comedian sitting in a boat 2,300 miles up the Amazon, eating an all-British ice lolly. Perhaps those Lyon's Maid lollies have some special hallucinogenic qualities.

One of the crew was the Peruvian naval officer, who was an expert at navigation, with the flat bottomed, shallow draft gun-boats of the river fleet.

Every time we cut across a sandbank or mud bar he closed his eyes, until by the end of the trip, he got used to it and cheered us on, with a frenzied olé every time Don carried out this spectacular manoeuvre.

A couple of weeks after I got back, a Peruvian friend rang me, with a message:

Our river navigator had, in a moment of lapsed memory, tried to repeat the same manoeuvre with a gunboat.

The Admiral was not at all pleased!

One final word, to reduce the whole business to a manageable banality. When I arrived back in Britain, one of the London Airport porters said to me: 'They're putting round some rumour that you've been up the Amazon in a hovercraft. I told them straight, mate – even you're not bloody mad enough to do that!'

29. The Golden Silents

A couple of days after I had flown back to London, I took the still pictures of the expedition into the offices of the magazine, which was going to run the hovercraft story of the Orinoco journeys. The Editor was most upset when he saw them, as, of course, they would pre-empt his series – so I offered them to him in exchange for money to buy some much-needed medical supplies for the Indians of the Selva. He offered me £85.

Wordless with fury, I took the pictures straight down Fleet Street, to the offices of the *News of the World*, where the Features Editor, John Jowett promptly promised to pay £900 – to meet medical supply bills.

I can never thank all the people who helped me to get those desperately needed supplies to the eager army doctors in the Selva.

A young medical supply salesman, who was introduced to me and heard my story, very kindly got in touch with companies, like Glaxo, who promptly let us have large quantities of the medicines, for a fraction of their cost. For example, 200,000 tablets of sulphaguanazine, which is an anti-gastroenteritis specific, we bought for below the packing price, plus gallons of 'Savlon' and an anti-leprosy drug called Avu-Sulfon, which provided us with about 80,000 more tablets at below cost. One day, even a man on a plane from Paris, expressed interest in my efforts in the course of conversation, and sent me a large case of special disposable surgical gloves and dressings.

The whole issue, which by now provided quite a transportation problem, was dealt with by the efficient and knowledgeable Booth Line. From Liverpool, they carried the entire shipment for nothing, right up to Iquitos and into the safe hands of my friend Pat Nichols, who passed them straight through to the Army Medical Service for distribution to the jungle people.

When I came out of the offices of that first magazine, I was in despair. Now, through the generous efforts of people I'd never met before, the whole project had become worth while.

The short article came out on the *News of the World*'s front page, complete with a photograph of the hovercraft, rushing up the Amazon and then was sold by the newspaper, to the American adventure magazine *Argosy*.

Even *Flight International* carried an article on the expedition and showed several photographs, which I had taken of the machine and the team, so at least, I could say thank you to everyone, indirectly, in print.

Then I closed the book on it all until I wrote the words in this one.

A few weeks later, I was touring the northern clubs, when I got a phone call from Michael Mills, asking me to meet him and Tom Sloan, the next day at the B.B.C. Television Centre.

This meant flying down from Newcastle, first thing in the morning, and catching a plane back, to make the show that night. But Michael was an old friend and I knew he wouldn't put me to this trouble, needlessly.

When I got to the B.B.C., Tom was his old cheerful and aggressive self, and was obviously keen for me to work for the Corporation again.

With Richard Evans, a patient and painstaking film maker from the Ealing studios of the B.B.C., we watched some random clips of old silent movies. From the off, I sat entranced, as my childhood flooded back to me. I was back at the cinema with my brother as we roared our heads off at the wonderful antics of these great movie clowns.

When we had finished, Tom said: 'Would you help make these pieces of silent film into programmes and link them together in a studio?'

'How many films have you got, and who is in them?' I asked him.

Richard thought that they had about a quarter of a million feet of film, featuring Buster Keaton, Laurel and Hardy and some early Chaplins, as well as the Keystone Cops and Ben Turpin, plus a whole long list of every silent screen favourite I had ever seen.

Best of all was that most of the material, especially the Keaton pieces, had not been seen on British television before.

I knew I had to link the film extracts in some different manner from the usual method of a joky commentary, and I suggested that we did it in front of an audience.

The only other way seemed to be to do the same sort of links that Bob Monkhouse had already successfully used in *Mad Movies*.

There were objections to using the Ealing studios, with an audience, because of fire regulations, and Tom, Michael and Richard were dead against the then accepted funny links.

Something stirred at the back of my mind and I turned to Tom.

'Where did you get the idea of these programmes, in the first place?' I asked him.

'I was at the National Film Theatre, watching a programme of Buster Keaton films, and judging by the audience's reaction, I thought this idea would be worth trying,' said Tom.

'That's it!' I said. 'That's the missing link. We'll do it in front of an audience of movie buffs at the National Film Theatre. The way I'll handle it is to explain to them how the tricks and gags were done, and give them some of the background material on the stars who made them.'

'Great!' said Richard, who, like me, was an aficionado of the silent era, and the others duly agreed.

The main difficulty was in convincing the National Film Theatre to let us have facilities for filming the audience and links, and showing the silent films, in the afternoons. But, as the whole project would take nearly a year to get ready, the B.B.C. went to work on the administration side, and I went along to the N.F.T., to sell them the idea.

When I told the management there, what an opportunity it was to reinstate Keaton, and the other silent movie greats, back in their true place in the public affection, they agreed that we could go ahead.

There followed months of dashing to Ealing, to view film clips with Richard, as I alternated cabaret dates and club appearances with pantomimes and summer seasons, racing back, time and again, to help solve the inevitable problems of turning these gems of film comedy into coherent programmes.

Richard and I decided that we must group them, under general headings, like 'The Great Chases', 'Thrills and Spills', or any other good attractive blanket idea that would help us to link these widely differing fragments into half-hour shows.

In this, the editors played an enormously important part and never once resented my instinctive choice of the length of a particular piece, or the pace of the editing.

300

Richard co-operated with great enthusiasm, and amassed an enormous amount of background facts and figures, from which we could lay out the basic scripts. I've certainly never enjoyed anything more than working with such keen and enthusiastic collaborators.

When we finally came to try our hand at the public showing, I knew we had the makings of a world-class series.

There were difficulties, of course. The first three shows that we did from the National Film Theatre went off superbly well, but were badly lit and one of the cameramen wasn't up to standard Michael wasn't happy with the decor, either, but Tom was wildly enthusiastic, and we went ahead.

I was horrified to discover that tickets for the studio audiences for the series had all been issued to the same people.

In other words we had, as near as dammit, the same audience for every show.

Part of my plan had been to warm up the audience with my variety and cabaret material and to get them in a receptive state before we showed them the silent clips, which were backed by a music track, but had no sound effects, as such, laid on the sound track.

The 26 half hours were made back to back, that is to say two at a time, which meant I had to keep the audience warm for the whole two hours taken up by the actual recording, with its various delays and inevitable hitches.

No comedian in the world has 26 hours' material to draw on, and the audience was a very hip one, made up of silent-movie fans of all ages, so I couldn't get away with corny stories. The only way out was to change the whole concept into an informal party atmosphere.

So I asked them how they were, what had they been doing? – anything to keep their interest going. I even introduced them to each other and asked them questions about the silent films, to test their knowledge.

Once I got some of their names in my head I found that the answer to the problem was to use all the old Summer seaside show 'joey-joeys'. I made them argue out who-did-what in which film – divided them into pro-Keaton or pro-Chaplin groups, and made them shout out the names of their idols, to see who won by volume of sound alone. In other words I treated them like a huge family audience at a Christmas pantomime.

Thank heavens, they loved it and even brought me grapes and sweets. I think this extraordinary atmosphere, that became accidentally generated by my desperate remedies for the ticket situation, was one of the secrets of this series' world-wide success.

It would have been a fatal mistake to try and be funny between the short extracts, as no one could possibly 'top' them.

The jinx continued, though. Right in the middle of the series there was a strike at the B.B.C. We had, for some reason, to carry on doing the shows without an audience.

That meant I now had to guess the studio reaction and Richard had to cut in and out of our audience footage, of which we had, luckily, a great deal.

I took a deep breath and, after watching several play-backs of how the audience had reacted to my links, I carried on filming at the theatre – looking to right and left, as though I was including the whole non-existent lot of them, acknowledging their absent applause and even waiting while I timed their totally absent laughter.

I must have looked a raving lunatic up on that stage, in front of the cameras, bowing and smiling away while I tried to calm down an invisible full house – but then, it's a mad business anyway!

It was difficult, to say the least, and I was truly grateful for all those years of experience, on my part, and the great editorial skill, on Richard's and his team's part, which saved us from a short six programme series.

Despite it all, what a final product we had! Through it came shining the true worth of Buster Keaton and his contemporaries, as fresh as when those beautiful pieces of comedy were made.

Stan Laurel showed himself to be an able and inventive clown even before fate teamed him with Oliver Hardy. Laurel was actually directing Hardy when James Finlayson, the eternally-irate Scots comic, scalded himself with some boiling soup and had to come out of the picture, leaving Hal Roach with the golden opportunity to join Laurel and Hardy in that marvellous comedy wedlock.

This extraordinary story was confirmed for me by both Laurel himself, on the two occasions I had met him, and by Hal Roach as well, when I interviewed that great producer of comedy films on the Golden Silents series.

Roach told me that, Laurel and Keaton, who were both prize products of their music hall and vaudeville backgrounds, were by far the most inventive comedy minds of that whole era.

Dick Van Dyke also told me that he and many other comedians used to go to see Stan Laurel at his Malibu Beach apartment house, in the latter years of his life, and spend hours discussing comedy and how to perform it.

Stan Laurel, who was kind enough, together with Oliver Hardy, to compliment me on my original approach to comedy, told me that his own approach was always instinctive first and then he would develop the situation along logical lines later. But first, he insisted, the original thought was instinctive.

I was fascinated as he explained to me how he would develop a gag from just a vague flash of inspiration – like trying to get a donkey into a hayloft – and then the painstaking process that followed, as he slowly and logically built up the whole sequence.

Strangely enough, Professor Einstein said much the same thing about his theory of Relativity: that he had first conceived it in a flash of inspiration or, as he called it, intuition, and then set about the long task of proving it by logic.

Chaplin, as usual, was balletically wonderful, with his grace and cheek making up for the sometimes almost coarse routines and gags. We had sixteen of his early pictures, to choose from, and took the most scintillating of his beautifully timed comedy business.

Since my very young cinema-going days, I had watched with wonder the tremendous talent of Charlie Chaplin and always looked forward with joyous anticipation when his credits flashed up on the screen. But when it came to the final count of sheer belly laughs per sequence, somehow, Buster Keaton always scored more heavily with me. The world seems divided, by no means equally, into Charlie Chaplin and Buster Keaton fans, yet they all seem to unite when it comes to Laurel and Hardy. Everyone loved them.

Ben Turpin, too, came across as far more than just a cross-eyed droll when we could once again enjoy his superb acrobatic skill and joyous satire.

Chester Conklin, the Keystone Cops and all of the silent movie stars, like Charlie Chase, sparkled once more, and brought a new and lasting enjoyment to millions of homes around the world.

It was all a vindication of my belief that well-conceived and well-made visual comedy is timeless.

Richard made up montages of similar bits, such as a thirty-second sequence of different comedy falls, or a minute of incredible chases and crashes, explosions and chaos. During all these excerpts, it became obvious what terrible risks the performers had taken, because using a double then was almost unheard of.

Keaton had in fact broken his neck during one fall. He continued, quite unconcerned, without even knowing how near to death or total paralysis he had come, till a later X-ray showed the fracture.

Another time, while making *The Electric House*, a marvellously inventive piece of gadgetry, built into a complete animated house, he broke a foot when it got caught in a moving escalator.

Having seen all his pictures, except the sadly destroyed *Three Ages*, of which only a fragment remains, it is a constant source of wonder to me that he wasn't smashed to pieces a dozen times over.

Only his almost psychic timing, as an acrobat, and incredible physical fitness saved him – plus perhaps, a guardian angel like mine, in a perpetual state of nervous exhaustion.

Oliver Hardy also took some incredible falls for a heavy man. Starting as a type cast villian, Hardy had slowly progressed into the wonderful chubby, complacent and pedantic character that captured the public's hearts.

When I met these two great comedians, on their last tours of the British music hall, I was delighted by them. A whole lot of British comedians had put on a special show in their honour at the Savage Club. As it was real music hall, I was thrilled to take part.

I was immensely excited, as I could hardly believe that these idols of my childhood should actually take an interest in my efforts to amuse.

Both of them were exactly as they had appeared to me as a child – they even had the same mannerisms and voices that they projected on the screen.

Oliver Hardy, who at any moment I expected to twist his tie between his fingers, beamed seraphically on his partner, as Stan Laurel explained to us, in very nearly the same tone of voice that we all knew so well, the intricacies of screen comedy timing and the all-important use of the two-shot – that is the camera shot where both the characters can be seen at the same time.

'Without that,' he grinned, 'it would be Laurel – or Hardy – but never Laurel and Hardy!'

Sadly, we were unable, because of contractual difficulties, to include the gems of Harold Lloyd's great stunt movies, but I was lucky enough to have met him too and, had found him to be as friendly and unassuming as his horn-rimmed-spectacled image.

Bob Monkhouse had invited me along to meet Harold Lloyd, when the great American stunt comedian came over to show a release of his *World of Comedy*, which was made up of many clips from his movies.

Lloyd told me he had started life, as an athlete and boxer. He moved into film making before he was 20, when he had made a large number of short subject films with a character he had created called Lonesome Luke.

I have seen a number of these and the inventive sight gags in them often crop up later in his feature films.

An intrepid stunt man himself, he was only doubled on a very few occasions: once, for example, in long shot while supposedly climbing the face of a high building.

I asked if the sequences, at apparently great heights, were faked.

'Well,' he said slowly. 'They weren't quite as high as they looked – say two hundred feet rather than three hundred.'

'Did you use a net?' I asked him point blank.

'Not exactly,' he smiled, 'but there were precautions of course – you see the camera platform was underneath me.'

'Oh, I see,' I said, thinking this was the explanation of his seeming lack of fear of great heights. 'How far underneath you was the platform?'

'About thirty feet,' he said simply.

A very intelligent man, whose tricks were carefully and imaginatively conceived he showed me his missing fingers and wryly explained that he had only the limited use of this hand, throughout all those hair-raising stunts of his, due to the explosion of a prop bomb that he was holding while having some publicity photographs taken.

Hal Roach came over to be interviewed, once the series was well under way, and we just managed to get this material in the can, before the audience ban was put on us.

As a matter of fact Michael Mills and Richard Evans had phoned me urgently, asking me to rush over to Ealing, as they were both very worried that Roach, who had just been upset by a V.I.P. at the B.B.C. would pack up and leave.

I broke every speed limit to get there, because here was the man who, above everybody else, held the key to so many secrets of the silent comedy era.

I dashed up the steps of the editorial block at Ealing and gasped out: 'Mr Roach, I've been waiting more than forty years to shake your hand!' And I meant it too.

His great grin spread across his large humorous features as he held out an enormous paw to engulf mine. Then this big bear of a man pointed at me and said: 'This guy is the living image of Chaplin, in his middle years.'

And that, plus my own obvious unbounded enthusiasm, seemed to decide him to stay and co-operate fully – much to our relief, because he had, in fact, at that moment, considered flying straight back to the States.

Once he realised I knew my subject and had actually been a music performer myself, he opened up his giant storehouse of comedy memories and we spent our entire time together, in absorbing discussion and laughter.

His stories about the business were legion, my favourite being about the filming of a Laurel and Hardy gem, called *Little Big Business*.

The whole film revolves round the two of them being Christmas tree salesmen, trying to sell a tree to the difficult James Finlayson, who, in shutting the door in their faces, damages the top of the tree.

Laurel, politely rings the bell and the subsequent argument degenerates into a slanging match, then into physical violence and finishes with Finlayson wrecking their Ford Model T, down to the last nut and bolt, while Laurel and Hardy completely break up his entire house.

It is a marvellous gem of an admittedly violent piece of comedy.

Roach produced it and the designer had suggested that, rather than go to the expense of building a house on the outside studio lot, the company should hire a downtown-Burbank villa and send the owners on a two-week vacation, during which time they could shoot the picture and then the carpenters and painters would make good the damage.

A house was duly found and the owners agreed. Later that month, the film production teams turned up in Burbank, and the shooting commenced around the empty furnished house.

It was only as Laurel and Hardy were completing its partial demolition, with a fire axe, that the horrified owners turned up and Roach realised that it was, in fact, the wrong house. He ruefully admitted that after paying the damages it would have been considerably cheaper to have built the whole thing in the studio.

During the interview with Roach at the National Film Theatre, Richard had invited, without either of us knowing, those two stalwarts of the Hollywood era, Ben Lyon and Bebe Daniels.

Ben was still his sprightly and handsome self, but Bebe had tragically been affected by a stroke, which had left her weak and ill. Nevertheless, she insisted on coming to see the show and Richard told me, halfway through, that she was in the audience.

Not wishing to embarrass her, because I realised she was sensitive about not being her usual intensely alive self, I hesitated to introduce her. Roach sensed, immediately, that something was amiss and asked me, point blank, what it was.

I explained the situation while the audience was watching one of the pieces of film.

Roach became very excited, because he had discovered Bebe Daniels and, in fact, we had an actual piece of film of her in her first comedy screen role, under his direction.

When the lights came on, Roach virtually took over and insisted on Bebe being recognised by the audience. She stood up, with Ben at her side, and her face was radiant.

Then we showed the piece of film, to enormous applause, and Roach went down into the audience to embrace her. Without any shadow of schmaltz or phoneyness, it was a very moving moment, and Ben told me afterwards it was the finest medicine, that Bebe could have had.

The whole series made me realise, that, if I could have chosen my job, and the era of doing it in, I would have been blissfully happy as a gag-writer with Keaton, or any of the top comedy teams of that wonderful decade.

Everyone must have their own favourite moments, among that wealth of material, but here are a few of mine.

The startling cyclone sequence, from *Steam Boat Bill Junior*, when a complete side of a house falls on Keaton, who passes safely through the open window frame, is a classic.

This was done, in a cyclonic wind from an aircraft engine, by building a two-ton wooden frame of a planked building and exactly calculating the angle that the open window space would occupy as it fell. Had the building been lighter it would have moved in the wind and hit Keaton. It is instinctive to see, as I have the still frame of film where the window sill misses his head and shoulders by inches. At that moment the expressive face of Buster Keaton shows a stoic resolve, right through its so-called immobility.

Actually, of course, Keaton's face registered many subtle shades of emotion, mainly through his eyes, which many top actors have told me is the whole secret of successful screen acting technique.

Keaton's masterpiece, to me, will always be *The General*, that superbly funny version of the great train chase, that actually happened, when Union spies stole a Confederate train, during the Civil War. I once showed this film to an expensive audience at a Variety Club event. I had suggested showing the film and inviting Miss Florence de Jong, who still plays piano for silent films, as she did when she was a teenager.

The cinema was jam-packed with people of all ages. After *The General* had finished, the audience stood up and gave its star, long dead, an ovation that, by my watch, lasted for five minutes.

The strange, baby-faced Harry Langdon, who had faded into almost total obscurity, also sprang back to laughter-packed fame. His comedy was of the gentlest kind, yet aggressively physical and very inventive.

We also showed a cyclone sequence of Langdon's, which was every bit as dangerous and original as Keaton's, and extracts from *Long Pants* and other Langdon pictures, that proved to an entirely new generation that this man, whose clever work was nearly forgotten, had so much to offer to our comedy starved world today.

Two of his comedy routines I will always laugh at. The wonderful scene where he tries to attract the attention of a policeman, sitting on a basket trunk, not knowing that this is really a theatrical dummy. The gloriously funny fight he has with himself, which so many mime artists have used since, fails to get the cop's attention. Then, when his back is turned, the dummy is taken inside the theatre and a real policeman sits on the basket, just in time to get the brick which Langdon, in disgust, chucks at him.

The other is the marvellous long-distance walk sequence from *Tramp, Tramp, Tramp,* which had every fall-gag in the book in it. The particular one I love is where Langdon is hanging over a terrific drop, hundreds of feet below, with his belt caught on a large nail, sticking out of an old fence. He produces a hammer and bangs the nail in more securely, extracting nails from further along the fence to hammer them in to his belt as well. These nails are the ones securing the fence to the uprights and the whole thing sways out over the precipice with Langdon firmly attaching himself. Eventually it gives way and he toboggans down the steep slope, to end up ahead of the other long-distance walkers.

Langdon, like Keaton, only used dummies as doubles where he would obviously be killed in a trick gag, but in this case he did it himself.

The Chaplin films still stood the test of time and *Easy Street* remains far and away my favourite. The huge villian was played by Eric Campbell, who featured in many Chaplin films. His fight, with the newly recruited Chaplin cop is as fresh and as funny as when it was first screened, before the nineteen twenties.

Chaplin eventually gases the giant, by shoving his head inside a gas lamp, which the huge Campbell has bent over to show his enormous strength, and he finally K.O.'s the villain by dropping a kitchen stove on his head.

Even if it was made of cardboard and balsa that stove must have nearly brained the massive actor.

The Cure, where Chaplin plays an alcoholic being dried out at a health spa, is again wonderfully funny, especially the sequence where the liquor, which has been smuggled into the spa, gets accidentally tipped into the spring and all the spa visitors get smashed out of their minds.

Laurel and Hardy's Academy award winning, short subject picture about two sailors, on a weekend pass, who hire a car and carelessly bash another one in a long queue of automobiles, is another of my special favourites. The resulting argument builds, in typical Laurel and Hardy terms, until it encompasses an orgy of auto wrecking. It was the same sort of technique that they worked in their great custard pie fight, which starts with Hardy kicking Laurel's leg and being kicked back, then kicking passers-by, from where it takes off into a universal trouser rip-off of anyone passing, climaxing in the great pie fight.

Let's face it, you've really got to see it to appreciate it, which gives the whole key to the success of this timeless comedy – it is essentially visual. Whereas a spoken gag is only funny the first couple of times you hear it, a sight gag is a joy for ever.

The series became a national cult and played pretty well right round the world. It was, undoubtedly, the most interesting work I had done for years – but, obviously, the real kudos goes to the stars of the *Golden Silents*.

A dear old man at Felixstowe stopped me one day.

'Mr Bentine,' he said. 'I must say how much I loved the old films – you must have enjoyed working with them!'

Thinking he meant the films themselves, I agreed and thanked him, but he continued: 'I recognised you under all those disguises – I could tell by your laugh.'

I tried to explain that the films were silent and the laugh he might have heard was mine, which is distinctive in tone, joining in with the audience, but he wouldn't have it – he was totally convinced that I was in every film.

I thanked him again, for his interest and appreciation, and he turned to go, then looking back over his shoulder he added: 'By the way, Mr Bentine, considering how long ago you made them – you carry your age very well!'

30. Clown – crying

At this time clubland circuit of northern England was booming and I decided to really concentrate on developing my cabaret act.

For this Alfie Ravel, the small and talented musical clown, whom I had originally met in pantomime years before, joined me.

Alf's shrewdness was backed up by an original line of everyday dialogue which he referred to as: 'a special kind of conversation.' His props he called 'the miracles' and he could keep me chuckling for hours with his reminiscences.

My favourite one was when he was working in a high-class circus cabaret in Germany and the Herr Direktor's advice to him was: 'If der audience don't laugh, kick der midget up der arse!'

I nearly used that immortally Teutonic phrase as the title of this book but my nerve failed me.

It was he and his long experience of the business in this form that persuaded me to tour the working-men's clubs, as they were known.

These ranged from the large asbestos-boarded, timber-framed halls, through converted cinemas, bought cheaply during the television-caused local picture slump, to lush fun-factories modelled on their Las Vegas prototypes.

The less fancy ones featured hot pies and peas and the psuedo night-clubs offered scampi and chips. They boasted such names as 'La Ronda', Spennymoor, 'La Bamba', Darlington and even 'Las Vegas', Castleford, which had a doorman dressed up as a matador.

In all of them there was a rousing Northern welcome if they liked your act – and total silence if they didn't.

Thank God they loved mine, as I played them all from 'The Paradise Club', over a garage in Guisley, to 'El Latino', South Shields.

I always found 'prop' comedy a more certain way of holding the diffused attention of a cabaret audience, who are too distracted by food – and often too much drink plus the bird-in-the-hand and other hindrances – to concentrate on the poor bastard standing up there in the din and bright lights of the tiny, badly sited platform that usually does service for a stage.

However, in the case of the Batley Theatre Club, one of the best designed and biggest in the North, the audience reaction could be overwhelming – and everywhere somehow I managed to hold those elusive but potentially wholehearted audiences for an hour or more. The deafening applause at the end was part of the incentive to come back again – together with the generous fees that were available.

The North of England is like that. If they like you they'll pay handsomely for you and even let you know they appreciate your sweat-streaming efforts at the end.

As many of the clubs had gambling facilities, sometimes payment would be in cash. This was, in a way, a nuisance because it meant carrying this sum in notes over the weekend when the banks were closed. One club even had its own system of banking. To my amazement, as Alf and I walked back to our hotel in a northern seaside town, we saw two huge bouncers leave the club carrying money that we had seen earlier being counted into leather bags.

Crossing the Promenade at this early hour of the Sunday morning, they swished their way through the shingle and sand to the water's edge where one of them flashed a torch seawards.

An answering twinkle of light replied to their signal and shortly afterwards a rubber dinghy appeared – the money was transferred and the boat was rowed off into the just breaking dawn. Presumably the Club banked in Ireland or the Isle of Man. Alf and I didn't stay to inquire.

In my cabaret act I played the invisible flea circus, which was now an ingenious prop that took up most of my estate car – and a double-ended furry animal called a Woofenpouf, whose genealogical traits I fully exploited. I also used the sink plunger, vacuum cleaner pipes and other props, finishing with a Russian astronaut's medical examination, in which Alfie was the intrepid astronaut. I played a very Russian doctor, in a language reminiscent of my short extemporary performance with Eddie Gray and the lady Pekinese fancier.

That piece of broad visual nonsense, with Alfie straining hopelessly to fill a graduated medical glass behind a large hospital screen, stopped the show every night.

From the clubs I adapted the act to fit the more sober but

still broad tastes of the seaside summer season public, all round the British coast. Finally, with Alf's experienced help as a fine children's entertainer, I slowly mastered part of the art of Christmas performance – though this is so tricky to do that on more than one occasion I failed to get across to that ultra-difficult audience.

Pantomime in Britain is not really very old in conception but is highly stylised and has to be adapted to a first house or matinée of very young people and to the evening performances before the more sophisticated adults.

The secret is never to play down to the children and to make them do the work, with frequent appeals for their co-operation and participation, and plenty of sight gags.

The flea circus always worked marvellously with both houses.

Armed with these new comedy weapons I played dates ranging from South Africa to Hong Kong, always accompanied by the business-wise Alfred.

In South Africa I met the brilliant and liberally minded Professor Blakeslee, a retired physicist/astronomer, who was fascinated by my father's researches, and who carried on his remarkable work at Witwatersrand University into a busy retirement investigating the field of paranormal psychology.

Flying to Hong Kong seemed pretty hair-raising as we swooped low down between a great double block of apartment buildings filled to bursting with busy people who must all be stone deaf.

On the way from the airport the taxi driver, a friendly and anything but inscrutable soul, left me open mouthed with astonishment when he found out that I was a comedian. He reacted in the time-honoured manner that I had come to expect on any taxi ride into any town where I was appearing, from Bradford to Los Angeles. Grinning broadly he came out with: 'You know what they say about Hong Kong? If you please them here you can please them anywhere.'

It was while crossing from Kowloon to Hong Kong that I found out how to make pressed Peking duck.

Just buy two ducks Kowloonside and board the ferry. By the time it pulls out from the quay you can't move a muscle for the passengers packed patiently around you.

When you disembark Honk Kong side, your ducks will be squashed flat.

Hong Kong found me playing the beautiful Mandarin Hotel

by night and attempting to help the wonderful work of Professor Hodgson by day.

This astonishingly original orthopaedic surgeon had developed, along with his splendid team, a tremendous leap forward in the treatment of scoliosis – or as it is known to semi-laymen like me, curvature of the spine.

At Sandy Bay Children's Hospital, built by his own loving efforts, I also met Professor Arthur Yow and doctor Jack O'Brien; the one, a splendid young Chinese surgeon, and the other, a brilliant and typically ebullient Australian one.

Together with Sister Barbara, an Irish nun of immense charm and determination, I visited this tiny and efficient hospital and was held spellbound by the miracles that they were performing daily with these terribly handicapped and beautiful children.

Douglas Freebody, one of Britain's leading orthopaedic surgeons and my across-the-road neighbour had asked me to look up his good friend 'Hoddy'.

The Hodgson-Yow-O'Brien team had developed a halo-pelvic traction splint of revolutionary design. This was virtually an exoskeletal structure that fitted round the skull of the child patient like a halo and was attached to a hip-girdle by extending rods.

The whole extraordinary metal structure was fitted in one operation and supported the cruelly deviated spine while, daily, it was used to straighten out the patient from the distorted travesty of childhood into the beautifully normal posture that nature intended.

The miracle of this transformation was then made permanent by the insertion of a titanium prosthetic support, which was fitted internally to the spinal column, to keep the child painlessly and properly proportioned for life.

My knowledge of medicine is still very sketchy but just sufficient for me to realise the benefit that this remarkable operation could bestow. I wondered how I could help spread the news of this wonderful technique. Overnight, the answer came to me, not without praying, and I contacted my old friend Raymond Baxter, who presents the ever-original and fascinating *Tomorrow's World* programme, on the B.B.C.

Ray replied to my enthusiastic cable and, within weeks, a full visual report of this operation and its techniques had been seen by over ten million people in Britain – so my visit to Hong Kong had done a bit more than just supply my financial needs.

I also learned what prejudice can mean to progress, when an

eminent orthopaedic surgeon back in Britain said: 'Mr Bentine, I appreciate your semi-educated enthusiasm, but you must realise that this method will only work with Oriental children, who are much more stoic than Occidental patients.'

To which I, automatically and tactlessly, replied: 'Professor, do you subscribe to the popular theory that the vagina is orientated sideways East of Suez?'

This unthinking remark won me a withering look and the bum's rush from a Harley Street consulting room.

Unexpected support came from the lovely Ingrid Bergman who listened to my description of the splint and then told me how one of her twin daughters had been given an alternative operation in which this straightening-out process, or distraction, as it is called, was carried out in one terrifying session.

That sounded reminiscent of the Spanish Inquisition and, semi-laymen though I am, I could see the advantages of the Hodgson-Yow-O'Brien method.

I was delighted later on to meet Professor Robinson, the leading orthopaedic of the famous Johns Hopkins Hospital in America and learn that he had adopted this revolutionary splint for cases of automotive whip-lash, the horribly descriptive phrase that covers car accidents, where fractures of the upper or cervical area of the spine are common.

By this time I was also heavily involved with LEPRA, that marvellous organisation based on the old British Empire Leprosy Campaign, that helps, so effectively, to deal with the problem of mankind's oldest known disease from which there are, incredibly, still some 15,000,000 sufferers.

Through the *Golden Silents* fan mail, I had received a letter from a leading ophthalmic surgeon, who wanted to know if he could buy copies of the programmes, to show as an inducement to his outpatients in Malawi who were suffering from leprosy.

The B.B.C. administration could not let him have the copies, because of the world copyright system.

Shamed by this, I invited the eminent eye surgeon to lunch, to apologise for the failure to get what he required and he brought along the head of LEPRA, Francis Harris.

They explained to me the horrors of the leprosy patient situation in the world – a horror based on the appalling ignorance that most people have of this crippling disease and one which I shared with the rest of the public.

LEPRA was about to become international and Francis offered to provide a leprosy survey in Peru, which was something I had already been asked to help with by General Benavides.

One thing led to another and a LEPRA team came to my house and showed us a wonderful prize-winning film of their work with leprosy outpatients in Africa.

With them they brought the very tall and very brilliant Doctor Colin Macdougal who, through another strange series of coincidences, I was able, eventually, to fly to Peru. There, with the help of the Peruvian Ambassador, H. E. Señor Adhemar de Montagne and my ever willing co-operative family, this outstanding and enthusiastic clinician made a complete survey and report of the whole country's leprosy problems, which far exceeded the World Health Organisation's previous efforts in this area.

Through this and LEPRA's generosity we were able to send a Peruvian doctor to Mexico, to be trained as an expert in leprosy control and he is now working with the Peruvian Government and LEPRA in a combined attack on the problem.

Dimly, in these fields of medical research, and in my own faltering attempts to help people, like the extraordinary Maureen Mawhinney in her work with handicapped children, I could begin to see what my father meant, when he had told me that my own destiny lay in using my show business and semi-scientific background, to further the efforts of other more highly skilled researchers.

* * *

Mind you – I sometimes wonder what I am going to get involved in next.

Gratefully I realise that life for me, and no doubt for my long-suffering family, is seldom dull, though of necessity there are short periods of peace among all the frenzied activity.

These quiet moments seldom last longer than a week or so and many of them have been spent with Sam and Marty Kershen on short and much-needed holidays in various parts of Europe where our happily shared and often juvenile explosions of mirth help to release my pent-up emotions.

On one of these family excursions to Rome I was describing the idea of the new children's puppets I had just designed. Based on the Bumblies I had dreamed up a race of small people, whose faces are only partly seen and half hidden under their appropriate character hats.

Sam suddenly said: 'My dad used to have a funny way of saying, "What's the matter with you – have you got potty?" '

316

The phrase stuck in my mind and the Potties were born, eventually to graduate on to the television screens of Britain and, later, many other parts of the world.

I knew I had got the basic designs right when, after the second series of *Michael Bentine's Potty Time*, a small and lovely little Chinese child shyly said: 'I like the Potties.'

And to my delighted question: 'How lovely. What do you like about them?' she blissfully replied: 'They are all Chinese!'

One remark like that, coming from the completely honest mind of a child, makes all the effort worth while.

These Potties, now in their second series, have rather taken me over, in that they use up most of my energy in devising and creating them and developing their fascinating Potty world.

As I am essentially non-political by nature and instinctive in creativity, they furnish me with a long-needed outlet for the seething mass of ideas and images that can pass through my mind.

I suppose that they are really a projection of my own experiences in life. When I see them explaining to me their problems and Potty solutions to their own difficulties, I'm sure it is really me trying to work out my own puzzlements.

Originally given the opportunity to come to television, through the efforts of Johnnie Downs of the B.B.C. Children's Department the Potties are now being produced by Thames Television. From our small beginnings, they have spread out to be enjoyed by literally millions of children and, surprisingly, by even more adults.

The Potties have also helped me to get out of my system the horror and shock of the passing of my son Gus and his friend Andy whose disappearance in a light plane for nine dreadful weeks, till they were found dead in the machine in a wood in Hampshire, will I'm sure never be allowed to be fully explained.

The accompanying scandal of the frequent misuse of and general permissive attitude towards private planes in Britain, had shaken me completely. I can only hope that the passing of these two innocent victims of this appalling situation has shaken up the people concerned.

Just before the whole ghastly business occurred I had been involved in trying to alleviate some of the suffering cause by the shattering earthquake in Peru, which had wiped out over 55,000 people in a matter of minutes.

I was rehearsing a summer season show in Southsea, when news of the *terre-moto* was phoned to me by Clementina. As the details of the catastrophe came through in their full horror, the Peruvian Ambassador, who had only recently arrived in Britain, also telephoned me, to ask for my help.

I had already arranged with my producer to hold up the show, while I hurriedly packed up to leave for Lima when Señor Adhemar de Montagne got through to me. I promptly phoned David Attenborough at the B.B.C., to see if an appeal could be made.

He was most sympathetic and contacted the Disaster Emergency Committee – then phoned me back and asked me to make the appeal myself.

I wasn't prepared for this at all and explained that I was off to Peru by the first plane, but both David and the Ambassador insisted that I stayed.

Dashing up to London I collected the copy of the film I had made of the Peruvian mountain people. Chris Brasher, the Olympic athlete, and now a B.B.C. producer, met me, and we ran the appropriate sections for him to choose from.

There was no time to write a proper script and I just stood in front of a camera and said whatever came into my head.

As the film of the actual disaster areas, which had been flown to us straight from Lima, came up on the monitor screen before my horrified eyes, my voice must have betrayed the emotions which took control of me.

I don't remember what I said but, at the end, I know I was weeping openly.

I begged Chris to let me do the video-taping again but he gently refused, realising that I could never complete it and that the appeal, to be effective, must be made then and there.

The Ambassador was still loath to have me leave for Lima, because he felt that I could help more in Britain.

I never did go in the end, but I was able to be of some use, in co-ordinating many of the problems raised by Oxfam and other organisations involved in the relief of the disaster area.

The R.A.F. was quite wonderful and responded to my desperate request for help, by transporting the badly needed medical and concentrated food and blood supplies. In fact they laid on a whole series of sorties, by Britannia and Hercules transport planes, flying out more than 150 tons of these vital requirements within a matter of days.

There wasn't much sleep for any of us, but then all you had to do, when things got a bit too much, was to visualise the appalling

318

conditions at the other end of the operation, and just how much help was needed.

Later the R.A.F. also flew out three complete pre-fabricated schools which the Anglo-Peruvian Society provided. These are now supplying some of the educational needs of the slowly recovering disaster areas.

A journalist later went out to Peru, after all the hard work and effort by so many devoted people had been done, and wrote a scandalous article, in which he criticised the other end of the rescue operations – hinting at the inefficiency of the Peruvian Government and their tardiness in moving the supplies up to the site of the earthquake,

Perhaps if this merciless critic had done a little research, he would have realised that the sheer magnitude of the problem had swamped Peru's limited resources, which of course were stretched beyond endurance. Better still he might have helped, in some small way, at the time.

Supplies from all over the world had lain on Lima's airport for weeks until they could be moved up into the mountains, for the simple reason that there was no one and no transport left to move the stuff. Everything and everyone was already fully engaged, up to the limit of their capacity.

I learned something else during all the relief operation; that the generosity of the British people is unrivalled anywhere in the world.

One small infant school, in Felixstowe, for example, raised more than £120 by the efforts of children in making and selling sweets and cakes.

This was in direct contrast to a cheque for ten pounds that I received from a huge agricultural and fertiliser firm for opening their annual fête.

But the bulk of the very large support for the appeal came from the people of Britain – old-age pensioners, who could ill afford the money, and folk of every race, colour and creed, who sent in sums ranging from pennies to hundreds of pounds.

All through it the summer season went on and I lived most of that time in a sort of waking, working dream.

Then, one day, the Ambassador rang me to say that the Peruvian Government wished to give me a decoration.

Surprised and embarrassed I didn't quite know what to say until it suddenly struck me what I should do. I asked if I could accept the honour on behalf of the British people.

Later that summer, at a simple ceremony in the Ambassador's

home, with an alarming amount of publicity, the Peruvian Ambassador presented me with the Condecoration, that had last been received by my Uncle Ricardo as vice-president of the Republic.

Clementina and the family were there and I felt slightly dazed by the whole procedure.

The next month, the Anglo-Peruvian Society held a ball at the Savoy; the guests of honour being Lord Louis Mountbatten, Lord Carrington, other distinguished dignitaries and an Anglo-Peruvian clown – me.

I hate social occasions of this sort and was feeling terribly uncomfortable in full evening dress from Moss Bros. with tinkling miniature decorations and the new large and impressive Condor of the Andes at my throat, when I felt a heavy hand descend on my shoulder.

Turning round, I saw the smiling face of a musician from the Savoy orchestra, with whom I had done so many shows.

' 'Allo, Mike,' said my musical friend. 'You doin' the cabaret 'ere tonight, mate?'

Sic transit gloria mundi.

*   *   *

Well – there you have it.

For better or for worse, as near as I can remember it all, these are some of the things that I've experienced in a life that now for the first time I have looked back upon and found quite surprising. I've had to leave out a lot of incidents and a lot of interesting people so if you are not included in these pages – I haven't forgotten you.

One more thing: do watch out for that long banana skin – I do.